News From True Cultivators

News From True Cultivators

Letters to the Venerable Abbot Hua

by

Heng Sure Ph.D.
and
Heng Ch'au Ph.D.

English translation by the
Buddhist Text Translation Society

Buddhist Text Translation Society
Dharma Realm Buddhist University
Dharma Realm Buddhist Association
Burlingame, California U.S.A.

News From True Cultivators - Letters to the Venerable Abbot Hua

Published and translated by:

Buddhist Text Translation Society
1777 Murchison Drive, Burlingame, CA 94010-4504

© 2003   **Buddhist Text Translation Society**
          Dharma Realm Buddhist University
          Dharma Realm Buddhist Association

First edition 1983
Second edition 2003

09 08 07 06 05 04 03 02 01 10 9 8 7 6 5 4 3 2 1

ISBN 0-88139-425-4

Printed in Malaysia.

Addresses of the Dharma Realm Buddhist Association branches are
listed at the back of this book.

Library of Congress Cataloging-in-Publication Data

Heng Sure, Bhikshu, 1949-
  News from true cultivators : letters to the Venerable Abbot Hua /
Bhikshus Heng Sure and Heng Chau ; translated by Buddhist Text
Translation Society ... [et al.]
      p. cm.
  ISBN 0-88139-425-4 (hardcover : alk. paper)
  1. Heng Sure, Bhikshu, 1949---Correspondence. 2. Heng Ch'au,
Shramanera--Correspondence. 3. Hsuan Hua, 1908---Correspondence.
4. Buddhist monks--Correspondence. 5. California--Description and
travel. 6. Spiritual life--Buddhism. I. Buddhist Text Translation
Society II.
Title.
  BQ739.C2 H46 2003
  294.3'092'2--dc21

                                                    2002002193

Contents

Preface

Three steps, one bow – three steps along the side of the highway, then a bow to the ground, so that knees, elbows, hands, and forehead touch the earth, then rise, join the palms together, and take three more steps, then begin another bow. Hour after hour, day after day, for two and a half years, this was how they made their pilgrimage. In China, devout Buddhists sometimes undertake the arduous and prayerful practice of three steps, one bow, for the last few hundred yards of a journey to a sacred site. But this was California, and these two pilgrim-monks were young Americans. Dressed in their robes and sashes, carrying no money, armed with nothing but discipline and reverence, they walked and bowed 800 miles along the narrow shoulder of the Pacific Coast Highway. Progressing a mile a day, they bowed from downtown Los Angeles north along the coast, through Santa Barbara and along the Big Sur, through San Francisco and across the Golden Gate, then 100 miles farther north to the City of Ten Thousand Buddhas, a newly founded religious and educational center in Mendocino County. As they bowed, their prayer was that the world would be free of disaster, calamity, and war.

The silent monk in the lead was Heng Sure. Originally from Toledo, Ohio, he had found his way in 1974 to Gold Mountain Buddhist Monastery in San Francisco. There on a side street of the Mission District, an eminent Chinese monk, the Venerable Master

Hsuan Hua, was living in obscurity as he carried out his pioneering work of transplanting the Buddhist monastic tradition to the West. Moved by Master Hua's virtue and wisdom, Heng Sure joined other young Americans in taking a monastic name and the full ordination of a Buddhist monk.

During his subsequent studies, Heng Sure read of a bowing pilgrimage made in the 1880's by the Venerable Hsu Yun ("Empty Cloud"), who was the most distinguished Chinese monastic of his generation. Master Yun had bowed every third step across the breadth of China; it had taken him five years. Heng Sure knew that Master Yun had been patriarch of the Wei Yang Lineage of the Chan School, and he knew that his own abbot and teacher, Master Hua, was the current patriarch, having received the lineage transmission from Master Yun in 1949. Inspired by this close connection, Heng Sure asked Master Hua if he could undertake his own pilgrimage of three steps, one bow. Master Hua approved, but said, "Wait."

Heng Sure had to wait a year. What he needed, Master Hua said, was the right companion and protector. It was to be Heng Chau. Originally from Appleton, Wisconsin, Heng Chau had come to Berkeley to study martial arts, and he had become an adept in several traditions. When his tai-chi teacher finally told him, "Chan is higher than any martial art," Heng Chau crossed the Bay to study at Gold Mountain Monastery. He soon heard about Heng Sure's vow, and he asked if he could bow with him. Within a week Heng Chau took novice precepts and made a formal vow to bow beside Heng Sure, as well as handle the logistics of cooking, cleaning, setting up camp, and talking with strangers.

Thus the pilgrimage began. Master Hua saw them off as they left Gold Wheel Monastery in Los Angeles on 7 May 1977. To Heng Chau, the martial artist, he said, "You can't use your martial arts on the pilgrimage. Heng Sure's vow is to seek an end to calamities, disasters and war; so how can you yourselves be involved in violence? If either of you fights – or even indulges in anger – you will no longer be my disciples." For protection from the dangers of the

road, Master Hua instructed them to practice instead the four uncon-
ditional attitudes of the Bodhisattva: kindness, compassion, joy, and
equanimity. It was by no means the last time that the two bowing
monks would need their teacher's advice.

On the road, the two pilgrims followed their monastic discipline
strictly – eating one vegetarian meal a day; never going indoors,
sleeping sitting up in the old 1956 Plymouth station wagon that
served as their shelter. In the evenings after a day of bowing they
studied the *Avatamsaka Sutra* (*Flower Adornment Sutra*) by the
light of an oil lamp. They translated passages into English and
attempted to put into practice the principles of the text in their day-
to-day experiences on the road, as their teacher had encouraged them
to do. The monks guarded their concentration by avoiding
newspapers, by leaving the car radio silent, and by keeping to a strict
meditation schedule. Heng Sure held a vow of silence for the entire
journey, and it became Heng Chau's job to talk with the many people
who stopped along the highway with questions. Occasionally the
visitors were hostile, and some threatened violence, but the greater
number were curious, and often the curious became the monks'
protectors, bringing them food and supplies until the monks had
bowed their way out of range.

Everything important that happened on the highway – the
mistakes and the growth, the trials and remarkable encounters, the
dangers and the insights, the hard work with the body and in the mind
– the pilgrims reported in letters to Master Hua. He would answer in
person by visiting them from time to time, giving them indispensable
spiritual guidance, admonishment, humor, and timely instructions-
both lofty and mundane.These letters are the contents of this volume.
They were not written with the thought that they would be published.
Rather, they were a medium in which the two monks attempted to
speak to their teacher as openly and sincerely as possible about their
experience on the road. As such, the letters preserve an unadorned
account of an authentic spiritual journey.

The Venerable Master Hsuan Hua

A Brief Portrait

"I have had many names," he once said, "and all of them are false." In his youth in Manchuria, he was known as "the Filial Son Bai"; as a young monk he was An Tzu ("Peace and Kindness"); later, in Hong Kong, he was Tu Lun ("Wheel of Rescue"); finally, in America, he was Hsuan Hua, which might be translated as "one who proclaims the principles of transformation." To his thousands of disciples across the world, he was always also "Shr Fu" – "Teacher."

Born in 1918 into a peasant family in a small village on the Manchurian plain, Master Hua was the youngest of ten children. He attended school for only two years, during which he studied the Chinese Classics and committed much of them to memory. As a young teenager, he opened a free school for both children and adults. He also began then one of his lifelong spiritual practices: reverential bowing. Outdoors, in all weathers, he would make over 800 prostrations daily, as a profound gesture of his respect for all that is good and sacred in the universe.

He was nineteen when his mother died, and for three years he honored her memory by sitting in meditation in a hut beside her grave. It was during this time that he made a resolve to go to America to teach the principles of wisdom. As a first step, at the end of the period of mourning, he entered San Yuan Monastery, took as his teacher Master Chang Chih, and subsequently received the full ordination of a Buddhist monk at Pu To Mountain. For ten years he devoted himself to study of the Buddhist scriptural tradition and to mastery of both the Esoteric and the Chan Schools of Chinese Buddhism. He had also read and contemplated the scriptures of Christianity, Taoism, and Islam. Thus, by the age of thirty, he had already established through his own experience the four major imperatives of his later ministry in America: the primacy of the monastic tradition; the essential role of moral education; the need for Buddhists to ground themselves in traditional spiritual practice and authentic scripture; and, just as essential, the importance and the power of ecumenical respect and understanding.

In 1948, Master Hua traveled south to meet the Venerable Hsu Yun, who was then already 108 years old and China's most distinguished spiritual teacher. From him Master Hua received the patriarchal transmission in the Wei Yang Lineage of the Chan School. Master Hua subsequently left China for Hong Kong. He spent a dozen years there, first in seclusion, then later as a teacher at three monasteries which he founded.

Finally, in 1962, he went to the United States, at the invitation of several of his Hong Kong disciples who had settled in San Francisco. By 1968, Master Hua had established the Buddhist Lecture Hall in a loft in San Francisco's Chinatown, and there he began giving nightly lectures, in Chinese, to an audience of young Americans. His texts were the major scriptures of the Mahayana. In 1969, he astonished the monastic community of Taiwan by sending there, for final ordination, two American women and three American men, all five of them fully trained as novices, fluent in Chinese and conversant with Buddhist scripture. During subsequent years, the Master trained and oversaw the ordination of hundreds of monks and nuns who came to California from every part of the world to study with him. These monastic disciples now teach in the 28 temples, monasteries and convents that the Master founded in the United States, Canada, and several Asian countries.

Although he understood English well and spoke it when it was necessary, Master Hua almost always lectured in Chinese. His aim was to encourage Westerners to learn Chinese, so that they could become translators, not merely of his lectures, but of the major scriptural texts of the Buddhist Mahayana. His intent was realized. So far, the Buddhist Text Translation Society, which he founded, has issued over 130 volumes of translation of the major Sutras, together with a similar number of commentaries, instructions, and stories from the Master's teaching.

As an educator, Master Hua was tireless. From 1968 to the mid 1980's he gave as many as a dozen lectures a week, and he traveled extensively on speaking tours. At the City of Ten Thousand Buddhas in Talmage, California, he established formal training programs for monastics and for laity; elementary and secondary schools for boys and for girls; and Dharma Realm Buddhist University, together with the University's branch, the Institute for World Religions, in Berkeley.

Throughout his life the Master taught that the basis of spiritual practice is moral practice. Of his monastic disciples he required strict purity, and he encouraged his lay disciples to adhere to the five precepts of the Buddhist laity. Especially in his later years, Confucian texts were often the subject of his lectures, and he held to the Confucian teaching that the first business of education is moral education. He identified six rules of conduct as the basis of communal life at the City of Ten Thousand Buddhas; the six rules prohibit contention, covetousness, self-seeking, selfishness, profiting at the expense of the community, and false speech. He asked that the children in the schools he had founded recite these prohibitions every morning before class. In general, although he admired the independent-mindedness of Westerners, he believed that they lacked ethical balance and needed that stabilizing sense of public morality which is characteristic of the East.

The Venerable Master insisted on ecumenical respect, and he delighted in inter-faith dialogue. He stressed commonalities in religious traditions – above all their emphasis on proper conduct, on compassion, and on wisdom. He was also a pioneer in building bridges between different Buddhist national traditions. He often brought monks from Theravada countries to California to share the duties of transmitting the precepts of ordination. He invited Catholic priests to celebrate the mass in the Buddha-Hall at the City of Ten Thousand Buddhas, and he developed a late-in-life friendship with Paul Cardinal Yu-Bin, the exiled leader of the Catholic Church in China and Taiwan. He once told the Cardinal: "You can be a Buddhist among the Catholics, and I'll be a Catholic among Buddhists." To the Master, the essential teachings of all religions could be summed up in a single word: wisdom.

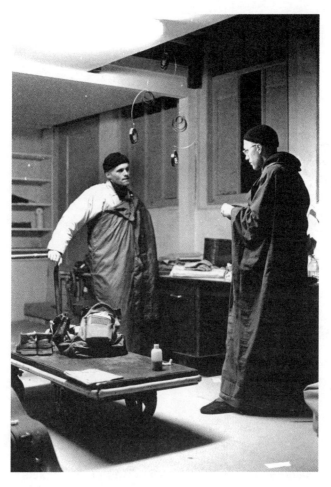

Planning the pilgrimage, Heng Sure and Heng Chau converse in Gold Mountain Monastery's work loft.

Heng Chau comments: "We connected! The long unspoken link between us surfaced. We knew each other, and a mutual vow made long ago was ripening. Suddenly I found myself absorbed in planning an incredible expedition with Heng Sure that on the one hand I knew I couldn't pass up and on the other I equally couldn't imagine getting clear and free enough inside and out to go."

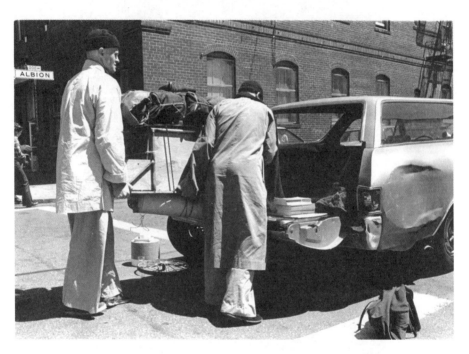

Packing gear into the old station wagon, the monks do final preparations before beginning the pilgrimage.

The Master instructs: "Bowing once every three steps is not the kind of method that anyone wants to do, because it's so dangerous. So at all times you want to be very careful… When you come to curves or narrow lanes, you can bow alongside in the grass off the road."

First bows to begin the pilgrimage at Gold Wheel Monastery, South Pasadena.

May 1977

Gold Wheel community send-off. Circumambulating the bowing monks while reciting the Great Compassion Mantra.

May 1977

Heng Ch'au, the Dharma Protector

May 11, 1977

Dear Shr Fu,

Homage to the Venerable Master,
May he lend his compassion to all beings!

This work is very much like a Ch'an session. Constant mindfulness is hard work and we are making slow and steady progress. Three steps, one bow.

Heng Ch'au is a good protector. He has already saved us from one nasty situation which he will tell about below. Many lay people have protected us and show us great care. I am not talking very much at all. This is a wonderful chance to practice my vow to speak only words in service to the Triple Jewel. I am forever grateful for the opportunity to cultivate the Way.

Heng Sure

* * *

Keeping our wonderful protection requires carefulness. We've met relatively few obstacles so far, but many tests.

Our first day out we started bowing along a row of bars in a tough neighborhood. Lots of drunks and macho toughs. Our first solo, we were really less than confident. Wet and muddy from the streets (it had just stopped raining, a small clearing when we started bowing), we were not an awesome sight. On the second bow the action started.

A huge drunk tapped me on the shoulder from behind, "Hey what you making with this?" I feebly tried to explain through his stupor. He's seven inches from my face. He slowly pulls one of those sentimental, wavy-haired, hippie pictures of Jesus out of his wallet. He keeps shaking it in front of my face, waiting. I gracefully exit to stay close to Heng Sure. A souped-up car whizzes by full of drunk and violent men, "You queers have until sundown to be out of this neighborhood!" We're only three minutes out and already so much flak.

We trudge on. Many groups of people forming ahead as the word quickly spreads. "You'll never get anywhere that way, ha! ha!" laughs someone.

"Hey, Joe, they're blessing your gas station! ho! ho!" mocks another.

Some pass us like we're old popsicle sticks. They are indifferent, as if in T.V. samadhi. But each group dissipates as we bow into them. How we must seem to them!

They test us verbally—no response. "Hey, think I'll kick 'em in the ass when they kneel down!" No response. A larger, older group of men gather at one corner. The leader stands a good 6' 5". His sidekick has been running in between us, patting us on the heads, posturing, and trying to provoke us. No response. Heng Sure is constant—pushes forward. I close the gap. Suddenly they make way, telling the lingering one, "Let 'em be, they ain't doin' nothin'." We bow through. I feel the two leaders stalking from behind. It's hard to put down all my years of martial arts training, but I know there's no real protection save sincere cultivation. We keep bowing, walking... Finally the hulk pulls alongside and politely asks, "Pardon me, Sir, may I ask what you're doing?" I nod, finish a bow and explain.

"Wow, that's something! Don't he talk? You've got the hard job. I can dig being peaceful. All the way to Ukiah! What's this

Buddha about?" etc. They are moved. Something soft and genuine peeks out. The edge is gone. Ice melts to water. "Peace to you guys," he says and crosses us with his blessing as he walks away. "Take care."

We are beat! Time to find a camp. The clouds are back. It's starting to rain. Forgot toilet paper.

2:30 a.m. Parked across from a tortilla factory in South Pasadena. I woke up reciting mantras. I hear footsteps shuffling and quiet voices. A shadow passes by the right side of the car. Bang! An arm forces itself through the vent window, trying to open the door. Dogs outside barking wildly. I yell, "Hey!" I can make out four dark figures moving away from the car. They re-group down the street. A little later I hear rocks hitting the pavement around us. I wipe the moisture off the window and see them, now with night sticks or bats, coming for us, buzzed on something, throwing rocks and charging down the center of the street to attack us. I jump the seat, grope for the ignition and start the engine. Engine won't turn over. Panic sets in. I recite Gwan Yin's name and try again. Varoom! the engine roars. I pull out. One of them jumps at the car trying to stop us. We made it!

Went to Gold Wheel Temple and slept in driveway until 4:00 a.m. Adrenalin exhaustion. A hard day, this one.

We are accidentally killing many little bugs and ants under our bowing hands and feet. Every day we feel stronger, more mindful. Dreams within dreams bowing through L.A. It's inconceivably wonderful, Three Steps, One Bow.

Peace in the Way
Heng Ch'au

Lincoln Heights baddies

May 14, 1977

Dear Shr Fu,

We continue to bow about one and a half miles a day, averaging five hours of bowing and one and a half hours of 20-minute rest periods in between each hour. We rise at 4:00 for morning recitation and finish by 6:00 p.m. to wash up and recite evening recitation as always. The day also includes a *t'ai chi ch'uan* lesson from Dharma Master Ch'au in the morning and short reading and translation of the *Avatamsaka Sutra* at night before we recite the first lines of the Shurangama Mantra forty-nine times and then pass out. We are living in one of the upasaka's old Falcon van, sleeping out on the streets of L.A. and washing in the park. Our lunch comes from several Dharma-protecting upasikas. The upasakas and upasikas are watching over us with care. They are working to make our trip go smoothly—getting letters from the police, giving us coins for parking meters, etc. The other morning when it rained, we bowed in the Woo's garage and ate lunch there. We bowed through a tough neighborhood called Lincoln Heights. We reached the front of Lincoln High School just as classes finished. We were immediately surrounded by forty or fifty jeering, shouting, swearing rowdies. When they saw their words couldn't move us, they started to laugh and before long they began to bow along behind us, until we had fourteen boys in line bowing to the *Avatamsaka Sutra*. They all grew more respectful after about six bows—the toughest ones couldn't keep it up—and they went away, silent and sober. No more trouble that day.

The next day at 10:00 I had the sudden awareness that somewhere the demon armies were working up another test for us, a challenge that would appear before long. Friday morning as we neared the end of Lincoln Heights at 10:15 I sensed something up ahead, but I have taken my glasses off and have glued my eyes to my nose for the rest of the journey, so I don't see many details on the road. Heng Ch'au told me later what he saw. A gang of five older men gathered at a taco stand on the corner. One of them was a real demon—ugly, with a misshapen body like a pear. He was jumping around and pointing at us and in his hand he carried a five-foot, sharpened, twisted metal whip. He moved a trash can in front of our path to block the walk and he began to beat it with his whip, making a great noise and denting the sides of the can, all the time pointing at us and trying to provoke his buddies into a similar rage. Heng Ch'au says he was a genuine, big-league baddie, beyond the reach of reason or words. As I bowed along I didn't see any of this, but suddenly I had the strong feeling of invisible aid, a wonderfully good, powerful presence. I had a great feeling of calmness and light.

Heng Ch'au says that as I bowed right into the middle of the group at the taco stand, the leader suddenly went out like a light. He lost his anger and he grew very obedient, like a small child. The others sat motionless at their tables as I bowed around the garbage can below their feet and walked on across the street to bow on the other side. A young, clean man stepped out of his doorway and asked politely, "Can you tell me about your religion, please? I'm very impressed by what you are doing..." and Heng Ch'au told him briefly what the trip was for. He explained quite well.

I can't say for certain who was there leading us through the streets of Los Angeles, but it certainly felt like there were some special responses that morning.

If there is a living being who has a thought of hostility towards the Bodhisattva, the Bodhisattva also views him with kind eyes. To the very end he has not the slightest anger.

Avatamsaka Sutra
Ten Transferences Chapter

Disciple Heng Sure
bows in respect

* * *

Some false thoughts and recollections: a group of disciples brought picnic lunch and change for the parking meters. I can't begin to fathom Chinese social rituals and protocol. In Chinatown an old couple (Mandarin) exclaimed, "Why, they're foreigners!" No, I thought, we are just bringing over the quality stuff you forgot (Buddhism). In fact, until we are all enlightened, we are all foreigners.

Heng Sure's pants are back, fixed and patched with a bright Hawaiian floral print. The long robe helps cover the patch and keep a proper deportment: The kids in Lincoln Heights would have eaten us up for such an inconsistency. People are skeptical, they scrutinize everything we do—from our shoelaces to where our eyes wander. No room for mistakes or indulgence.

Steering the Middle Way with offerings is hard. When we get "junk," we fix it up by rinsing off the oil, diluting the sugar, and sewing the holes with patches. When we get "gold," we tarnish and cover it. Think we'll dye the circus hobo pants Bhikshu brown and gray.

Lay disciple: "Well, you'll be out of L.A. in a month."

Monk: "Oh?"

Lay disciple: "Yeah. I figure the hardest part is over (Lincoln Heights). Chinatown is a little better, and Beverly Hills, no problem."

Monk: "The hardest part is inside. It's never easy."

Lay disciple: "Oh." (smile of recognition)

Bowing: Sometimes after countless ups and downs, coming and going on the cement, there is simply nothing. Sounds, conversations, hecklers, restaurant smells, cigarette butts—no problem. At times, even the "me" gets lost, unimportant, blended into it all, yet untouched and separate. Patience and humility comes easier after bumping noses with ants, in between lumps of welded chewing gum and broken bottles. It's just fine. The place to be now. Cleaning house, inside-out.

Chinatown:

1) Least Buddhist of all. Animals being slaughtered openly ("fresh").

2) On main corner: We are bowing. A parade funeral replete with marching band playing "Will We Not See You Again," motorcycle cops, crowds, small local circus on the right, a big strawberry cake appears in front of us on a chair, a Chinese T.V. newsman taking pictures. We bow through and under. Only a handful notice.

3) Bowing two feet from swimming fish in market window tank. Waiting to die. Both of us. Blub, blubbing with their mouths, us quietly reciting. Both watching each other in our "tanks".

4) Crazy lady who has been following us cackling, sneaks up behind and kicks me right in the acupuncture point in groin. Keep bowing, wondering where we met before and where we will again. Feeling sick.

5) Drive around corner and pass through an intersection to park. A few seconds later crash, bang bang! a terrible accident. We missed it by seconds. A Chinese street gang swaggers by. What a fine way to cultivate! Much peace in the Dharma from two "foreigners."

Disciple Heng Ch'au
bows in respect

Where do you think you are, Mecca?

May 18, 1977

8:00 a.m.

Dear Shr Fu,

We appreciate the wonderful weather that the dragons are sending Los Angeles. It's not too hot and not too cold.

We are very tired in body, but very happy in mind. Every joint, muscle, and limb is speaking its own pain-dharma but this will gradually disappear as the work progresses and our bodies adjust. We fall asleep every night after reciting the Shurangama Mantra, totally exhausted, but the next morning wake up at 4:00 feeling energized and ready to work again. We have increased the bowing time gradually each day: yesterday was six and three quarters hours. The problem in the city is trying to find a parking place for our Bodhimanda/van, and then walking back to the bowing site. It really eats up the rest periods.

Although we are tired, it helps keep us mindful. It is a small problem and it feels good to be working.

Yesterday we received lunch offerings from the L.A. lay disciples and each time it is a humbling experience. We have no merit and virtue of our own. We are simply borrowing the Venerable Abbot's merit to receive the treatment we get. Truly, if it were not for the faith these lay people have in the Venerable Abbot, this trip would be impossible. We would have starved already, or been robbed and beaten each night we stop to rest.

By returning the light this way it makes clear the responsibility for us to be left-home people at all times—to learn how to behave correctly with lay-people, with other left-home people, with Americans, with all people. It is time for us to learn how to stand up for Buddhism on our own, to take responsibility for the teaching we have received and to do it correctly.

Proper conduct is hard work, just as hard as bowing and we are happy for the chance to learn it.

* * *

6:00 a.m.

Dear Shr Fu,

One of the laymen is going to Gold Mountain today so this will be a quick note.

We are making slow progress—about ten city blocks per day. We are now in the center of downtown L.A. and although the buildings are large and the sidewalks are broad, we find it a tougher neighborhood than Lincoln Heights or Chinatown. The rich people do not want us on their sidewalks and they radiate a kind of depersonalized hatred at seeing two monks being repentant beneath their feet. A well-dressed woman in her forties stamps by, inches from our heads and fingers and shouts through clenched teeth, "Where do you think you are, Mecca? That is disgusting in the United States!" Heng Ch'au isn't talking to people who don't ask sincere questions, but his answer to this woman could have been, "Yes, you're right. And that's just the problem. Until it's no longer disgusting, this country is in trouble."

Sleeping at night in this city is a very tense business. We try to find spots to park our van near to the bowing site but last night another thief stuck his hand in the open window. He went away quietly when we shut the window. We are awake at the time and ready to do morning recitation, but it is still an unsettling experience. Heng Ch'au tells me I woke up last night and began talking in my sleep about "waiting for the *hu fa*'s (Dharma Protectors) on the corner of the block by the bank." He says I talked in Chinese for three minutes before going to sleep. I was rattling away while sound asleep.

Our appetites have decreased. We are eating less and bowing more. Our pace is slow—the same speed as when we request the Sutra-lecture Dharma at Gold Mountain. This is a wonderful method of cultivation.

Disciples Heng Sure and Heng Ch'au
bow in respect.

Moonies in Beverly Hills

May 24, 1977

Dear Shr Fu,

We are just about to pass through Beverly Hills—making slow but steady progress. When the traffic is fast and the people are dense it is easy to speed up your bowing without noticing. So we have made a conscious effort to slow down our bowing to a mindful rhythm and the result is we have become invisible to many people. Los Angeles moves so fast that we look like trees, rocks or parking meters to the majority who breeze by in their cars; those who see us roll down their windows and scold us, swear at us, honk their horns, scream, laugh, some even slow down to give advice ("get up," "go home," "get off the street").

Sometimes we get praise from people. Some think we are Moslems or Hare Krishnas or Moonies, and every so often someone recognizes us as Buddhists. The children are open to us, fascinated and pure.

Although we could not be with the Master on Buddha's birthday, Heng Ch'au and I wish to bow nine times to the Master on this occasion. We are ever mindful of our good fortune to have met the proper Dharma here in the West.

The Master's great compassion and vow-power have made it possible to bring good medicine to living beings; our lives have a useful purpose and a positive direction to travel. Cultivating the Way is a priceless treasure!

When we are sincere, the results are immediately visible—anger disappears from faces—the tension dissolves from street-corner groups that gather to stare at us, and even the heat in the air seems to cool slightly. If we are false-thinking or have any anger or fear in our own minds, then nothing happens as we bow into a crowded area; or worse, the tension builds up and people get hot or uptight as we pass and we reap the results in increased cursing, anger, and fear from the crowd. The pressure makes a rare chance to cultivate.

The Dharma Protectors make it possible and the pressure makes it real, good, hard work. There is a lot of magic on this trip and the Master's presence is always close by.

Mindfulness of a cultivator

May 25, 1977

This experience is rich in learning, tests, and exposure to all kinds of people and situations. Heng Ch'au and I talk about the states we encounter and apply the principles we have learned to solve our problems. Each time we trace a problem back to a flaw in our own perception of reality, to a hang-up, an affliction, or an attachment, we know we have found the source of the problem and then the state almost immediately resolves itself.

The mindfulness of a cultivator is not easy to maintain all the time—especially these three: patience with all states, compassion for all beings, even the demons who come to provoke us, and also a sense of shame—keeping my faults and shortcomings in front of me at all times, in all places.

When these three dharmas are ever before my mind, a kind of vajra resolve takes over, people seem to look right past me and see the *Avatamsaka* instead. This is what I'm working for, I have to make my conduct clean and pure all the time. The job now is to learn how to behave properly as a Bhikshu. This work will not be wasted!

Too much hate in this world

May 29, 1977

Please do not worry about us—Heng Ch'au and I are doing okay—we've hit a regular pace—and bow about 5½-6 hours each day. We start bowing at 7:00 a.m., take one hour off at 10:30 to write and repair our gear or meditate—start again at 1:00 p.m. and bow until 6:00, taking twenty-minute stillness breaks each hour. At 6:00 we find a spot to park the van for the night, wash up, meditate, and prepare for *wan k'e*. We listen to the *Avatamsaka* each night— I recite and translate from Chapter One—we haven't got a tape recorder yet, so we haven't been able to listen to the tapes of the Master—and then we say the Shurangama Mantra forty-nine times (the short version) and then rest, as tired as young boys after a full day outdoors. I forgot to add that we get up at 4:00, do *zao k'e* and exercise, and then prepare to start by 7:00 a.m. As we leave the city behind we will be able to add more bowing hours each day.

Our bodies have adjusted to the work slowly. We are exhausted each night and ready to go again each morning. We took off our gloves last week because we felt it was insincere. These sidewalks are pretty smooth and we don't need gloves until we get into glass and gravel on the highway shoulder. We took off our sunglasses, too, because people thought we were hijackers. I started using kneepads several days ago after I developed a deep, aching bruise on my left knee from so much bowing. With the knee pads I can bow all day—we did 6 hours and 20 minutes yesterday. As soon as the bruise heals, I'll take the pads off. Heng Ch'au is still wearing his hat to cover his leaving-home burn scars, but they will be all

healed within a week. We have stopped all useless talking—
plugged that leak.

The two of us are really looking forward to the Master's visit to
L.A. next week. We long to hear the proper Dharma-wheel turned
the way young babies rely on their parents. Our thoughts turn to the
Venerable Abbot and to the Avatamsaka Assembly the way bees
turn to honey.

We have bowed through Beverly Hills and we are nearing
U.C.L.A. in Westwood. By next weekend we should be out of
Santa Monica and on Highway 1, ready to trade our van for a cart
and to start the long road north to the City of Ten Thousand
Buddhas. Each time I think of *Wan Fwo Ch'eng*[1] I visualize a
bright torch in the gloom. The Master's vision of a Buddhist city
based on true, wholesome principle is the very best medicine for all
beings. Sometimes while bowing along through L.A., I feel myself
at the point of tears—happy tears at the hope and the goodness in
store for the West. We *can* turn our lives around and go towards the
good and we now have a road to travel on, a road that will carry us,
our parents, our friends, young and old, back to a place of purity
and light, balance, and harmony. I wouldn't care if the road from
L.A. to *Wan Fwo Ch'eng* was 70,000 miles instead of 700. I'd still
feel it to be my sacred trust to bow and pace every step of the Way.

Disciple Heng Sure
bows in respect

* * *

---

[1]   The City of Ten Thousand Buddhas

Dear Shr Fu,

Broken rules, broken mirror.

Heng Sure and I have been going by the principle: if we hold the rules and precepts we will be okay. The other day we took too long after lunch and were ½ hour late getting back to the bowing site. As we dawdled getting our trip together at a gas station, a black van came roaring by and smashed our side mirror. The retribution mirrors the offense—broken rule, broken mirror. Now, every time I have to crane my neck out to check traffic because of no mirror, I am reminded of that mistake, realizing it could be my head next time.

Bow, bow, bow—all the time bow. I have so much arrogance I don't even see it until I start bowing. Like breathing—so unconscious, automatic. It's only when you stop breathing that you realize how vital it is. Only when I start bowing do I realize how huge my arrogance is. The bowing lifts that weight off my body. Lightness always follows bowing—bowing in the magic circle.

Some conversations. Two older women circle us. They're friends, it seems, but at odds.

1st woman: "Ridiculous!"

2nd woman: "Bless you."

1st woman: "Ridiculous!"

2nd woman: "Bless you."

Three hyped-up teen girls buzz up, spewing questions, "What are you doing? Where are you going?"

Monk: "Same place you are—nowhere."

Girls: "Why do you have to do it so low to the ground?"

Monk: "So we don't get lost—if we get too high, we get lost."

Girls: "Where do you sleep—a motel?"

Monk: "In sleeping bags."

Girls: "Why don't you drive to this Buddha City, it would be faster?"

Monk: "Too easy. Anybody could do that."

Girls: "Are you with the Hare Krishnas?"

Monk: "No."

Girls: "They shave their heads, too."

Monk: "That's as far as it goes."

Girls: "Well, I don't get it. I mean, why are you doing it?"

Monk: "To clean up our act and hopefully to get rid of all the hate, bad vibes, and disasters on the planet."

Girls: "Good luck."

More conversations: A little girl coolly glides her hotwheels to a stop inches from Heng Sure and with wide-open eyes asks, "What are you doing, Mister?" I explain. Later as we stop for a break she comes cruising up again. "Why did you stop?"

Monk: "We didn't stop."

Girl: "But you're not bowing."

Monk: "We're still bowing inside."

Girl: (quietly and thoughtfully) "Oh." An older girl with an edge, "What is *this* anyhow?" etc. I'm getting nowhere with her. Finally she says, "Well, you believe in what you do and I in what I do. You won't convince me and I won't change you."

Monk: "What do you believe in?"

Girl: "I believe in God."

Monk: "So do I. *All of them.*"

Girl: (emphatically, bothered) "But I believe in *one* God only!"

Monk: "Does your one God only believe in you?"

Girl: "Well, ah, ah, ah—take care of yourselves..." she mumbles away, talking to herself.

Monk: "*You*, too."

Flashy car squeals up, "Yoohoo, yoohoo, hey—hey you guys. What are you doing? Are you Krishnas?"

Monk: "No. Buddhist monks."

Girl: "What?"

Monk: "Buddhist. Buddhist monks."

Girl: "*Oh, Buddhist.* Wow! Far out! Great! I love it. I *love* it!"

An older man: "They're in a fraternity. That's part of the hazing they have to go through to join the fraternity."

An old woman watched us with a skeptical and discerning eye for about half an hour. Finally she said, "*Okay*, God bless you," and left.

"I think we passed," added Heng Sure. A young photographer, sincere, came and asked to take pictures and for information. "You know, there is something very beautiful around you," he said. "I can see and feel it."

Two very old ladies out on a walk, leaning on each other for support, stop and patiently watch, waiting for a chance to talk. Timidly, one asks, if they can disturb us.

Lady: "Well, I don't care what religion you are. I think it's wonderful praying like this. We really admire you."

Monk: "There's too much hate in the world. If we can change our hate into peace…"

Lady: "Well, I am sure whoever bothers you will find a little peace."

A *windy* day, this one!

Disciple Heng Ch'au
bows in respect

We are trying our best to go home

June 8, 1977

Dear Shr Fu,

We drove ahead to check out the road: sheer cliffs on one side and private beach homes on the other—barbed wire fences and menacing warning signs protecting it all. Like this until Malibu, maybe further. Reluctantly we decide to keep the van for a while. "Don't force it... accord with conditions."

There's so much to learn about being a monk: deportment, rules, ceremonies, when to speak and when to shut up, who to talk with and who to avoid. It all comes slow and hard. Usually I learn quickly but here it's not simply a question of imitating, but of transforming from the inside out. In other words, the understanding has to come from within. Can't fake it. The heart and mind have to change, and that takes time, a good teacher, hard work, and patience. In the meanwhile, I blunder along from sloppy mistakes to gross errors. A phony monk would be transparent to anyone, especially himself.

Heng Sure has been plagued with a battle of diarrhea all afternoon. No complaining—just hanging in. He's dead asleep now, propped up against the spare tire. After lunch the hoots and hollers began again. A car pulled up, "Hey, you guys want a joint?" plus some obscenities about Jesus. The police (that is, the Los Angeles County Sheriff) stopped to watch but did not question us. A lot of little miniature dogs came charging up to their fences as we passed, doing their guard duties in pink ribbons. And everybody jogs here. From the time we get up until we fall asleep we hear the constant footfalls of tennis shoes and huffing all around us. People are pretty mellow and accepting. We wind through like a trickle of water along the gutter after a light rain: unobstructed and unnoticed.

I hope all is well at Gold Mountain. We do miss the Sutra lectures. Every night we read from the *Avatamsaka* at the same time you do.

Today we are very tired and sunburned. We bowed close to the road (no sidewalks, small shoulder) in alternate fashion to be more visible. Our flowing robes are real traffic-safety assets: very noticeable along with the bald heads. From the beach someone yells, "Go home, baldies!" I thought to myself, "We are trying our best to go home—to *truly* go home."

At the last five minutes of the day on this busy, dirty stretch of road a man and woman walked up. The man bowed once, stuffed something in my hand and said either, "peace" or "please" (diesel trucks too noisy to hear clearly), and walked away quickly. It was a $50 bill—half a Buddha for the City of Ten Thousand Buddhas.

Disciple Heng Ch'au
bows in respect

24

Easy to say and hard to do

June 10, 1977

Dear Shr Fu,

We are parked in Will Rogers Beach, with the Pacific waving on the left and the metal river of Highway 1 flowing on the right. As we bow we make our own rhythmic waves, and the mountains come down to the shore in a graceful, waving motion, as if they, too, are bowing in the Dharma-body of Vairocana.

The chance to cultivate the Buddha's Middle Way on a journey like Three Steps, One Bow is truly wonderful. One might hope for such a chance and not find it. I have written in the log about making the most of this chance and I will send it (a long essay) when the book is filled. Briefly, it says that to cultivate the Way successfully one cannot be casual or part-time or anything less than totally, completely, sincere all the time. You can't pretend, or fake it, or take vacations. You have got to really *want* to walk the Bodhisattva path, and *want* to make the total control of body, mouth, and mind a natural, genuine way of life that comes from the core/nature. Nothing else will do the job. To try to act virtuous at one time and then forget it the next time is not the Buddha's Way. In order to be truly worthy of your teaching, Shr Fu, in order to be worthy vessels of the Dharma, our cultivation has got to be right on, all the time. For me this means that when bowing I bow without any false thoughts, without any desires or hopes or wishes. And then when the bowing is done, to act selflessly, to seek nothing, to have no selfish thoughts and to move only in accord with principle, so that every situation reflects the training and the consciousness of a cultivator at Gold Mountain. Our attitude out here on the road is that we *are* at Gold Mountain, not different.

That is the ideal and it is easy to say and hard to do; and it will take a total transformation of my nature to make it real. Nothing else will suffice. And going slowly as we are, there may be just enough time to crack the "black lacquer barrel." Not a minute too long, and this fact makes me really ashamed. The daily bowing lets me see that I have enough greed, hatred, and stupidity for any three people. And that means I've got to work three times as hard to change; but if I'm going to be of any use to the Triple Jewel, that's where the work is at.

Disciple Heng Sure
bows in respect

* * *

False Thinking Hurts.

Bowing along the Pacific Coast Highway this morning (June 7), I started to false-think about a letter I needed to write. Suddenly there was this sharp pain in my head—like an electric nail being driven in. Immediately, I started reciting again and the pain vanished within thirty seconds.

This happened once at Gold Mountain in front of the Gwan Yin altar. The pain was like a bolt and almost knocked me down. As I started to recite, it subsided.

It seems when it is quietest outside, it is deafening inside. Bowing along this serene, foggy, misted, coastal park, you would think concentrating would come easy. But for some reason, my mad mind churned at a high rpm: trying to remember names of old friends, favorite foods, past travels, my family. Some were "good" false thoughts and some were "bad". It didn't seem to matter. The point was, they kept coming and coming, just like the waves breaking and crashing on the beach below. Constant motion: the ocean and my mind. To actually stop the "mad mind," I can't imagine. "Patience, patience, got to have patience."

It's at this point I can feel it wanting to shoot out. My energy and tension builds up and if I don't pay close attention, anger pops out, or my eyes start attaching to sights, my ears notice and dwell on sounds, I feel irritable and impatient—the "fire goes up", and if I'm sloppy, more bad karma is set in motion. In some ways the ghetto gangs and hostile construction crews are easier to bow through than a peaceful park. Outside danger forces total inner concentration: outside pleasant, then inside is free to lazily drift and scatter.

Disciple Kuo T'ing (Heng Ch'au)
bows in respect

Looking "dumb" in T'ang dynasty robes

June 11, 1977

Dear Shr Fu,

Bowing through the grease and oil, broken glass and grime of the asphalt does a messy number on the robe and *yi* (sash)… grease "monk-*yi*'s."

At the Beach.

From behind, a little voice, "Hey, Mister, aren't you *un*barrassing yourself?" We keep bowing. Again, "Hey, Mister, what are you doin'?" "We're Buddhist Monks. We're praying," I answer him. "What are you doing?" "Watching you be dumb," he answers without hesitation.

Looking over to my left I see oodles of people in swimming suits playing volley ball, sunbathing, swimming, surfing, sailing, eating—just plain old Saturday afternoon good times at the ocean. I start looking pretty "dumb" to myself sometimes. Baking in this hot sun under T'ang Dynasty robes, picking glass and gravel out of my hands and forehead… that water looks so inviting right now. Anyway, I've done all that, the beach and sunbathing, so I'll keep at this cultivating stuff somemore. The water still looks inviting though, and we still look "dumb". Then I remember my vows and how clear and happy my heart was when I made them; and suddenly the bowing and the gravel and the broken glass feel right at home. Never been happier, never looked more "dumb". The *Avatamsaka* says, "…all happiness in the world is suffering." We are finding the converse is just as true: all the suffering of cultivation is happiness.

Disciple Heng Ch'au
bows in reverence

* * *

Labor Day Weekend.

Dear Shr Fu,

> _Don't be pleased if gods, dragons,_
> _and Bodhisattvas come,_
> _Don't be angry if demons_
> _and externalists come._

Some days it's hard not to feel overjoyed. I feel full of happiness today—I can barely contain it. It's a feeling like the Buddha's birthday, the Master's birthday, and Ullambana all rolled into one surprise gift—a visit out of empty space by the Venerable Abbot and fourteen Gold Mountain cultivators and friends.

What was the occasion? Just another exercise of the Bodhisattva practice of forgetting oneself for the sake of others. Where else in the world are there people like these who got up at 4:00 a.m. and drove 350 miles south from San Francisco to Santa Barbara just to bring lunch and support and encouragement to two members of the family on an extended work leave? Inconceivable! How did they ever find us—half-hidden in the shade off a lonely highway outside Santa Barbara? How did Heng Ch'au and I both know that something special was coming that day? This morning he said, "Let's stay out and be visible today." Why did I clear a sitting area under a certain eucalyptus tree hours before they arrived—the same tree we all sat beneath? How did three cars speeding along, dodging tickets and asking the way from passers-by, manage to

Venerable Master and disciples travel from the City of Ten Thousand Buddhas to visit the monks at the bowing site.

Fall, 1977

The Master and disciples receive offerings at the noon
meal and share Dharma with the donors.

Fall, 1977

arrive at the same time—just before lunch hour? *Only* through the power of goodness could the small miracle we saw today come about. We all witnessed a feat of spiritual engineering, the kind of thing that happens all the time at Gold Mountain.

Seated in the van as usual at lunch time, we had recited the offering praise and had dished out a bowl of rice. Before I could eat the first spoonful I saw Heng Ch'au's eyes pop open and heard his voice squeak, "Shr Fu!" I thought to myself, "Impossible. But wait! You've learned to appreciate the impossible!" "Shr Fu!" he said again. I turned to see the Venerable Abbot, dressed in blazing golden robes, walking through the pools of sunlight to our car.

There they all came walking—three carsful of people aglow with inner light: monks, nuns, novices, and laypeople—they looked closer than blood relatives, hard-working, well-comported heroes and heroines of the Way: such a rare and wonderful assembly of people!

We all sat for lunch and listened to stories and instructions. We laughed and shared food and offerings with our Dharma friends, then up and away the assembly went on the long ride back to the city. They just came down to give us light. Wonder of wonders. I felt made of wood—stunned. I wanted to give thanks, to acknowledge the work and the kindness of everyone—I had to let my heart and my eyes speak for me.

Sitting next to the Venerable Abbot is like sitting in a cool, clear pool of liquid light. No thought bothers your head (whose head?). The Great Compassion Mantra seems to recite itself—just as regularly and as normally as your heart beats. Perceptions are clear, sharp, and relaxed. No worries exist, no pressures. Even if I'm being taught or scolded it feels like sweet dew. I'm sure that sitting in the Buddha's Dharma Assembly is much like this.

Then, inconceivably, the Master rubbed my head, then rubbed Heng Ch'au's head. I feel energy moving through my center, to my toes and back again. "Is it ripe yet? Is it ripe? Is this melon ripe yet?" he asked, laughing, as he thunked our foreheads with his fingertip.

Bowing later that afternoon, as if on air, we looked up to find a mammoth white cloud, the only cloud in a bright blue sky, as big as the Sierra Madres below, moving northwest and shaped exactly, perfectly like a dragon in full flight. Every detail was there: tails, ears, claws, and as the afternoon turned to evening, the dragon moved further north. We felt that he was hovering over the caravan of cultivators on the road back to Gold Mountain.

So there are days when it is difficult not to feel overjoyed, and Labor Day, 1977, will live in our memories as long as the tall eucalyptus stands, the "White Flower Tree" that shaded our lunch along the Flower Garland Highway. To share affinities with cultivators whose lives are dedicated to making others happy with no thought of themselves is truly a life worth living.

Disciple Kuo Chen (Heng Sure)
bows in respect

* * *

Dear Shr Fu

Sunday, while bowing, I had a vision of everyone at Gold Mountain having a chance to do their own bowing once every three steps. Laypeople and left-home people, all got to pursue to the "limits of empty space" our own particular Dharma. Each person's face and presence was glowing and serene. So happy were the faces! No face showed any concerns or doubts, just smooth, genuine, lit-up joy! It was really neat! Each person was different, yet all reflected the same purity and trueness. There was a closeness felt; a big family of Dharma friends shining on each other.

And then on Monday, the very next day, who drives up? The Master and the four-fold Great Assembly! I wanted to hug everybody and give something. A few tears dropped into my noodles as I looked around at all the faces and goodness sharing and shining as we sat under some eucalyptus trees that minutes before were just another stopping place for us.

Bhikshuni Heng Yin stretched up on tiptoes to carve and commemorate the occasion on a high eucalyptus tree with a Swiss army knife as a visitor named Malcolm sitting with an untouched plate of food in his lap stared incredulously. Malcolm had brought out a melon to share with two monks in a quiet lunch and then everyone drove up. The Master gestured for him to join in with irresistible and inclusive kindness. I felt a bit like Malcolm: speechless and overwhelmed by the awesome virtue of the Assembly.

As fast as you came, you left. "No big deal," said the Master. A huge, mile-long dragon cloud hung in the otherwise totally cloudless sky for hours, and the joy and light you brought to our hearts and work will see us through many bowing miles.

But something more incredible happened. The Master knew the exact section of the *Sixth Patriarch's Sutra* we had read that very morning. His comments and allusions to it were right on the nose! Not only that, but the Master also knew my deepest thoughts and troubles of the last few days. I hadn't told anyone, not even Heng Sure. "So how did I know?" the Master laughed and asked. And the same for Heng Sure. After everyone left, we were like ten-year-olds again, smiling and ready to tackle the Labor Day highway. "Together we will go to Perfect Enlightenment. I hope so. I hope so." Much peace in the Way.

Disciple Kuo Ting (Heng Ch'au)
bows in respect

Lay disciples come often to the bowing site, bringing food and encouragement.

Fall, 1977

Two "monks" assault a teenager

June 16, 1977

Dear Shr Fu,

We are three miles outside of Malibu and making our way along the gutters and driveways of the Pacific Coast Highway. Kuo Shih and Kuo Hsiang Woo are coming out this Sunday with the little cart which we parked at Gold Wheel, and they'll drive the green van back to South Pasadena. Outside of Malibu it looks like the countryside opens up and we will be able to find spots to pitch the tent at night and camp. The trip should change in flavor at that time—no more leap-frogging through the traffic to a parking space and then walking back to resume the bowing. But through the populated parts of the trip, through L.A., the van was the only way to go. Now that we're on open road with the traffic flying by, the truth of the proverb "*When you get to the mountain, there's sure to be a road*," is really evident. What looks to the eye like a totally impassable section of road for monks and pedestrians, looks very different from your knees. Bowing space always appears, naturally and effortlessly before us. It's pretty amazing. People come up and say, "You bowed through there? Where?" I hope it is the same when we encounter the superhighway.

Gold Mountain Buddhists have already got a good reputation with the law authorities—for being peaceful, law-abiding, rule-following citizens. Not far from here in Topanga last week there was a bad incident: two robe-wearing, shaven-headed young men who fit our description assaulted a sixteen-year-old boy and held him at knife-point for an hour. Two L.A. Sheriffs stopped us, frisked us, did a whole series of check-outs for warrants, I.D.'s, etc., etc. When they decided that we were not the ones they wanted, they relaxed (they said they thought the assailants were Hare Krishnas) and asked a little bit about our trip. The cops were efficient, and they left wishing us well. Three days later (yesterday afternoon) we were suddenly surrounded by four more squad cars and a paddy wagon. They came out of nowhere and swarmed like moths around a lightbulb. This group didn't know about the first check-out, and approached us very hostilely and warily, saying, "Do you have your knives on you?" Heng Ch'au answered, "We are not allowed to carry weapons, it's against the rules." "Oh, are you Buddhists or Krishnas?" "We are Buddhists!" "Oh, yeah, it's you guys. Okay. No problem. Say, do you do that bowing all day?" Heng Ch'au said, "Yes. We get up at 4:00 and pray and meditate and bow until 10:00 p.m. We eat one vegetarian meal a day." Whistles of admiration, grins, and slow shakes of heads from the cops: "Wow. Only one meal a day? Okay, see you later. Watch out for cars. Good luck."

Shr Fu, the visit to Gold Wheel Temple gave us a great deal of inspiration and turned our work in wonderful ways. To witness the Master's selflessness, his virtue and compassion brings us great delight. At Gold Mountain it is easy to rely on the Master's constant presence and his every-day example of virtuous conduct. Away from Gold Mountain, out here on the road, meeting with people from all directions, we get a keen appreciation of the Master's consummate skill and eloquence, his mastery of human-nature and his penetration of others' conditions and potentials. Most uncanny in the Sage is the strength of water: it never contends at any point. It yields, takes the last place, the lowest place, accords with all conditions but never struggles. This is easy to speak of, exceptionally difficult to practice and most awesome to witness. I find myself asking: "What would Shr Fu do in a situation like this?" The answer: "Don't false think! Never mind! What are you going to do? You can't climb on your teacher's conditions all your life. Stand on your own feet! Use your own wisdom! Accord with conditions and do not move! Turn the light back, be patient and 'don't get angry *swo pwo he.*' Be like water. The soft overcomes the hard."

I wrote an essay on responses, and one of the paragraphs goes like this:

> *So have I had any responses? No, nothing magical. I'm too raw, too much a beginner with too many karmic debts to pay back; but on the other hand, amid mundane dharmas I have had a response. I've clearly seen the foundation of my cultivation and the purpose of my life. This is a response. I don't know how to fly or even how to run. I don't yet know how to walk, but I'm practicing bowing and slowly, surely, under the patient and compassionate guidance of a good and wise Teacher, I am learning how to stand on my own, and how to stand for Buddhism.*

Jotted this down while waiting out a case of diarrhea on a very hot afternoon:

THREE STEPS, ONE BOW / GOLD MOUNTAIN CULTIVATION IS:

no talking	no drinking	only prayer
no looking	no smoking	only shame
no joking	no lying down	only reflection
no watching	no relaxing	only others
no listening	no hiding	
no self		

Disciple Heng Sure
bows in respect

A narrow escape at Highway One

November 16, 1977

Dear Shr Fu,

Sometimes the practice of the Bodhisattva Path is very "conceivable". We're perched on a sandy field of scrub oak and dry, dry grass. The Lompoc Federal Prison is over the hills to the West, and Vandenberg Air Force Base lies to the north. A more cheerless, bleak, November landscape is hard to imagine. The bowing is over for the day and the wind which has been whipping the hilltops since noon now has some real teeth in it. I've lit the oil lamp to write these lines that occurred to me just moments ago as the sun fell, red and windswept.

A Bodhisattva's work is never done; there is no 9 to 5 day in the job of cultivation. There is no Monday to Friday workweek, no retirement with bonus at age 65. The *Avatamsaka Sutra* tells us that living beings have no end, they are infinite and boundless, yet the Bodhisattva has vowed to save them all. Therefore, his work does not end. A Bodhisattva saves himself, too, and by cultivating the Proper Dharma, he gains wisdom, compassion, and expedient power. This wisdom allows him to get involved in the gritty, muddy middle of the mundane world and work to save others right where they live and suffer most. However, the Bodhisattva has broken all attachments to his self. He no longer has desires, so his work for others gives him more happiness and satisfaction than a lifetime of leisurely vacations and selfish pleasure-pursuits. The Bodhisattva rests in his work and works while he rests. Life is work and work is bliss—a truly wonderful state of mind.

Just as I wrote the last line, out of the darkness came a knock on the car window and a tight voice said, "Uh, hey, we're stuck in the sand, can you give us a tow?" Heng Ch'au did not hesitate, but stepped outside, and found two unhappy men. He said, "Sure, be right there." We repacked the lamps and meditation gear and drove through the ruts and flying sand to extract a pickup truck and put it back on the road. Reciting the Great Compassion Mantra has become automatic whenever we aren't bowing or reciting ceremonies. Its strength lifted the truck out with ease, our Plymouth providing solid muscle as well. We walked through the headlights back to the car.

"Thanks, you guys, a real lifesaver," said the men greatly relieved.

"No problem," replied Heng Ch'au.

A small matter and easily accomplished, but it added cheer and light to this desolate central California coast.

At other times the events that occur in the practice of the Way are truly inconceivable. We see so little of what is actually going on in the world behind the facade of the senses. We just piece together bits and echoes of the actual reality. Bowing along on a Friday afternoon I suddenly sensed the Venerable Abbot's presence right in my heart. He sat in full lotus, reciting a mantra, apparently, and this image calmed my mind profoundly. Suddenly, fifty yards ahead I heard the sounds of screeching tires and a huge cloud of dust billowed up. Heng Ch'au later described the scene: apparently a driver fell asleep at the wheel and ran off the road. His car climbed six feet up a sharp embankment then turned, still speeding along, and zoomed straight down towards two cars and a truck that crowded the lanes below. Somehow, unbelievably, the car slipped between a van and a truck, missing both by a hair and continued on down the road, leaving several ashen-faced drivers badly shaken, but happy to be alive. Had the cars collided we would have been right in the middle of the scene—King Yama would have had a busy day receiving new souls from Highway 1. As it turned out, the

Master's image faded from my mind moments later. What is really involved? Who saves all these lives from four hundred miles away, invisibly, without expecting a thank you or any recognition at all for the effort? I have no doubts that it was the Venerable Abbot's presence manifesting in the nick of time that prevented the collision on the road. Prove it? There's no other way to explain how the falling car shoe-horned its way back on the road. How many times have things like this happened in the lives of disciples: narrow escapes from certain death, when Gwan Shr Yin Bodhisattva appeared before people at the critical moment and then disappeared again after all was safe?

As we work to make our hearts a pure place, I've found myself always returning to the basics. For instance, the first thing a new Buddhist learns is how to put his palms together in respect. Joined palms indicate singleness of thought. As the work of cultivation is on the mind-ground, singleness of thought is most important. I noticed that my joined palms mudra has grown rather sloppy, with gaps between fingers and thumbs. Standing next to the Master last week at Gold Wheel Temple before he spoke Dharma, I watched him bow to the Buddhas. I was deeply moved. When the Master joins his palms there is a totality about it—a perfection that can only come from singleness of mind. I tried my new, improved, palms-together while bowing and the mindfulness to the external form *did* quiet my mind inside. The false thoughts were easier to subdue when my palms were fully joined, without gaps or leaks. Back to basics.

Witnessing the Master's bowing is a humbling experience, a good medicine for arrogance and a model for people and gods. His bowing is a completely magical transformation: when the Master bows he disappears. His total lack of ego is revealed, he seems to become one with the Buddhas he bows to. I don't know the Master's state when he bows or at any other time, but something very pure and special happens when he bows before the Buddhas. There is just bowing. It looks as if there is no bower and no one bowed to, it is simple and profound reverence; wonderful to watch.

Back on the road I am learning to bow correctly, from the beginning. Lower the ego to the ground as far as you can, with heart fixed on the Eternally Dwelling Triple Jewel, and then rise up and put your palms together with a single mind on the way to the City of Ten Thousand Buddhas.

Disciple Kuo Chen (Heng Sure)
bows in respect

* * *

Dear Shr Fu,

I am in Lompoc at a gas station waiting for the car. Open, empty country is ahead with no towns and few gas stations for "bowing miles". So I am in town getting supplies and needed repairs for the weeks ahead. Heng Sure is bowing in an isolated field-plateau in the hills overlooking the Federal Prison on the fringe of Vandenberg Air Force Base. This is where we camped last night. The mechanics have advice and humor on the roads ahead and wish us luck.

Shr Fu, it's funny, but lately on this pilgrimage I am finding it more and more natural and honest to be quiet. It isn't that there are no thoughts or feelings. I am happy and full, but not of conversation words. So it is difficult to write because this is a new and unfamiliar place. The words of the Sutras, especially the *Avatamsaka*, are what I like best to hear and repeat. They echo in our hearts all day and are part of this quietness. Other noises and sounds come and go, but the sounds of the Sutras stay, speaking directly to our experience and circumstances. The sounds of the Sutras are natural and blend with the stillness of the wind and trees.

There is a subtle, peaceful merging of these principles and our minds. As we read to each other from the Sutras our faces and eyes light up, saying, "Hey! Yeah! That's it. That's the way it is!" heads nodding, faces smiling in agreement. It often feels as if we have another person with us—a wise and infallible friend who

Heng Chau bowing near Vandenberg Air Force Base.

October 1977

understands our deepest thoughts and feelings—the *Avatamsaka Sutra.*

What we experience, the Sutra explains; what the Sutra explains, we experience. When we get to a place in cultivation neither of us has been before, invariably in the evening the Sutra glows, explaining and expounding on that state. Inconceivable! And there is so much to enter and explore!

As we bowed through the small town of Vandenberg Village at sunset Tuesday, a crowd of some thirty people gathered around—watching, discussing, wondering about us. A little old man stepped out of his house, respectfully walked up and made an offering. With a kind smile and a gesture of his arm to the north he said without words, "Hope this helps you on your way. Keep going. Good luck." Suddenly the tense and uncertain crowd that had quietly watched this dispersed. In a matter of minutes they came streaming back laden with money and food offerings. Old people and young, little kids and grandparents, all smiling, giving, and wishing us well. The power of giving and gathering in by *one* person turned a practically hostile crowd into happy well-wishers.

Driving back from the gas station I found Heng Sure smiling and full of light and peace, bowing in a wind-blown, empty field off Highway 520. As we quietly sat inside the old Plymouth eating a lunch of bread, fruit, nuts, and vegetables, I realized we had bowed ourselves into another world—a crystal pure, and happy place—and we were only beginning. My mind went to Gold Mountain and shortly the Master and entire community. Face after face manifested, squeezed together in the car, all happy, all leaving the Saha dust together. This was home: the eternally dwelling Triple Jewel without a place or limit.

Someday every face we have seen while bowing once every three steps—the police, the kids, mechanics, deer, ants, the old people and prostitutes, reporters, wind, rocks, and clouds—will be one face. All will return and rely on the eternally dwelling Triple Jewel within our true self nature. All living beings have the

Buddha-nature. All will become Buddhas. A very happy day, today.

A woman runs across four lanes of high-speed freeway traffic, slips and slides down a steep embankment to offer homemade cookies and $5—full of smiles all the way.

Much peace in the Way,

Disciple Kuo T'ing (Heng Ch'au)
bows in respect

In the Buddha Hall at Gold Wheel Monastery after receiving instructions from the Venerable Abbot.

November 1977

Returning to Los Angeles for instruction. Bowing in front

old Wheel Monastery, South Pasadena. November 1977

Off by a hair's breadth, off by a thousand miles

January 21, 1978

Dear Shr Fu,

San Luis Obispo is now behind us. Morro Bay is twelve miles ahead and then, nothing but miles and miles of winding coast line to San Francisco. The San Luis passage felt special, rather like a gateless toll-gate. Many big tests of resolve and concentration. We were very aware of the Ch'an Session going on at the City of Ten Thousand Buddhas and felt like our work was a highway Ch'an. Ch'an sessions mirror our cultivation. If the daily work has been carelessly done, you find out right away in a meditation intensive. The pressure reveals the cracks and flaws. Instead of a harvest, the session becomes a trip to the repair shop. City-bowing is the same. All the bad habits that we overlook or fail to smelt out appear as we bow in the city. The false and the hidden aspects of our minds suddenly appear in the spotlight. The verse goes:

In the country, smelt it down.
Test its temper in the town.
Pass or fail we still go on
To contemplate the noumenon.

When cultivators truly use effort, tests are constant, both in the country and in the city. As Shr Fu's disciples we know that, "Everything's a test to see what you will do. Mistaking what's before your face, you'll have to smelt anew."

Heng Ch'au related a test he faced: in Pismo State Park, with not a soul around, he looked for several seconds too long at a beautiful double rainbow in the eastern sky. In a flash his head was filled with images of old desires and habits. In that single glance, he "fell back on the wheel," as in the verse:

When you see things and understand
You transcend the world.
When you see things and are confused,
You fall onto the wheel.

Off by a hair's breadth at the start, D.M. Ch'au missed the mark by a thousand miles in the end and had to resmelt anew.

I faced and failed a similar test. In this case, it was more like being off by a whale's breadth, but the result was the same confusion.

One evening, near Vandenberg Air Force Base, a familiar van swung over and parked ahead. It was the Gold Mountain Chevy van. I didn't have my glasses on, but I'd know that car anywhere. It was at the end of a long day of bowing and my ego was looking for any excuse to leak out. "How wonderful! A surprise visit from our family," I thought. I projected that it was a Bhikshu bringing new Sutra, or food, or maybe a message from Shr Fu. I had the whole greedy scene worked out in my head in no time. "Funny that no one has come out of the van, though; I wonder what they're waiting for? How come Heng Ch'au hasn't walked by me to greet them? Oh well, just finish this day's work and then take your reward. There, the van door's open. Who is it?" I thought. "Howdy fellows, have you accepted Jesus as your personal Savior?" Oh no! A Christian preacher who happens to drive a green Chevy van! Back to the wheel to smelt anew.

The smelting process is just like the daily work in the monastery. Be on time, don't rap, eat just enough and no more, stay mindful of your method, walk the Middle Way at all times, subdue your self at every turn. If the smelting has been patient, vigorous

San Luis Obispo
January, 1978

and sincere, when the city streets appear below our knees the intensity and temper of the metal is measured. The strengths pass the test; the weak spots go back to the furnace for another round. Just as in a meditation session, cultivation goes on as usual, only more so. With the focus on reciting and sitting, the fruits of daily work roll into the storehouse. The barren trees must be pruned back for the next growing season.

This is an example of an inner dialogue that arises during the smelting. "Have I subdued my desire for fame? How's my concentration as reporters from two local papers click, click, click their cameras for hours? Do I move off my center and start to pose? On to the wheel I go. How about food? Am I still attached to flavor and getting full? Let's test it out. Here come Shramanera Kuo Yu's grandparents, Bill and Pat Irelan, with a tray of hot, home-cooked cornbread. All six organs move at once and the mind is filled with clouds of false thoughts. Back to the foundry. Say, what am I cultivating, anyway, besides greed for hot cornbread? How about sleep? It's 8:30, the Sutra's been recited and I am exhausted in every fibre. My bad habits make me impatient; I'm right on the edge of taking a deep dive into sleep. It's time to meditate, but what's the use? I'll only nod out. Shr Fu! What am I gonna do? I'm at the end of my rope. The deeper I go into my mind, the more muck and garbage I turn up. There's no lotus here; there's just mud. Well, I can't go wrong asking my teacher, even if I'm a hopeless case. His compassion is deeper than my stupidity. Try him again. I'm working to stand on my own feet, but this is a time of need. Here's the *Forty-two Sections Sutra*; just open it up to see what it says":

> *Shramanas who study the Way should get a hold on their minds and be vigorous, courageous, and valiant. Not fearing what lies ahead, they should destroy the hordes of demons and obtain the fruits of the Way. Having the strength of precepts, samadhi, and wisdom in order to break through and destroy your beginningless habits and your beginningless pretentions, and all your other faults is analogous to destroying the*

multitudes of demons… Don't turn back halfway. Go forward vigorously and with courage. Only go forward; never retreat. Only advance; never retreat.

Amazing. It's just as if the Master were sitting right here! Then I heard in my inner ear the Master's voice say, "Kuo Chen, you lazy bug. How can you possibly think of sleeping when you haven't done your homework? Do the work just like you wear clothes, just like you eat. Did you skip lunch because you were too tired? No! Well, how can you not meditate? Everyone else is working hard in the Ch'an session, what's your excuse?"

I sat upright, folded my legs into full lotus and sat. My fatigue and my doubts vanished bit-by-bit, like the valley fog before the morning sun. "Pass or fail we still go on to contemplate the noumenon." Who can doubt that drawing near to a wise advisor is 100% of the Way?

Morro Bay	13 miles
Monterey	135 miles
San Francisco	249 miles
City of Ten Thousand Buddhas	one single thought

Broken precepts begin with false thinking

January, 1978

Dear Shr Fu,

Sunday, 3:45 a.m. Up for morning recitation, scramble for sweaters to keep out the morning chill. The highway's deserted and quiet, only the sound of the moon and a softly gurgling creek before we start with the Shurangama mantra.

5:00-6:30 a.m. We write and read Sutras, fill up the kerosene lamp. Sit in meditation.

6:30-7:00 a.m. Do t'ai chi—slipping and sliding on eucalyptus-tree berries.

7:15 a.m. Drive to bowing site on mountain pass in Santa Lucia Mts. Cold, clear, and light wind. Sun rising over the mountains.

8:00 a.m. Four disciples from Los Angeles come out bundled up and ready to bow.

9:00 a.m. A man named Richard quietly joins the bowing procession in front of state Prison outside of San Luis Obispo. "I just saw you and felt sincerity and a bond. So I decided to join in. Is it okay?" Richard said he did a little yoga, t'ai chi and some Ch'an meditation, "and this bowing looks and feels like the same." He made an offering and then left about 10:00 to go back to work. He is a gardener. He's planning to come to the City Of Ten Thousand Buddhas this spring when he has a month vacation.

10:30 a.m. Stop bowing, transfer merit. Drive to field off freeway for meal offering.

10:45 a.m. Run out of gas (no gas gauge).

11-11:30 a.m. Meditate.

11:30-12:15 Meal offering and meal. During the meal a stranger reverently walks up and with folded hands, does a half-bow and offers a bag of fruit and long-stem red roses.

1-2:00 p.m. Gwan Yin praise, Great Compassion mantra and *Avatamsaka Sutra*, translated by Heng Sure. (Tushita Heaven Chapter).

2-6:00 p.m. Bowing. On the way back to the bowing site, I am in a false-thinking samadhi about how to get the extra food offerings to the City of Ten Thousand Buddhas. I spot a turtle right in the middle of the freeway, craning its neck, bewildered. By the time I woke up and thought to liberate it, we'd gone too far. Had to turn around and drive back. We got back just in time to hear and see the turtle popped and splattered by a big, pink Cadillac that ran over it. We feel the turtle's life end right in our stomachs. There is a big lesson here: "Off an inch in the beginning, off by a thousand miles in the end." Had I been according with conditions and not in one place with my body and in another with my mind, I would have been decisive and stopped the car as soon as I saw the turtle stranded in the road. Instead, my false thinking "samadhi" about food caused me to be off by a few seconds and that made all the difference. Bodhisattvas are supposed to liberate and rescue living beings, says the Bodhisattva Precepts. Lesson: broken precepts begin with false thinking and cause disasters and sufferings.

3:00 p.m. A man walks across the heavy traffic to make an offering, saying, "I never knew such a place existed in California (referring to the City of Ten Thousand Buddhas). I want to help out."

4:00 p.m. A woman stops her car outside the prison gate and approaches. "Will you please accept this?" she asks humbly handing me her book of food stamps. "And could you in your prayers include my husband? He's in there," pointing to the prison. "Bless you, God bless you."

5:30 p.m. "Go home you bald-headed farts," from a passing car.

5:40 p.m. A man walks up to us on a narrow and tricky ledge. He almost falls but keeps coming. Handing me a money offering, he says, "When there is veneration, even a dog's tooth emits light." He turns and leaves.

6:00 p.m. We transfer merit, bow to the Triple Jewel and the Master.

6:30-7:30 p.m. Sit in Ch'an.

7:30-9:30 p.m. Recite *Amitabha Sutra* and praise. Translate *Avatamsaka Sutra*.

9:30-10:30 I do some Shao lin exercises and then do standing meditation outside to wake up and to chase out the cold.

10:30-11:15 p.m. Recite mantras and bow to the Patriarchs.

11:15-12:30 p.m. Read Vajra Bodhi Sea and sit in Ch'an.

12:30 Blow out kerosense lamp, hear a "who, who" from a solitary night-owl, and fall asleep.

Much peace in the Dharma,

Disciple Kuo T'ing (Heng Ch'au)
bows in respect

56

Amitabha!

February 22, 1978

Dear Shr Fu,

Back to the Nature.

Best wishes from Three Steps, One Bow to the Venerable Abbot and the Great Assembly. We are in Harmony. Harmony, California, population 18. Halfway between Cayucos and Cambria. Every day the hills get greener, the sky looks bluer, the people get fewer, the morning fog grows thicker. The landscape includes long snakes and long-haired cattle on winter forage. A passing biology major from Cal Poly confirms that what Heng Ch'au saw on Sunday *was* a mountain lion.

On the advice of a Dharma-protector we have begun to eat the green weeds that grow beside the road. Gathering wild food is a good dharma. It's free, like the Buddha-nature. Before we discover that the Buddhas of all time and space come from the mind, we run all over the Dharma Realm looking for the Path. Then we hear it's been inside our true mind all along—all we have to do is uncover it. Ah! Wild food is the same. The fields look full of weeds until someone says, "Hey! That weed you're standing on tastes like the finest supermarket greens, better, even, 'cause it's free and fresh and abundant." Ah! the field of weeds becomes a nutritious garden. The challenge now to the cultivator is to not think of his stomach every time he looks at the ground. Three Steps, One Bow has given us a new appreciation of much that we have overlooked or taken for granted. It deserves mentioning as an inexhaustible storehouse of food for pilgrims and mountain hermits of the future. We don't trip out into extended food-gathering—we can identify five or six varieties of plants that grow nearly everywhere. In five minutes we can pick a potful (watch *carefully* for insects—this is their world, too!), then wash and boil them for two minutes. Done. What's more, we have been looking for more bitter foods to dispel "fire-energy" that comes with meditation. Dandelions and mustard green have just enough natural bitterness to drop the fire without being too bitter to swallow.

Our lives grow more natural and more simple as we bow away the artificial views and habits we learned over the years. The natural and simple truth: all conditioned things will die. Our bodies are temporary unions of earth, air, fire, and water. No amount of natural food will keep the body healthy when it comes time to die. The back-to-nature movement is on the right track, but if it stops with roadside weeds and granola, it hasn't gone back far enough. Buddhist disciples are part of the truly important movement in the modern world—the "back-to-the-'true' nature" movement. The true self-nature does not perish; it is our birthright as living beings. By cultivating the Path that all Buddhas have walked, we return to the biggest Nature there is.

> *The 'wind and light of our original ground' have a special and wonderfully delightful flavor that is quite inexhaustible. If we wish to try its taste we must simply purify our minds.*
>
> Water and Mirror Reflections
> by Venerable Master Hua

You might say the Master is talking about the Bodhi plant—the one we most want to identify, eat, and share with all our Dharma friends. This plant is not in the edible-plant field-guides, because it's special—it grows on the mind-ground. Our teacher shows us where to look, how to recognize it, and how to harvest it. Here is the way it could be listed in *A Buddhist Flora*:

Species: Enlightenment.
Variety: wonderful.
Habitat: within the true heart of all living beings.
Distribution: throughout the Dharma Realm.
Season: eternal.
Description: see Flower Garland Sutra for references.
Wonderful beyond words.

More Car Stories.

Our Plymouth cave-on-wheels is not an ordinary car. We suspect it is a dragon, maybe a transformed disciple of the Master's who volunteered to work on Three Steps, One Bow. The car is always protecting our Dharma and speaking it for us, too. Some nights under the bright moon it just plain looks like a dragon with a beard and tail. It should have collapsed a dozen times by now, but it keeps right on rolling. Once during the heavy storms in early February, the car refused to start. We were parked right on the highway shoulder. The gas station man couldn't start the dragon—nothing worked. The car sat tight while we bowed in ankle-deep puddles. We had planned to drive into Morro Bay that morning to dry the gear out at a laundromat, but no dice—the car was wet. Suddenly a familiar blue bus appeared beside us with three golden figures strapped to the seats. It was Upasaka Kuo Tsai, who had come down to take us and the three Buddha images to L.A. Had we gone to the laundromat he never would have found us. "Well, let's give the car one more try." Vroom! It started like a champ and away we went. "Do you mean to say the car knew someone was coming and deliberately held you there for the rendezvous?" "Well, how else do you explain it?" There are all sorts of strange marvels in the world—countless, inexhaustible, measureless, and unfathomable—and they all proceed from the zero in the mind. How inconceivable! Amitabha!

Disciple Kuo Chen (Heng Sure)
bows in respect

Bowing between winter storms near Morro Bay.
February, 1978.

Venerable Master Hua and cultivators from Gold Mountain Monastery visit the bowing monks.

Nipomo, Central California,1978.

Buddhism in America

February 23, 1978
Harmony, California

Dear Shr Fu,

I wrote a short essay this a.m. about some things that have become clearer to me about Buddhism and America while doing Three Steps, One Bow.

Buddhism in America

Morro Bay, California

This country was settled by people from all over the world— every race and color imaginable. They all shared one thing: the United States, which stood for a chance to start over, an opportunity to change old habits and renew. They were all looking for a paradise they had lost. Leaving their homes and the familiar, they came in search of a pure land and to reclaim their natural innocence. Dreamers and idealists, these people were seekers of stillness and after ultimate peace and freedom. This is still true today and people are still coming to America for liberty and Eden.

But we haven't found it yet. Why? You might say one reason is we weren't looking in the right places. It's a lot like the story in the *Dharma Flower Sutra* about a wealthy man whose son was discontent and wanted to run away from home. But before he left, his parents, fearing he would become a drifter and penniless vagrant, secretly sewed a wish-fulfilling pearl in their son's clothing. The son left and sure enough became down-and-out. But he didn't realize that a priceless pearl was sewn in his clothing so he couldn't benefit from it.

Americans are a lot like the wealthy man's son. We are always unhappy at home and itching for freedom. So we have run outside: pursued wealth and sought "more, better, and bigger"—cars, homes, and highs. Yet all this worldy accomplishment that has made this the richest country in the world has not produced paradise. Our material success has brought little freedom or security. We are as restless and uprooted as ever, maybe even more so than two hundred years ago. The harder and faster we search for the "pearl" outside, the further from home we go. "Off an inch in the beginning" we are "off a thousand miles in the end." Morro Bay is at "the end" in lots of ways and a good example of why Buddhism is taking root in Western soil.

Virginia and John McKenzie, of Morro Bay, and their four kids are a typical American family. College graduates, they made their home in South Pasadena and began to live the good and promising life. "But it wasn't just if you had a color T.V. that mattered," related Virginia, "it was *how many* color T.V.s you had that counted." Something was missing and more success over the years failed to correct it. "So we sold the T.V.s and the Cadillac, bought an old station wagon, and moved to the mountains." They lived there for three years and learned a lot. "I learned how to save rubber bands and felt like I was in kindergarten again." But the kids needed "school and scouts" so they moved to Morro Bay as a compromise—a city, but not polluted and upside down like L.A., they thought.

In a short time, the oil corporations and gas and electric companies set up huge plant facilities. The "developers" flowed in, parceling and building, until Morro Bay swelled in size and headaches. "The freeway is getting closer, and this 'nice, quiet community' has a serious drug problem with its children. We are very concerned." Said Virginia, "Our kids are good kids, but when *it's right in* the schools...".

The McKenzie family read about the City of Ten Thousand Buddhas in a San Francisco paper and saw us bowing. They have spearheaded a campaign of support and are "just really happy for a chance to give." They send out gas, water, and food regularly. I explained briefly about how the Sangha are "fields of blessings," people give *through* us not *to* us. Giving is a way to plant good seeds and nourish what Buddhism represents: enlightenment, compassion, ending suffering, and ultimate wisdom. "That's neat!" said Virginia. "Like planting seeds, kind of. I don't understand a whole lot. All I think of when I give is up there (City of Ten Thousand Buddhas). I see all those fine faces, wonderful land, and good buildings and what they are being used for and I 'send it up' to help it grow." She gestures like a cheerleader. Of the five precepts, she said, "Boy, holding precepts would take a big weight off your back, wouldn't it?"

Cliff and Vicky are a young married couple who live in a high-rent, crowded condominium development community called Baywood in Morro Bay. They aren't happy or settled. "We've been looking for something that expressed and meshed with our thoughts and feelings—inside, you know? Success and traditional religions just don't make it. This wasn't 'home' for us," they explained. "A lot of people talk about the Path and the Way, but we haven't found anybody really doing it." When they found out we were part of a whole community of lay and left-home, *practicing* Buddhists, "I couldn't wipe the grin off my face for days, I was so happy," said Vicky.

They came out with their friends to make offerings, and joined in our Sunday afternoon Gwan Yin praise-recitation and chanting the Great Compassion Mantra. Last week Cliff was driving home during a bad storm. Heavy rain and high winds were pushing his little car all over the highway. A flock of birds struggling with the storm got tossed in front of Cliff's car. "I looked out the rear-view mirror and saw a bird roll across the highway. I had hit it!" said Cliff. "I knew the bird was dying. I felt I needed to do something to help. Then for some reason, without thinking, I said 'Namo Gwan

Shr Yin Pu Sa' about five or six times. I remembered Gwan Yin helps in times of suffering and sickness. Then something strange happened. Suddenly the skies cleared and the wind died down. It was sunny and safe all the way home," said Cliff.

"When he walked in the door he was glowing and happy," said Vicky.

"I know it had to do with reciting Gwan Yin, but I don't know how or why. I've never had anything like that happen to me before. Strange, huh?" related Cliff.

They all took copies of the Great Compassion Mantra that a layperson from L.A. had donated, and they were full of questions and sincerity for the Buddhadharma. "What's the pure Dharma body?" "Where can we start to read?" "What's a Bodhisattva?" "What else can we do?" "Who is Amitabha Buddha?" and so on.

The last two peregrine falcons in the country are carefully protected on the landmark of Morro Bay—a high rock island that rises up out of the middle of the Bay. The city itself is a bird refuge and people are very aware they live on the edge of the edge of the continent. There's no more room to expand or to run over the next hill for greener grass. As a country, this is where it is at: we have run out of room to run outside. The "great evasion" as one historian called our running away from ourselves, is coming to a natural limit and we are spiritually a thousand miles off the mark.

But Americans are optimists and resilient. They don't despair. Practical and self-reliant, they pick up again and try to avoid the same mistakes. This is repentance and reform. People we meet are not ashamed or afraid to admit they got on the wrong track and want to start again on the right foot. Open and energetic, a lot of folks are ready to leave the "brave new world" for the Flower Store World. They are ready to "return the light and illumine within." But where to begin?

"...where was there ever a man of wisdom who got to see and hear the Buddha without cultivating pure vows and walking the same path the Buddha walked?"

Avatamsaka Sutra
Tushita Heaven Chapter

The Master has stressed, "Make Buddhism your personal responsibility." This is what really counts: each person "trying his best" to put down the false and find the true. What moves and inspires people is practice—pure vows and walking the road. Talk is cheap. There are a lot of people like Heng Sure and myself who realize we have not really done our own work, that we have been on the bandwagon and have been taking a free ride. We have nearly exhausted our blessings by just enjoying them. Like the son of the wealthy man, we have run out of conditions to climb on and have to start from scratch.

The City of Ten Thousand Buddhas is so important. It is a pure place where we can cleanse our hearts and souls of defilement and ground our lives in morality and virtue. The City of Ten Thousand Buddhas represents hope for countless living beings to end suffering and find true freedom. It is becoming a symbol, like the Statue of Liberty, of opportunity and refuge: a chance to finish the Real Revolution for Independence by liberating the mind-ground.

Many people we have met share this conviction and are very excited about the orthodox Dharma and the City of Ten Thousand Buddhas. In a very real way, the American Revolution for independence was never completed. Americans feel this sense of "unfinished business" in their hearts and minds. Our history and behavior continues to be a restless search for our natural roots and ultimate liberation. Who would have guessed the "pearl" was sewn right in our very own clothing?

What is the "pearl"? Is it our affluence and prosperity? No. The pearl is the bright substance of our everlasting pure nature, our true unchanging mind. We have been saying that Buddhism is new in America, but this is not really accurate. Like the pearl, Buddhism has always been here. We just didn't know where to look. So now the Monk in the Grave has come to America and reminded us all about the pearl sewn in our clothing—the pearl that grants all wishes, "Your very body is the enlightenment-ground, and your mind is the Pure Land," said the Sixth Patriarch.

Stan, a native of Boise, Idaho, is in his late 70's and lives in retirement now with his wife in Morro Bay. He still wears logging shirts and comes on strong, straight, and honest, "We read about you in the paper and about what you're doing up north in Ukiah..."

"The City of Ten Thousand Buddhas?"

"Yes, that's it. Well, all I got to say is the country needs more people like you." Stan made an offering and invited us to stay at their home while we were in the area. I explained our vows wouldn't allow that, but it was a kind offer. "Well, it's been an honor knowing you. My wife and I are very interested in what you folks are doing. This is what will make the country strong. Good luck and thank you."

The Monk in the Grave did not come here in vain. Virginia McKenzie wanted to thank someone. We said that the best thanks was practice, and we told her of the words over the exit door of Gold Mountain Monastery: "Try your best."

"Boy, that's it, isn't it?" she exclaimed. "And if you make a mistake, try your best to try better!"

Much peace in the Dharma,

Disciple Kuo T'ing (Heng Ch'au)
bows in respect

Is this it? Is this all there is?

March 16, 1978
North of Hearst Castle

Dear Shr Fu,

Spring came all of a sudden today and we took off layers of clothes for the first time since November, it seems. Hot sun and visits by swarms of insects.

It's so clear that everything is made from the mind alone. Last month I dug through my clothes bag looking for a pair of warm socks. The light, hot-weather socks would not do. Too cold. Today I sorted through again. The heavy wool socks looked like pure misery on such a hot day. They were no longer attractive. At the bottom of the bag were the light socks. Ah! Perfect. Had the socks transformed in four months. Not a bit. It was all my mind's doing, making big discriminations, and seeking comfort for the skin-bag. Being a living being can sure be complicated and troublesome.

Heng Ch'au and I have had a big realization over the past few months that the Venerable Abbot is here among us. We reached this awareness after experiencing Shr Fu's instructions coming true in our hearts time after time. Such clarity and precise timing! Wherever we wander on our initial attempts to walk the Middle Way, whatever state arises in our meditation, we find the Master has foreseen our direction. Then either he points to an open door and/or by using some effortless expedient means he delivers with a message or a gatha to steer us away from a certain path, or to another straighter, higher road. This is hard to communicate in words, but we both feel the Master's presence as we work. It's tangible, reliable, and constant, as long as we use effort. The power and the wisdom of a Good and Wise Advisor is inconceivable.

Many cultivators throughout history have worked really hard, but fell into attachments to form or to emptiness and stopped their progress simply because they had no such teacher to guide them. Heng Ch'au and I bow to our teacher each day on the highway, morning, noon and night with ever-deepening respect for him and with a profound sense of wonder at our incredible good luck to have met a Good Knowing Advisor in this life.

Disciple Kuo Chen (Heng Sure)
bows in respect

* * *

Dear Shr Fu,

It's spring. Suddenly there are warm winds and soft sounds. The bitter and cold winter storms are gone, leaving behind flowered green meadows and easy, flowing creeks. The birds are looking for mates and building nests. It's that time and the earth's "natural" energy all moves in this direction: make your mark in the world, nesting (the home) and being creative.

And us? We are also returning to the natural—the original natural, the unconditioned self-nature. Life after life we yielded to spring's desires and pleasures. Life after life we went "with the flow" and returned to the nest. But the nest (home) became a cage and soon the ultimate questions arose: "Is this it? Is this all there is? Mating and dying, dying and mating? Birth, dwelling, decay, emptiness all in the blink of an eye? Is there no more than eating, sleeping and wearing clothes? How and where do you look?"

> *If there are those*
>   *who don't know how to get out,*
> *Who do not seek liberation*
>   *but only cry and are dazed,*

The Bodhisattva manifests for them
  the giving up of his country and wealth,
And constantly happy, he leaves the home-life
  and his mind is tranquil and still.

Avatamsaka Sutra

Yesterday, Heng Ju and Kuo Kuei Nicholson stopped by and Kuo Kuei commented, "Tomorrow is a special day."

"Oh?" I said.

"Yeah, it's the day Shakyamuni Buddha shaved his head and rode off on a white horse—his left-home day." What a powerful image of purity and freedom: the Buddha shaving his head and riding off on a white horse to cultivate! Shakyamuni Buddha had one of the finest nests. So why leave it?

The home is a place of greed and love,
  bondage and fetters.
He wants all living beings
  to be able to leave it behind.
Therefore, he manifests leaving home
  and gaining liberation,
And amid all desires and pleasures
  he accepts none of them.

Avatamsaka Sutra

This morning while bowing along the deserted, quiet road, I realized it has been almost a year since I left home and I'm happier every day. There is another natural urging that wells up inside of living beings. It is the urge for enlightenment and ultimate freedom. It is stronger and more basic than mating and nesting (needing a partner) and in time we all follow it. In time, we all realize it. "All have the Buddha-nature, all will become Buddhas." Some of us will mate this spring, some of us will cultivate. And that will make all of the difference. But, originally there is no difference, and sooner or later we all are "able to leave it all behind" and ride off on a white horse. So, "everything is okay," as the Master often says.

Everybody should be free and happy this spring and every day go toward the good. Lighten the heart and purify the mind and find ways to benefit others. In a year of bowing, Heng Sure and I are discovering that cultivation is right here in these simple basics. Getting rid of greed, anger, and stupidity is what matters and causes others to be happy and free. May we all go to perfect enlightenment together real soon. I hope so. Much peace in the Dharma.

Disciple Kuo T'ing (Heng Ch'au)
bows in respect

* * *

P.S.: The local Dharma Protectors have strongly urged us to leave Highway 1 and find an alternate route. The road apparently becomes very winding, narrow, and heavily trafficked. Our friends in the Forest Service are mapping out a new route for us through Ventana Wilderness and Los Padres National Forest. It will by-pass the treacherous section of Highway 1 up to Carmel. We should have it figured out whenever it's figured out. We have learned to not force or get attached to even the smallest things. Whatever happens will be as it should be and in accord with conditions, not our false thoughts. We will be on Highway 1 for another 4-5 weeks as best we can tell and will let you know as soon as we have a new route to the City of Ten Thousand Buddhas. There is no fixed way to get to the City of Ten Thousand Buddhas! All roads to it eventually return.

Seven miles of the most dangerous road

April 8, 1978

Third waterfall above Ragged Point, Monterey County

Dear Shr Fu,

Shr Fu, we won't be able to be with you on your birthday this year, but we will bow to you nine times here on the road and wish you many happy returns, with all our hearts. Here are some of the recent mind-changes on Three Steps, One Bow:

Heng Ch'au, Upasaka Kuo Chou Rounds, and I bowed around a steep rise and wham! there before us stood the next three weeks of our lives, etched in green stone and blue water: twenty miles of awesome rocks in the slanting, afternoon sun. The first sight of the sheer cliffs falling straight to the azure ocean took my breath away. We could see tiny flecks of sun-glare on glass: cars and campers rolling on a tiny thread of highway stuck on the mountainside, halfway between oblivion and nowhere. We were going to bow on this road? My first impulse was to follow an old habit energy and let my mind dive into a daydream, to avoid facing the reality.

But I couldn't do that. A new *yang* energy that's been slowly building took control and brought my heart back to focus on the work. What came to mind was this passage from the Sutra lecture the night before:

> *Although he causes all existence to be purified,*
> *He does not make distinctions amid all that exists.*
> *And he is caused to be happy, with a purified mind.*
> *In one Buddhaland, he relies on nothing.*
> *In all Buddhalands it is the same.*

Lunch with the Venerable Abbot at Gold Wheel Monastery.
April, 1978

Nor is he attached to conditioned dharmas,
Because he knows that in the nature of these dharmas
There is nowhere to rely.

Avatamsaka Sutra
Ten Transferences Chapter

I applied the Sutra passage to this situation: only hours before, I had been bowing on Huntington Drive, outside Gold Wheel Temple in L.A.; where were there any dharmas to rely on there? Where was L.A. now? When I was in L.A., where were these mountains, this ocean? How was this moment any different from that moment? I couldn't find any differences! So what was there to hide from? Why take a vacation in false-thoughts? It's nothing but the sad little ego looking for a way out of the pressure of slow, steady work on the mind-ground. What would Shr Fu say? "Everything's okay. No problem. Use effort. Fear is useless."

So, I took another look at the landscape before us. "Hey! What a beautiful, pure place to cultivate in. What a fine Bodhimanda!" My heart seemed to take wings and soar out into the clear air above the mud of my afflictions. When these boulders have turned to dust, I vow to still be on the Bodhisattva path, working to end the sufferings of all living beings.

Now we're concentrating on the basics: giving, holding precepts, patience, and vigor. Along with all the Master's disciples, we are working to give the world a City of Ten Thousand Buddhas, a place where precepts will be the ground rules for being a person. As for patience, well, there's lots of chances to practice patience on this mountainside. Kuo Dzai Schmitz is sharing the work with us this week, patiently enduring some of the most contrary weather of the whole trip.

We are traveling seven miles of the most dangerous road we've faced: poison oak that grows everywhere, venomous ticks that inhabit the underbrush, sunburn, the mad Big Sur wind, freezing rain that stops as soon as we put on our slickers and boots and then starts again when we change back out of our rain gear. This trip has taught us an appreciation of the monastic environment. How fine are walls, a roof, and a clean floor! I did not make the most of my chance to cultivate in the ideal meditative space of Gold Mountain Monastery. Now that I really want to do the work, all sorts of obstructions arise: each one becomes a test of patience, resolve, and *kung fu*: wind, insects underfoot, cramped quarters, rain and sun in excess, traffic—all these dharmas can help cultivators forge a vajra resolve. We transfer our work and wish that the City of Ten Thousand Buddhas will come into being quickly and easily, so that whoever brings forth the heart to cultivate the Way will have a pure place to realize their wish. They won't have to endure any hassles before they sit in meditation. I'm not complaining! I have never felt happier or stronger.

These clumsy corpses we walk around in are such a drag! We waste so much time looking after our bodies. The only sensible thing to do with them is to cultivate the Way. I like the Bodhisattva in the First Practice of the "Ten Practices Chapter": he makes a vow to reincarnate into a huge, vast body so that no matter how many living beings are hungry the flesh of his body will satisfy their needs. Then the Bodhisattva contemplates all living beings of the past, the future, and the present. He contemplates the bodies they receive, their lifespans, their decay, and their extinction. The Sutra says,

> *Again he thinks, "How strange living beings are! How ignorant and lacking in wisdom. Within (the cycle of) birth and death, they get countless bodies which are perilous and fragile. Without pause, these bodies hastily go bad again. Whether their bodies have already gone bad, are about to decay, or will come to ruin in the future, they are unable to use these unstable bodies to seek a solid body!*
>
> *"I should thoroughly learn what all Buddhas have learned! I should realize all-wisdom and know all dharmas. For the sake of all beings I will teach them*

equally in the three periods of time. According to and harmonizing with still tranquility and the indestructible Dharma-nature, I will cause them to obtain peace, security, and happiness."

I memorized this passage from the *Avatamsaka Sutra*, and it has given me heart to keep bowing through many situations, where my skinbag and my common-person's mind feared it could not go. One immediately useful application: when the heat and pressure builds in the legs from Ch'an sitting, all I have to do is review the Sutra's wisdom and I find strength to continue to sit without wiggling or dropping my legs out of full lotus.

"On the path to the worry-free liberation-city," as the Sutra calls it.

The biggest discovery of the month of March: "Where there's a will, there's a way." We are rich in methods to cultivate. What counts is resolving the heart on wanting to succeed. Then the Way opens.

Disciple Kuo Chen (Heng Sure)
bows in respect

Bowing in place in a Big Sur roadside turnout.
May 1978

How can you go wrong?

May 18, 1978

Dear Shr Fu,

As you often tell us, Shr Fu, everything speaks the Dharma. In this case, even thieves have become our good and wise advisors, helping us break our attachments. Your instructions at Gold Wheel were quite clear: "If you can't do a good job of putting down your false thoughts about the mundane, daily dharmas of food, clothing, and sleep, then your efforts will not carry you along the Way. Cultivate what is close by, cultivate the basics. Be patient with what you cannot endure."

In fact, I have not done a good job of putting down my false thoughts of the basics. I often keep my eyes fixed on the high, profound, distant Dharma and stumble over the daily matters that I take for granted. So what was stolen from the car? One-third of our food, our eating bowls, our alarm clock, and clothes. Really uncanny how if one does not do a good job of reciting one's own Sutra, Good Advisors will appear to point out the shortcomings and attachments. Clearly, effort must go first into everyday, ordinary concerns of existence: "The ordinary mind is the Way. The straight mind is the Bodhimanda!" As National Master Ch'ing Liang put it,

Truth and falseness interlink and mingle. It is the common mind which sees the Buddha mind. Cultivating both principle and specifics, one relies on basic wisdom to seek the Buddha's wisdom.

Avatamsaka Preface

I recall how as a child I was drawn to people who spoke principle. Those really "adult" grown-ups I met were people who knew the rules and built their daily behavior on a solid foundation of principle. The thing I like most about the Buddhadharma is the way everyone responds to its truth. People from all walks of life hear the Dharma deep within their heart of hearts. It never fails to bring out the best in all of us.

Disciple Kuo Ch'en came down yesterday and told briefly about his discovery of the Buddhadharma and what it meant to him. Kuo Ch'en took refuge with the Triple Jewel on the Master's birthday at the City of Ten Thousand Buddhas. He received the lay precepts on the Buddha's birthday just last week. He said, "I felt like I was home at last. In the sky I saw the most beautiful rainbow I've ever seen. And you know what else? I saw the end of the rainbow—the pot of gold—it was right there with us at the City of Ten Thousand Buddhas." Kuo Ch'en explained that "Before I met the Master and Buddhism, everything I did always let me down. Life was a long series of disappointments. I would carry out some new plan for success to its end and find myself nowhere again. Then, after I heard the Venerable Abbot speak Dharma, I looked into it for myself. I suddenly realized that my life is not worthless after all. I do have an important part to play in things—just keeping the precepts is a big job. What's more, I see now that all along, the problems I faced came from me, from my own mind. The answers to those problems come from the same place."

Kuo Ch'en was worried that his parents would have some difficulty accepting that their son was now part of an unfamiliar religion. Heng Ch'au said, "Be really patient with your folks. Don't try to convince them. You don't even have to talk about your changes. Just hold your precepts really tightly. You will get a good response according to your sincerity. The precepts naturally clear up and help us go to the good. Your parents want you to be happy, and when they see you growing more pure and light every day, they will naturally come to recognize the true principles of the Buddhadharma. Most of all, don't force anything and don't get angry!

That's really important. After all, you're not killing, you're not using dope or liquor, you're really happy. How can you go wrong?"

Every time we see a fellow disciple of the Master's we recognize a quality of light and goodness shining from the eyes and the heart. It makes us truly glad to be working within the Dharma and trying our best to "step by step, make the tracks for the good."

Disciple Kuo Chen (Heng Sure)
bows in respect

California Highway Patrol looking c

or the monks' safety. June, 1978.

I could chew one verse for weeks

June 18, 1978

140 miles South of San Francisco on Highway One

Dear Shr Fu,

The *Avatamsaka Sutra* is really wonderful. It is a flawless guide and a light for every state of mind we experience. Moreover, it's a manual on how to survive on the road. For everything that comes up, from wild animals to car breakdowns, we turn to the Sutra for the answer. People who have never heard Sutras (as far as they can remember) come out time and again just to listen to Heng Sure make the Chinese characters come alive for them. They feel there's something special, almost magical, about the Sutra, and they are all really impressed that someone could sit down and take these ancient characters and translate them into words they know— words that sink deep into their hearts. Said one man, "Why has no one ever done this before in the West?! I can't understand it. This (*Avatamsaka*) is the most far-out thing I ever read or heard. It says it like it really is. I could chew one verse for weeks and still not exhaust it." He was really glad when he found out about *Vajra Bodhi Sea* and the *Avatamsaka* translation and commentary in it.

Today the *Avatamsaka* gave me the answer I sought in two situations. The feel or the spirit was in my heart, but the Sutra was able to put the light on it and make it bloom. The more we bow, the closer our hearts mesh with this Sutra. And the closer our minds merge with the Sutra, the easier and cleaner our lives become.

Layperson: "It's cold and windy out here. When it rains it will be difficult for you."

"Every day is a little happier. The weather doesn't matter," I said.

"Oh, you're almost *there* then."

"Almost where? Until everyone is *there* and someone else isn't, then how can we be there? As long as there is suffering in the world and until all beings get the peace and happiness they seek, our work isn't complete."

> *All of the most wonderful happiness*
> > *that the Bodhisattva obtains,*
> *He transfers to all living beings.*
> *Although he transfers it to all living beings,*
> *He is not attached to transference itself.*
> *The Bodhisattva cultivates this transference,*
> *And he gives rise to a measureless*
> > *heart of great compassion.*
> *The virtue of transference that*
> > *Buddhas cultivate—*
> *I vow to cultivate it fully to perfection.*
> *Not for himself does he seek benefit.*
> *He wants to cause all to be peaceful and happy.*
>
> > Avatamsaka
> > Ten Transferences Chapter

So there's a lot of work to do and no time to false think about why or "getting there" or even transferring merit and virtue. Cultivating is natural, you don't have to think about it or make plans or goals. When we can bow with a single mind, everything takes care of itself and differences disappear.

Layperson: "Someone said this is your *favorite* food, so we brought lots of it."

"We have no favorites. It's all the same." Whatever makes people happy is our favorite. What people delight in doing, what they like to give is what we like, too. "Do you need something, something special, perhaps?" is often asked of us. We answer,

"Whatever you want to give, whatever makes you happy, that's what we need."

The *Avatamsaka* says it clearly:

> *He attaches neither to self*
> *Nor what pertains to self...*
> *He delights in Dharma's true and actual benefits*
> *And does not love the reception of desires.*
> *He reflects upon the Dharma he has heard,*
> *Far free from the practice of grasping.*
> *He has no greed for benefits or offerings,*
> *And he only delights in Buddhas' Bodhi.*
> *With one mind he seeks the Buddhas' wisdom,*
> *Concentration undivided with no other thought.*

Avatamsaka
Ten Grounds Chapter

I have spent a lot of time and wasted effort seeking benefits and offerings for myself and trying to satisfy my desires. It's much simpler and wonderfully carefree to not worry about that anymore, and "With one mind seek the Buddhas' wisdom, concentration undivided with no other thought." When we concentrate, "everything's okay." Bringing forth a heart of "everything's okay" is repaying parents' kindness and the highest gift one can give to all living beings. Peace in the Dharma.

Disciple Kuo T'ing (Heng Ch'au)
bows in respect

* * *

P.S. *Vajra Bodhi Sea* is like having another sun in the world. It "produces a wonderful light which illuminates all things" (*Avatamsaka*).

Bowing on high cliffs overlooking Big Sur coastline.
June, 1978

But there's nothing left to climb on

July 20, 1978

Monterey, California

Dear Shr Fu,

We have arrived in Monterey—back in the city after three months of isolation among the rocks and waves of Big Sur. What a surprise! The differences I experience exist only in my mind. The Dharma Realm is one whole peaceful body. When my mind moves the wholeness is lost to view, self and others come into being, and Big Sur, Monterey, and the City of Ten Thousand Buddhas become names on a map, separated by miles of grueling steps and bows. When the mind is still and discrimination stops, then no matter where we are, we bow before the great Gwan Yin image in the Hall of Ten Thousand Buddhas.

The *Avatamsaka Sutra* says,

> *What, then, is the world? What is not the world? World and non-world are merely different names. The dharmas of the past, present, and future and the five skandhas, when named, bring the world into being. When they are extinguished, the world is gone. In this way, they are only false names.*
>
> Praises in the Suyama Heaven Palace

Words and names are creations of the mind. They are the tools of thought and just as false as can be. Why has the Venerable Abbot given us the constant instruction "Don't do any false thinking! Come up with a way to stop the flow of your false thoughts right there where they turn"? It's because our thoughts create the world we inhabit. They make the karma and the retribution we endure. As the Venerable Abbot says, "The Ten Dharma Realms are not apart from a single thought." From the hells to Buddhahood, we harvest the fruit of seeds we plant in our own minds. When we unite with the Way, we do it right in the same mind.

The Third Patriarch, the Venerable Seng Ts'an, spoke of words, thoughts, and the Way. He said:

> *The more you talk and think,*
> *   the further you are from it.*
> *If you can halt all speech and thought,*
> *   you will find it everywhere.*
>
> On faith in the Mind

"The person of the Way without thought is equal to the Buddha," said a recent Ch'an session verse of the Master's.

Disciple: "Shr Fu, I've been trying hard to get rid of all my common thoughts and have only Buddha-thoughts."

Master: "Okay, let's see, what's a 'Buddha-thought'? Come on, what's your answer?"

Disciple: "Uh, er, ummm, well, I know it's not false thoughts, and I have lots of those…"

Master: "It's because you have false thoughts that you don't know. What cannot be described, what is inexpressible, that is the Buddha. Anything that can be put into words is still superficial. The ancients said:

> *The mind wants to climb on conditions,*
> *But there's nothing left to climb on.*
> *The path of words and language is cut off.*
> *The place of the mind's workings is extinguished.*

As long as you still have thoughts, then that's when you have not realized Buddhahood."

Disciple: "Oh, so no-thoughts are Buddha-thoughts!"

Master: (No comment.)

* * *

He vows that all beings attain the body that is without fatigue and is just like vajra.

Avatamsaka
Ten Transferences Chapter

The Venerable Abbot is teaching me as much about my body as about my mind. On this bowing journey I am learning to recite a Body-dharma Sutra, trading in my *yin*, stooped, stiff, skin-bag for a straight, flexible, energized *yang* body. The bowing and meditation are making changes in my whole world. Cultivation is a wonderful fountain of youth. Every day that I hold precepts and subdue my false thoughts I feel myself grow younger, more honest, and more genuine. Naturally!

Cultivation subdues the body and mind. We regulate the body so that it can continue to work even when it's tired. We regulate the mind so that it doesn't create false thoughts.

Master Hua, Gold Wheel Temple—May 1978

Disciple Kuo Chen (Heng Sure)
bows in respect

The UFOs are coming!

October 28, 1978
Santa Cruz, California

Dear Shr Fu,

We just bowed past the city limits of Santa Cruz. Ahead is about 80 miles of empty coastline before San Francisco, and whatever our minds create. I am happiest when I bow a lot, sit long, and keep my mouth closed. I've noticed that those around me are a lot more natural and peaceful when I cultivate. Minding my own business and tending to my own faults seems to allow others room to grow and move without feeling hassled and obstructed. I've put my mind to not getting worried or angry, no matter what. I've eaten my fill of afflictions for too long. They just pollute the air and give me gray hair and wrinkles. This verse from the *Avatamsaka* really struck me as the right way to be:

> *He is quite free from contention,*
> *From troubling, harming, and from hatred.*
> *He knows shame, respect, and rectitude*
> *And well protects and guards his faculties.*

I recite this verse on and off during the day. Without fail it clears the shadows from my mind and leaves me feeling pounds lighter. I have never encountered anything more wonderful or true than the Buddhadharma.

In Santa Cruz we met Don Penners and his family. He is a local dentist who is selling his practice and moving to the city of Ten Thousand Buddhas to live and work. "We are all looking forward to the move. It's the best thing going in the world today. The Master's a great guy!" they said. When they first met the Master they were a little non-plussed. "Well, at first we weren't impressed. He looked so young and healthy—too much so to be a Venerable Abbot—so I crudely said, 'Who are *you*?' I thought he was one of the assistants. I've never seen anyone his age look so youthful and happy! We got no reply."

"In fact," the Penners went on, "The Master said *nothing* to us at all the first time. It was like looking into a big mirror. All we saw was *ourselves*. It was like the Master was empty inside. There wasn't any of the usual 'Hi, how are you... what you been doing?' It wasn't until later that we came to appreciate what a rare and valuable experience that was. We really got a clear picture of ourselves. It was quite something, frankly!"

We have met some strange people, too. One night while I was making tea on the back of the station wagon, two men pulled up to ask about the pilgrimage. One of them related during a perfectly straight conversation, "People think Jesus is coming again. But they're wrong. The UFOs are coming. They are out there watching us like a farmer watches over a corn crop. When they come, they are going to take some of us with them—alive, right out into outer space. The rest they will leave here on earth to blow themselves up with nuclear weapons and pollution. It says so in the Bible!" He insisted.

"Oh?" I said.

"Yeah, do you read the Bible?" he asked.

"Once upon a time..." I began.

"Well, *I've read it*! So what are you going to do?" He asked urgently.

"About?" I asked.

"When they come—the UFOs. Are you going with them or staying?" he pressed.

"We'll just keep bowing to the City of Ten Thousand Buddhas," I replied.

"You will? Well, I guess, but... well they are coming real soon. I know it..." his voice trailed off as he looked up at the stars.

There are a lot of different ways of looking at things. Heng Sure and I are slowly discovering that, with a proper mind, what is seen is proper; with a deviant mind, what is seen is deviant. Proper knowledge and views are essential, because however we look at things, that's what they become. As the Master wrote in a verse:

> As one plants causes, one reaps the fruit—
>   look within yourself.
> With reverence coming and going,
>   impartial is the Way.

All is well. There's no problem so big that a day of bowing won't solve.

Peace in the Dharma,

Disciple Kuo T'ing (Heng Ch'au)
bows in respect

Ripping band-aids off the old wounds

October 28, 1978
Above Santa Cruz on Highway 1

Dear Shr Fu,

> *Truly recognize your own mistakes,*
> *And don't discuss the faults of others.*
> *Others' faults are just my own;*
> *Being of one substance with everyone*
>   *is great compassion.*

Venerable Master Hua

An old friend of Heng Ch'au's saw us outside a housing project in Santa Cruz. "His face 'cracked' and after a brief talk, he left rather in a hurry," said Heng Ch'au. The next morning, just before *zao ke*, I was not yet on guard over my mind and I broke the rules by writing a casual, chatty note to Heng Ch'au. As I reached for the pen and paper, I knocked the lit stick of incense out of the censer and burned a hole in my jacket. This was a clue that I should be careful and check myself—what is out of harmony here? (But, I ignored the signal and went ahead to take another false step.)

I wrote, "Your friend must think you have not only fallen but have also burned out your circuits—crawling in the gutter in rags, with a friend who looks equally wasted," and gave it to Heng Ch'au to read.

Even before I saw the look on his face, I knew I had made a mistake. Heng Ch'au read the note and his expression showed disappointment. He said nothing. I had all of *zao ke* and the following hour of meditation to reflect on and repent of my stupidity. Since I had broken the rules once, now I had to do it again to announce my error and apologize. I wrote, "Writing that note was a real mistake. 1) It slanders the Triple Jewel, by calling our appearance 'wasted' and 'in rags.' That breaks Bodhisattva Precept #10, 'Do not slander the Triple Jewel.' 2) It plants doubt-seeds in your mind ('Does Heng Sure really feel that way about what we're doing?') 3) It maintains my old bad habit of holding a superior and critical attitude towards others. In fact, I don't feel burned out or fallen—of course I don't feel that way about you. The note was a sarcastic, uncompassionate slap at your friend. In fact, Bhikshu robes are the finest clothes I could wish for. Moreover, I wouldn't trade our work for any king's realm. Now I have to start being worthy of my robes and my vows. I can start by not writing such ignorant, bad-karma notes.

All I can say is that it was too early in the morning. I didn't have my thought-chopping sword drawn yet. An idle, nasty thought manifested as the note. Sorry for the hassle. "Others' faults are just my own."

Cultivating the Way to Genuine Good Health.

Cultivation is the road back to genuine health. Sutras are the medicine. The Venerable Abbot works like a good doctor, prescribing the most efficacious remedy for whichever of the eighty-four thousand types of afflictions obstruct an individual's way back to peace and happiness.

Originally, all the medicine we need for a complete cure of the big disease—birth and death—we already possess inside ourselves, but we don't see it, don't know how to use it, because of attachments to bad habits and upside-down false thoughts. The teacher-doctor comes in to tell us, 1) that we are sick; 2) that the cause of our sickness is looking outside of our own nature for happiness; 3) that there is a cure available; and, 4) that that cure is cultivation of the Buddhadharma.

Then, because the doctor is kind and compassionate, he gives us the medicine perfectly suited to our needs. But, it's up to us to be brave and take the medicine prescribed. At this point, practice of the Dharma becomes self-therapy, self-healing.

I have to remember that I am sick, must keep my faith in the efficacy of the cure, and must keep taking the medicine. The resolve for health follows faith in the doctor and the cure, and then steady practice allows the cure to happen. Faith, vows, and practice are the prescription for total well-being.

Our passage through Santa Cruz this month has been a mirror of the first stages of the Buddhadharma's cure. I reflected long on my past conduct in terms of the Master's teachings and the Sutra's model of Bodhisattva conduct. Bowing through Santa Cruz, it takes no effort at all to recognize that I am really sick. My past conduct reads like a checklist of the ten evil acts. I have done what demons do: killing, stealing, lust, lying, and taking intoxicants. It's not to say that I have changed since I began to practice good health. But, now I *recognize* how far wrong I've gone and how strong my habits are that still lead me away from health towards my old sicknesses. These habits are strong and not easy to change. But, I want to become a true disciple of the Buddha. No matter how much discomfort I have to endure, no matter how long I have to take the medicine, I am determined to get well again. The Master's state of happiness and health, and the radiant goodness of the Bodhisattvas that live in the *Avatamsaka Sutra* are simply wonderful—to realize their state of well-being is what I want most of all.

> *They vow that living beings forever escape their sick bodies and obtain the Tathagata's body.*
>
> Avatamsaka Sutra
> Ten Transferences Chapter

"Kuo Chen, your worst fault is being sticky with people, especially with women," said the Master, very clearly. This is called "recognizing the sickness." Step #2 is seeing how the disease appears in my behavior; and Step #3 is finding a way to turn it around. The Master's statement is, of course, right on. He pointed out the cycle of cause and effect that brought on my troubles. In this life I have harmed myself and caused a lot of suffering to others by my selfish misconduct. In the past I tied myself into bad relationships with women, which came to fruition in this lifetime as promiscuous, mutually harmful sexual behavior. Before I met the Proper Dharma in this life, I planted more bad seeds which are certain to flower in the future.

"If you can't transcend sexual desire, you will not leave the dust," says the *Shurangama Sutra*. If I don't end sexual desire completely, just cut it off for good, I won't be able to realize my goal of cultivation as a Bodhisattva and becoming a Buddha. I won't succeed. I believe in cause and effect. I see what I've done in this life, seen the bad I've done, because of past bad karma. I saw the blueprint for the future that I was drawing up for myself, and it wasn't a good one.

I want to change, and in the Dharma I've found a medicine to cure my illness. The medicine is called "Three Steps, One Bow and repentance and reform." Every day I repeat vows to end sexual desire, and I recite a wish that together with all beings I can return to the root and go back to the source of original purity. The vow has a part that says, "I vow that all negative affinities already established will come to fruition in a way other than sexual. I will never again have to endure sexual embrace in order to repay my debts. Any debts owed to me in this regard I now cancel." Does it work? Can I really uproot the bad seeds I've planted in this life so that I don't have to go through the same dance in the future that I endured in this life? I have faith that it will work.

Bowing past a shopping center parking lot in Aptos Village last week, I got an "offering of orange juice without the benefit of a cup," as Heng Ch'au calls it. Showered with sticky juice from a passing pick-up truck, I thought immediately of my vow.

Later that same afternoon I took a bath in a cup of beer that flew from a blue truck. I repeated the vow with a wish to transfer all merit and virtue of my work so that all beings might return to purity. The next morning I poured a cup of scalding hot tea into my Sierra cup, and reaching for the thermos lid, I tipped the whole cup onto my bare foot. The boiling tea covered my lap as I sat in lotus posture before doing *zao ke*. Scalding burns! And in my head, the memory of how much hot suffering I'd given to others through my lustful, casual, selfish behavior in the past. (Heng Ch'au's comments: "That's good tea, really wakes you up, eh?") Are these incidents actually my sexual karma resolving itself in another form, as I wished in my vow? I think so; I believe so.

Three Steps, One Bow is making my cure possible. Who throws the orange juice and beer? My Good Advisors. They may be people whom I've hurt in the past. Who are the teenaged Santa Cruz High School girls who shower me with rocks and curses that would make a truck-driver blush? I see them as my own behavior returning to me. They are my friends, my fields of blessings. As the Bodhisattva in the Ten Practices Chapter of the *Avatamsaka Sutra* says,

> *...as he sees a host of starving beggars coming to request his body's flesh to eat, "These are my good friends. I am really getting benefit. Without being asked, they are coming to help me enter into the Buddhadharma."*

I've just begun to see the extent of my illness. But this is a start, and with the good medicine I've got, bit by bit I will get well.

The Master explained the basic source of confused karma:

> *All the problems of the world come from the presence of the self. Without the self, who is there to be unhappy? Who is there to feel pain? The self is an illusion. You should have no self.*

That is the voice of the Good Doctor, ripping band-aids off the old wounds, not gingerly pulling at them, one scab at a time, the way most of us do. Shr Fu wants us to get better now! Until we all make it to Buddhahood, he's got to keep returning to doctor his unwell disciples. One of these great aeons, however, we'll all make it. The great hero's work will be done, and we will all be able to gather at the City of Ten Thousand Buddhas and "mutually shine upon each other's lotus thrones, in world systems like motes of dust."

Disciple Kuo Chen (Heng Sure)
bows in respect

The Monk and the Militants

November 8, 1978
Davenport, California

Dear Shr Fu,

There is an ineffable feeling of completeness and security in the life of a left-home monk. Having given up private home and personal relationships, the left-home person is at home in the world at large. His companions are all beings everywhere. His refuge is peaceful dwelling with the Supreme Knight, the Buddha, the wisdom-lore and the Enlightened Ones of the Sutras, and the selfless, pure, "field of blessings" Sangha members. Has there ever been any greater happiness and peace than this?

Several weeks ago I witnessed a wonderful story unfold which I've called "The Monk and the Militants". We were bowing in Santa Cruz when a reporter for the local college paper came up to interview Heng Ch'au. She was interested in our work and our vows. She was surprised that all our material needs come from free-will offerings.

The next day, after lunch, we bowed across Branciforte Creek and the reporter appeared again. She looked apologetic and flustered. Another student stood beside her, a hostile expression on her face.

"I feel embarrassed to ask you these questions, but I have to ask anyhow," the reporter said. The questions were all about politics and economics. They were pointed questions, and the language was angry, resentful, full of jargon and political rhetoric. It was clear that the reporter had been under attack by political classmates at school. They had pegged Buddhism as parasitical and exclusive and *san bu yi bai*[2] as an elitist and frivolous exercise, of interest and of benefit only to members of a rich, white minority in society.

The militants did not pick their opponent well. Heng Ch'au's answers left the students speechless: the reporter speechless with delight, her angry friend speechless with dismay. Heng Ch'au is not politically ignorant or naive. Rather he is experienced at the political-consciousness parlor game. Before he left home to become a monk he was a Doctoral candidate in the highly competitive History Department at the University of Wisconsin. He cut his political teeth during the red-hot sixties, the era of marches, sit-ins and consciousness-raising confrontations. It was precisely his disenchantment with the ineffectiveness and the narrow scope of the political answer to the world's problems that led to his discovery of Buddhism. In the Buddhadharma he found real solutions to the suffering that all people undergo. He left the home-life to study and practice the Dharma full-time as a monk.

Here are the questions and answers given that day as the monk met the challenge of the militants:

Q: What is the racial and class background of the members of the Sino-American Buddhist Association?

A: We come from the class of all living beings. SABA is truly international. The Buddhadharma cuts across all divisions of class,

---

2. Three Steps One Bow

race, sex, age, nationality, ethnic and economic backgrounds. It is the direct mind-to-mind language, the teaching of all beings, the teaching of the heart. It is the true classless origin of human beings. No one in SABA thinks in those divisive categories any longer.

Q: How can you avoid the reality of "those categories?"

A: It's all made from the mind. If you want to see the world as rich and poor, black and white, have and have not, then that's how it is. But if you take a step two inches to the left or two inches to the right or look over your shoulder, then it all looks different. If you are open to all possibilities, if you turn your head all the way around, then you approach the Buddhist view. Buddhism is the teaching of the mind and all its states. Both have no beginning and have no end.

Q: How can you feel comfortable taking the time to make a pilgrimage like this? Third World people have more primary concerns, like filling their bellies. Your pilgrimage is possible only in a country where everyone gets to eat his fill. Only then are you able to sit around and think of transcendental bliss.

A: No one who understands people could say that the only concern of any person or group of people is filling their bellies. That's just a handy label that rabble-rousers use to identify "the Third World" as they call it. In fact, Third World people are *people*, not bellies and mouths. They think of birth and death, where they came from and where they are going. All people think about it. We just returned from a trip through Asia and we visited some back-water places, where the Third World lives. People there met the Buddhadharma with an overwhelmingly positive response, as strong and as enthusiastic as anywhere in the U.S.A. Why? Because Buddhism is the language of the heart. Everyone recognizes it. It transcends the simple concern for a full belly. Buddhism is our original home. The rest is superficial.

Q: How are you adding to the world's production? Living like soft parasites in a safe monastery, how are you helping anyone?

A: People at Gold Mountain Monastery and the City of Ten Thousand Buddhas, and at the International Institute for the Translation of Buddhist Texts are deeply concerned with the suffering of beings everywhere. We believe that we must,

> *Truly recognize your own mistakes,*
> *And don't discuss the faults of others.*
> *Others' faults are just my own;*
> *Being of one substance with everyone*
>   *is great compassion*

But we don't just talk about it. So we eat just one meal a day. Some of the monks eat just one bowl of food per day. Why? Because there are people in the world who do not get enough to eat every day. We add to production by not being greedy and by decreasing consumption.

We do not solicit anything. All that we have and use are offerings given freely. We do not use money for food. We get our vegetables from what the markets throw away, or we grow it in our fields. We live on the scraps of the U.S.A. Any money that is offered is used to build Way-places and to print books. No one holds private property, it all belongs to the church. Our clothes are not bought. We recycle the clothes that other people no longer want. We are not concerned with stylish appearances. There are no water-beds at our way places. Most of the monks and nuns and even some of the lay people never lie down—they sleep sitting in meditation posture. We don't turn on heaters in our monasteries, no matter what season it is. We do nothing for name or for gain. We do not lead personal lives. The monks and nuns are celibate, they believe in eliminating all selfish desires. Now this is genuine revolution. Our Three Great Principles are these:

> *Freezing to death, we do not climb on conditions.*
> *Starving to death, we do not beg.*
> *Dying of poverty, we do not scheme.*
> *We accord with conditions but do not change.*

Unchanging, we accord with conditions.
These are our Three Great Principles.
We give up our lives to do the Buddha's work.
We rectify our lives to do the Sangha's work.
Our business is illuminating principles,
So that our principles are revealed in our practice.
In this way we carry out
The pulse of the Patriarchs' heart-transmission.

When we follow these principles, we truly help the Third World and all living beings. The answer to the world's suffering is not simply to give the Third World what the U.S. has. Rather we must turn our abundant blessing into merit and virtue through hard work and cultivation of our own natures. It's said that

To receive suffering is to end suffering.
To cash in blessings is to exhaust blessings.

The Buddhadharma teaches that the reason the world is in a mess is because our minds are a mess. If we want to clean up the world, we must first purify our own minds. We do not tell other people to wash their dirty clothes. Buddhists do their own dirty laundry. All of the problems in the world come from selfishness and the desire for self-benefit. The heart of Buddhism teaches us to have no self.

"Now if you have no more questions I'll get back to work bowing," said Heng Ch'au, and that ended the interview.

> *In this way, they tend toward true, real principles*
> *and gain entry into the profound place that is without*
> *wrangling.*
>
> *Avatamsaka*

Part II.

On Sunday afternoon, Heng Ch'au told me the story of his encounter with the students. He said, "I gave some thought to my answers and there was much more I could have said but that was not the time or place to go into depth. I would explain the principles of compassion and cause and effect. These two principles really expanded my own mind from my former materialist and divisive political views. My thinking used to be really narrow. It was purely intellectual. The materialist view is one-dimensional, it divides the world, it's based on fighting. Either side of the coin, capitalism or communism, is a dead end. There's no heart there. People are not as simple as mouths and bellies and greed for wealth. We are, by nature, spiritual beings.

"That's what lead me to change my mind. I looked into my own heart and realized that there was more inside than concern for my own benefit. How could I assume that that's all there is in others? Buddhism is based on kindness, compassion, joy and giving. It includes everyone, no one is excluded. Great compassion is grand and magnanimous; great division is petty and full of hatred. And, *everyone* has the Buddha nature."

What does our teacher say about class? He says:

All beings are my family,
    all the universe is my body.
Empty space is my school,
    the invisible is my name.
Kindness, compassion, joy and giving
    are my functions.

"After you hear this truth, who could ever be satisfied with class struggle and washing others' dirty clothes?" Heng Ch'au asked.

"I understand now that cause and effect determines the worlds that we live in. If we waste our blessings and don't cultivate merit and virtue, then even if we have wealth, we can lose it in this lifetime. If you do nothing but exhaust your blessings and follow greed, then in the next life you will certainly come up short. On the other hand, people are sunk in poverty this life because in the past they stole, wasted resources, were stingy and dishonest. This is what's really going on beneath the surface of the materialistic world.

"It's not difficult to see beyond the purely political view of the intellectual," said Heng Ch'au. "It's got no heart to it. Within it there is a really arrogant and superior attitude towards people. The basic assumptions are that poor people are worse off than rich folks and won't be happy until they have what the wealthy have and want. If you see the world that way, then that's how it is: a blend of greed and guilt. If the Third World does not want what we have, then how does it make us feel about our excess? Are two cars and a color T.V. and living the good life really our righteous share?

"In Asia I heard many people, particularly older people, say that as their countries 'modernized' and people moved closer to big cities, they all got more nervous as life got less simple. There was no time to enjoy life anymore. All people knew about was chasing the buck, desires grew and then simple things, simple thoughts no longer satisfied people. Families began to break down, headaches and problems increased as soon as First World culture was imported.

What's more, the Buddhadharma faces squarely the big matter of birth and death and its suffering. Poor people embrace the Dharma because they see the emptiness of life and the universality of suffering up close. They aren't cushioned from it the way the 'better half' is," said Heng Ch'au.

"The turning point in the encounter with the students came when I explained the actual practices of the members of SABA. Up to that point the interviewers assumed that we were just students, too, wearing funny clothes and playing the same political game. They assumed that we ate the same food, listened to the same music, danced to the same rhythms. When they heard about the bitter practices of SABA's 'Dharma-revolutionaries' the conversation quickly became very real. Great compassion is such a wonderful heart. As soon as you include all beings instead of dividing them up, discrimination and hatred just shrivel up," Heng

Ch'au said. "Like the Master told us in L.A., once you grasp any of the fundamental Buddhist principles, then there's no one you can't win over in debate. Who can refuse to stand inside the peace and happiness of the Buddha's light? The Buddhadharma is truly the highest of all teachings. It is 'without sophistry,' it 'goes beyond words and thoughts'. It's inconceivable!"

Disciple Kuo Chen (Heng Sure)
bows in respect

Don't cry, just die

November 13, 1978
Scott Creek, California

Dear Shr Fu,

Today the Master and a bus-full of bright-eyed Dharma friends came from the City of Ten Thousand Buddhas to give the bowing monks "a little gasoline" as the Master put it. How did we run out of fuel? I ran out of fuel by looking at women. Then I got sick. When the Master stepped down from the yellow dragon bus he started whisking away our obstacles and afflictions. "I heard from Kuo Chou you were sick. I asked him if you had died. He said no. So because you haven't died yet, I have come to see you. If you had died, I wouldn't have come. Do you understand?" The Master's strange words went straight to my heart. Finally, I understood. This is the whole story.

I should have left home the first time I came to Gold Mountain Monastery almost three years ago. I had returned to my true home and knew this was where I belonged. But I couldn't put down my selfish desire. So I turned my back on enlightenment and reunited with the dust. As a layman the purity and happiness I experienced at Gold Mountain was soon exhausted every time I went back home. Soon after I got all afflicted and hung-up, trying to act like a cultivator at home. I was trying to cultivate the Way and romance at the same time. It didn't work. At the peak of this self-inflicted crisis, with my girlfriend threatening to leave, I called Shr Fu expecting sympathy. The Master wasted no words or phony emotion. "So!? So she leaves. Good. No one is dying are they? Don't have any false thoughts or attachments." The Master warned me to be careful and act according to principle. I did not listen. I just couldn't cut off my desire and so things got worse and my "sickness" drained my spiritual strength.

When I left home, the Master remarked, "I believe you can leave home and cultivate the Way because you have put down your girlfriend. Be vigorous and advance!" Then Shr Fu addressed all the monks present informally and kindly, "You can't be sloppy or casual, especially now in America. This is the only way Buddhism will be established in the West. Most important, don't attach to women... that is the most important example for you to show America. You can't be too close to women or too far away or you're wrong. You are all my precious jewels. I won't sell any one of you. Don't waste your light-treasure!" Did I understand? No.

In the beginning of the bowing pilgrimage my false thoughts about women brought a hornet's nest of troubles. Bad dreams and demons, harsh weather and hassles all came because of this *mau bing* (sickness) of mine I believe. For example, in Santa Barbara, while false thinking about an old girlfriend, a lemon flew off of a passing garbage truck and hit me in the jaw, sending me to my knees. I said to myself, "Just a coincidence. If it really hit me because of my mind for women, then if I keep on thinking about them it should happen again." So I went on wondering if my old girlfriend had found another man and ZAP! Another lemon hit me square in the back, knocking me down again! Later the Master said, "Those sour lemons were from your sour thoughts about your girlfriend. Now that you know that your false-thinking isn't okay, don't do it any more." Did I understand? No.

In Malaysia I couldn't subdue my eyes or thoughts and got turned upside down. But this time my fuel reserves of merit and virtue were used up. I got so sick as a result of scattering all my energy by false thinking about women I nearly died. Shr Fu saved my life and brought me back from King Yama. While I was bedridden in Malacca, I saw clearly as never before, in my dreams and waking thoughts, that sexual desire is the root of birth and death. The Master would come to my bedside, rub my head and recite mantras, at the critical times, breaking the fever and purging toxins. All the while he kept smiling and asking, "Good, good. Did you die yet? Are you going to die?" In Singapore and Hong Kong the cause and effect of my false thinking and getting sick was uncanny and undeniable. Less than an hour after my mind would move I would become sick. The Master kept saying, "Sick again? Good. I hope you die soon." Did I understand? I thought so. But habits are stubborn and my ignorance deep. It is hard to 'die' even when you try your best. Never again I vowed, never again would I run out to beautiful forms.

When we returned to the U.S., Heng Sure and I began bowing near Santa Cruz. We went into town to contact the police and inform them of our journey. Surprise! The cop was a woman. I got turned and started smiling and rapping with her in the course of conducting our official business. That night I took ill again. Either my mind for women was going to die or I was. It now was clear to me that *all* desire was at root just sexual desire. Running outside one's own nature and seeking anything is death—the slow death of outflowing. Literally, the blessings and wisdom of the original nature dribble away until all that is left of one's bright Dharma jewel is dog shit. It is just like it says in the *Avatamsaka*:

> *Moreover, living beings are bound in a net of love.*
> *They are covered over with ignorance*
>   *and attached to their existence.*

They follow it and cannot give it up.
They enter into a cage of suffering
  and do the deeds of demons.
Their blessings and wisdom are exhausted
  and they forever harbor doubts.
They do not seek the place of peace and tranquility.
They do not know the path of escape,
  and without rest they turn
On the wheel of birth and death.
They constantly bob and sink
  in the suffering mud.

I've had a lot of time while slowly recovering in the back of the Plymouth to reflect on my "sickness" and how to get well. What I took for happiness in the world is really suffering; and what I once thought to be suffering (cultivating) is really happiness. Things aren't always what they seem. So it says,

> *I do not seek the unsurpassed Path for myself, nor do I cultivate Bodhi Practices in order to seek the states of the five desires or the many kinds of bliss in the three realms of existence. Why?*
>
> *Of all the happiness in the world, there is none which is not suffering...*

Avatamsaka Sutra
Ten Transferences Chapter

That is straight talk! In my heart, in ways no words could express, I now know this is so. This is what the Master meant when he asked when I was going to "die". His words were full of compassion and wisdom. It is the false mind that runs outside after desire that must die to cure the sickness of birth and death. The Master's words were the finest of medicines. "When your mind for women dies, then you can be free. If you can't kill it then you'll always be locked up in a cage. Do you understand?"

"Yes, Shr Fu," I answered, "I tried to, but I didn't quite pull it off."

"I'm a lousy teacher. I can't teach and transform my disciples. All I can do is talk unlucky talk and say I wish they would die," said the Master with a kind smile.

I write to tell the whole story so no one will think the Master's words were inauspicious. I am a lousy disciple. Even after the Master saved my life, I can't manage to "die". So, Shr Fu and all our Dharma friends braved the cold and rain to bring a little "gas" to the bowing monks. "Try your best," grinned the Master as everyone climbed back aboard the bus. A storm that had been gathering suddenly broke up and the sun shone down on all of us. I was so grateful I wanted to cry. Truly we are *all* one heart bowing to the City of Ten Thousand Buddhas! Then I had this thought, "Just try your best, Kuo T'ing. Don't cry, just die."

Like Bodhidharma liberated the bird in the cage, the Master has shown me a way to escape from the cage. But mistaking what's before my eyes I have flown back in mistaking the cage for a palace. No more. The beginning of returning to health is to know that you're sick. To be reborn in the Way one must die to the world.

Peace in the Way,

Disciple Kuo T'ing (Heng Ch'au)
bows in respect

Finding the false within the true

November 21, 1978
Ano Nuevo, California

Venerable Master,

The mother of heaven and earth
is said to be born from the Tao.
The sun and the moon are both bright,
moving in their orbits.
So it is with the basic substance
of all in creation:
It is infinitely wonderful.

Ch'an Master Hua

This poem came alive today, Shr Fu, as the sun rose on the rain-soaked coast. It's been raining for two days at Ano Nuevo. Everything in our world is damp. Moisture hangs in the air, saturating space without boundaries. It's wet outside the skin, wet inside our bones. The dusty hills have turned to dull gold, the sagebrush and the tall grasses have exploded in green. Everything is happy with the rain.

This morning the clouds blew away and the sun appeared. At nine a.m. there was a turning point; a transformation happened. The wetness began to flash, change, and disappear. You could see and feel the *yin*-moisture stage of the weather cycle reach its extreme and suddenly, dryness was born. Soon the water vapor left our slimy clothes, our sleeping bags, and the puddles on the ground.

Birth and change, *yin* and *yang*, happening all by itself, wonderful to see. All in its proper time. Nature is patient, the Tao contains all things.

Cultivating the Way has been called the great reversal. "Go towards the good," says the Master. "Return the light in every thought. Change your bad habits from evil to good. Find out your real self." This is what all Buddhist Sutras tell us. Because one who walks the Way turns back the energy that used to flow out in bad habits, soon the accumulated light will reach a flash-point. Like the sun transforms the wetness, the resolve to go toward the good and the practice of returning the light will carry one surely on to a new high road. There will be a birth of wisdom, a change of darkness to inner-light. The dross metal of the body transforms into vajra, the selfishness of false-thoughts transforms into the universal lamplight of Great Compassion. Birth, change, returning, transforming.

"If you want to find what's really true, don't look for it apart from the false," said the Master in Kuantan, Malaysia. "It's right within the false that you find what's true. And you have to be very, very patient."

"How do you find the false within the true?" asked a layman.

"Diamonds come out of the earth, don't they?" answered the Master.

The keys seem to be patience and faith. The three necessities for the Pure Land are Faith, Vows, and Practice. Faith can mean not pushing the Way, not forcing and seeking results overnight. The magic of the weather change at Ano Nuevo was in its perfect, effortless timing. It happened slowly and completely all by itself, wet changed to dry, *yin* changed to *yang*, all in perfect harmony. As the poem says, "The sun and the moon are both bright, moving in their orbits."

Even though we took a lot of wrong roads before we began to practice the Dharma, once we recognize our faults and resolve to change, we step inside the orbit of Enlightenment. Patiently, faithfully, "making tracks for the good, one step at a time," as the Master says, will certainly bring about the Great Reversal.

Now it's raining again and the autumn wind is whistling past our tin-roofed, four-wheeled Bodhimanda. Soon the sun will rise and the whole cycle will move on in its orbit. From empty space there is birth and change. "Infinitely wonderful."

Disciple Kuo Chen (Heng Sure)
bows in respect

Causes and conditions with Vairocana Buddha

November 23, 1978
Ano Nuevo, California

Dear Master,

It says in the *Avatamsaka*:

According to what living beings
practice in their minds,
The vision of kshetras follow suit.

I have found this to be really the case with dreams.

"Vow Power".

The Buddhadharma is vast and great, without bounds or distinctions. So are the Bodhisattvas' vows:

He further makes great vows, vowing within all
worlds to achieve Anuttarasamyaksambodhi without
leaving the place of the tip of a single hair; in every

place of a hair tip to make appear being born, leaving home, going to the Way place, accomplishing Proper Enlightenment, turning the Dharma Wheel, and entering Nirvana... in thought after thought, in accord with the minds of living beings to display the accomplishment of Buddhahood... With a single sound to speak Dharma and cause all living beings to be delighted at heart—vast and great as the Dharma Realm, ultimate as empty space, exhausting the boundaries of the future, throughout all numbers of kalpas without cease.

Avatamsaka Sutra
The Ten Grounds Chapter

In May of 1977 when we began from Gold Wheel Temple in Los Angeles, the Master noted in a lecture that all of us had been together with Vairocana Buddha in the past investigating the Buddhadharma. And way back then the Master said we should all go to America and investigate the Dharma there. "So now we are here together to fulfill our vows. Causes and conditions in the past create a strength of togetherness here, now, that stays through all circumstances. From limitless kalpas past, our conditions with one another are deep... Everyone is Vairocana. All around you, in front, behind, all around you is the Buddha. The pure Dharma body of the Buddha fills up all places."

All living beings are deeply related and connected. Who can say where we have been in the past or will be in the future cultivating the Way and fulfilling the vows of Bodhisattvas. Nothing is fixed. What we can see isn't always real, and what is real we often cannot see. The Master ended that lecture with this remark, "In the midst of a dream, we are all here doing the work of the Buddha."

Peace in the Way,

Disciple Kuo T'ing (Heng Ch'au)
bows in respect

On the Nipomo Mesa.

December, 1978

Pain to the extreme!

January 3, 1979
Below Half Moon Bay

Venerable Master,

He vows that all beings get pure Ch'an gates.

Avatamsaka Sutra

Patient Ch'an meditators know that when pain in the knees and ankles, legs and back occur after long hours of sitting, one reaches a point when the pain suddenly disappears. It's as if a gate opens and one passes through to another world, free of affliction. It's a wonderful experience.

On the way through the gate, however, it takes determination and patience not to be moved by the discomfort.

> *What others cannot endure, you must endure. While sitting in Ch'an everyone must go through the experience of leg pain. We all must pass through the stage of taking what others cannot take. And when we reach the point of bearing the pain that others cannot bear, then we can get good news. This is called "getting through the gate that is difficult to enter," and "breaking through the difficult barrier."*

> *Master Hua, Ch'an instruction*
> *December 1977*

In our station wagon I sit in the well where the back seat folds down. Heng Ch'au has to crawl over my knees to reach his seat in the back. Our meditation schedules are different and one evening he was returning from standing meditation just as I was reaching the point of extreme pain in the knees during Ch'an. I was really sweating. My body hurt a lot, but I was determined to take it. The happiness on the other side of the gate is quite fine.

> *Now we are in the Ch'an Hall and why don't we have any samadhi power? You hurt a little and can't take it... even to the point that in being unable to take it, you want to cry... you haven't broken through the barrier of pain. Now, we want to break through it. We break through these barriers and we can be at ease with the pain...*
>
> *Listen and Think*

I was at the point of extreme pain and because of my normal impatience I was debating whether or not I could make it through the gate. The pain had gone on for what seemed like aeons. In fact, it was more like half an hour, but I was ready to cry and moan. Had a fly landed on my leg, it would have been too much to take. Every cell was straining to hold on to full lotus.

> *...pain to the extreme, to the point that we forget there is ourselves and others.*
>
> *Listen and Think*

Heng Ch'au has a trick of closing the car door with his foot as he climbs on over my seat. He hooks his toes onto the door handle and pulls with his leg. The door swings shut without his having to turn around on the narrow door jamb. It's a nifty move, only this time it didn't work. Heng Ch'au slipped on the ledge and landed with all his weight right smack on my long-suffering knee.

Kerzatz! Pain to the extreme! Electric blue and white pain! So much pain that there wasn't any pain any more.

> *How can there be pain? There is no pain. No matter*
> *what it is you do, you should do it to the ultimate point.*
> *When you've cultivated to the extreme, your light is*
> *penetrating.*

Listen and Think

If I have ever emitted light, this was surely the time. I must have blazed like a torch for a few seconds. Tears ran down—tears of laughter. My nose watered and I could only laugh. It was such a ridiculous scene and the pain was just huge. Heng Ch'au apologized, he knows this point of pain in meditation, and he felt compassion for my misery. His comment, "Did I put you through the gate?" was right on. He had. As my eyes dried I realized that I was still in full lotus and I was on the other side of the difficult barrier. The pain was gone and my mind was quiet and still.

There was no Heng Sure and no Heng Ch'au. No Plymouth and no Ch'an meditation. It was really a tranquil state. Cultivating the Forty-two Hands and Eyes in this place of stillness was a brand new experience.

I don't recommend that Ch'an cultivators rely on externals to pass through Ch'an barriers, but sometimes unexpected expedients appear to take us across when our determination to endure the pain is solid and firm.

Disciple Kuo Chen (Heng Sure)
bows in respect

* * *

Dear Shr Fu,

It's truly as you say, "The straight mind is the Bodhimanda." I remember when I took precepts, it was said that each precept brings with it five Dharma-protecting Spirits. As long as one holds the precepts, these spirits protect one. But if one breaks a precept, they retreat, leaving one wide open to attack from the retinue of demons. Why do things go wrong with our lives? Why do we meet with disasters and bad luck? It's just because of not following the rules, not keeping the precepts. When the mind is straight, one's Bodhimanda is secure and lucky. When the mind is crooked, the Bodhimanda meets hard times. The Bodhimanda is just our own bodies and minds.

Out here, bowing, every time we break a rule or false think we get trouble. In the *Avatamsaka Sutra* it says:

As one thinks, so one receives in return.

This week, we really put our minds to working hard and keeping the rules. It was very peaceful and natural. The car, supplies, weather, our health—all effortlessly worked out just right and went well. Then I attached to a pleasant state in meditation and felt, "Hey, I've got something here." Within minutes, cars were honking and people were yelling at us. Strange people appeared, pale-looking and hungry for our light, wanting "to talk and rap." You see, after I got my state I got sloppy. I figured, "You don't have to start on time; relax, don't force it." So I got lazy and hung around the car making tea. Then I thought, "Well, I'm still hungry and that half an apple should be eaten." So I ate it, even though we have ended the meal. I didn't protect the Bodhimanda but left it open to strange energies and hassles with my false thoughts and broken rules.

I realized that all the disasters in the world begin in this way. There is no boundary or fence for our thoughts. They are free to purify or pollute to the ends of empty space. If I kept the rules and purified my thoughts, it could have benefitted a lot of living beings and improved the world. The Bodhimanda begins with a single thought and our own persons, but it has no end. The self and the Dharma Realm are not two.

When we were in Hong Kong, the delegation went to visit Western Bliss Gardens, a Bodhimanda the Master built years ago on the steep hills of that city. It is a very pure place. Even though Western Bliss Gardens is surrounded by urban noise, smog and pollution, as soon as you enter the gate, it's as quiet as mountain wilderness. The air is clean and the water that flows out of a rock is the purest I ever drank.

There's a Bodhi tree growing in a corner and I got the notion to pick a leaf from it to bring back to the U.S and carry with us on our pilgrimage. Clearly this was just greed and climbing on conditions. While everyone was inside, I ran over to pick a leaf. But every time I reached for one, I couldn't touch it. It was as if I was being restrained. Not only that, but every time I found a perfect leaf—just the right shape and size, etc.—when I reached for it, the perfect leaf suddenly revealed a flaw or didn't look like the one I wanted. This went on for about five minutes. Just as I finally found the leaf I wanted, when I touched it, I felt all sorts of itching and stinging on my legs. My socks were full of ants! They were biting and crawling all over my legs. I ran out from under the tree and started jumping up and down, shaking off the ants and scratching the bites. Then the Master came out and someone said, "Come on, time to leave." I never got the leaf, but I got a good lesson: greed and self-seeking bring disasters; and, "everything is made from the mind alone." The Bodhimanda is created by pure thoughts. It's not outside.

In the midst of a Hong Kong slum is a peaceful and well-protected Way-place. In the midst of the pure and peaceful California coast and countryside we can encounter hassles, weird people and feel insecure. Why? Thoughts. A pure mind can turn any place into a pure place. A defiled mind can transform even the purest place into mud. If I want a peaceful and well-protected

Bodhimanda, I should clean up my own mind and not try to steal it by picking other people's Bodhi trees.

Defilement and purity,
In measureless kshetra-seeds
Come about from living beings' thoughts;
They are held up by the strength of Bodhisattvas.

Avatamsaka Sutra

Peace in the Way,

Disciple Kuo T'ing (Heng Ch'au)
bows in respect

As one thinks, so one receives in return

January 24, 1979
El Granada, California

Dear Shr Fu,

Here's a rundown of the last two days' bowing to the city of Ten Thousand Buddhas:

Sunday, January 22: Quiet morning. Horseback riders trot by, "Hey, what you're doing is great. I'd do it myself if I had the time." And off they gallop. A young family in an old car stops. "We're going back to the East Coast, but we really feel like we have to see the Ten Thousand Buddhas place before we go."

"The City of Ten Thousand Buddhas," I say.

"Yes. There's something about it... we would not feel ready to travel back East until we have visited it. We are looking for a pure and holy place to christen our new baby and the City of Ten Thousand Buddhas feels right." The mother proudly holds up the little baby. "I chant Om Mani Padme Hum. I learned it from a Tibetan Buddhist monk in New Jersey. He was a good person, but there wasn't any heart there, you know? I mean, it was all very intellectual. We are looking for a method, a Path to really practice and walk. We saw a picture of the City of Ten Thousand Buddhas. It feels clean and has lots of light."

A man in the back seat asks, "What kind of Buddhism do you follow?"

"Buddhism is just the best in the hearts of all living beings. It has no country or sect. It belongs to everyone. Buddhism is the teaching of all beings. Nothing is excluded, we don't discriminate."

Big smiles and nods of agreement. "What system do you practice?"

"World Buddhism. All traditions, all schools are practiced and taught. Whatever suits you is available—Ch'an, Vinaya, Secret School, Pure Land, or Teaching—and someone to teach the method. All paths for all beings." More smiles.

"Got a map?" "Is it near Mt. Shasta?" "Far out, that's great."

After they left, two young Mormon missionaries in spotless vested suits walk up. "This is Elder _____ and I am Elder _____. We were wondering what you're doing."

"We're Buddhist monks on a bowing pilgrimage."

"Oh, Buddhists. We thought so. For what purpose?"

"To get rid of our faults and help the world." I am half expecting a sermon and conversion pitch, but they simply say:

"That's wonderful! We're behind you 100%. Good luck!" And they leave. Good vibrations there.

Tollgate.

As we bowed up to the last intersection out of town, a strange man appeared. He moved slowly, totally in control. His face was hidden from view behind a full beard and the shade of the tall black hat he wore. He circled us and then positioned himself in a field about 75 yards ahead and watched us. From a large shopping bag he pulled bottles of whiskey and beer and downed one after another like they were water. The vibes he put out were black and cold. As soon as I saw him, I found myself doing a couple of the Forty-two Hands.

After he settled in, strange things began to happen. Fire trucks and police cars went roaring through the intersection and then weird people started showing up. A car skidded to a stop inches from Heng Sure's head and then a woman offered him a ride. A man kept hollering from behind the black-hatted man, "What religion are you?" and laughing strangely. People in bizarre clothes and long scraggly hair walked by mumbling. The man in the black hat calmly watched over it all, nodding his head and laughing. Then he rang some bells that hung from his neck.

Immediately, five or six yelling and cursing men appeared on the embankment across the road from us. They were angry and violent. "This is devil's land here," said one. "May you be cursed!" cried another. "Wait 'til you get to Devil's Slide," threatened one with a menacing laugh. (Devil's Slide is a steep and narrow stretch of sheer cliffs and mountains about seven miles north. We've had many warnings about it.) They tossed some rocks but they missed us. The man in the black hat downed another bottle in one long swallow. Then he rang his bells and waved to the men. They climbed back over the embankment and disappeared, cursing and howling.

The black-hatted man approached to check us out up close. He laughs under his breath, "Heh, Heh, Buddhists, Krishnas, Buddhists, heh, heh..." I catch a glimpse of his face. It sends a shiver through me. I couldn't describe it except to say that it was full of delight for evil and harm, flushing red and full. He wanders over across the intersection and stands next to our car. He just stares and drinks. Without moving an inch, you can feel him directing the whole negative show with his presence. He gestures and the men and weird people return and start coming toward us.

This could be tight. Heng Sure and I have discovered that no matter what happens, we can come through it just fine if we don't let our spirits sag. If we don't let fear or anger or bad vibrations come into our hearts, we can slide through the tightest spots like greased fish. We are learning to counter-punch with kindness, compassion, joy, and giving instead of our fists, words, and false thoughts. "Everything is made from the mind alone... as one thinks, so one receives in return" (*Avatamsaka Sutra*). It's so true. Our survival has come down to not allowing an inch of doubt or *yin* energy to enter and pollute our minds. Put out light and the sun shines; put out darkness and it rains. The heavier it comes down, the brighter you've got to rise up and shine.

So here they were, all these hostile, strange people gathering to test our temper and resolve and maybe worse. What to do? Just the day before, we read from the *Avatamsaka*, and the verse came into my mind as we bowed into this tense "tollgate,"

> *It's just like the sun*
> *Which appears in the world*
> *But does not hide or fail to appear*
> *Because there are blind people who fail to see it.*
>
> *When the Bodhisattva takes on all this*
> *   grievous suffering,*
> *His vigor increases.*
> *He does not cast it off,*
> *He does not hide from it.*
>
> *He is not scared or startled.*
> *He does not retreat,*
> *He is not frightened.*
> *He has no fatigue.*
>
> *I do not seek liberation for my own body,*
> *But only to save all living beings.*
> *So that they all attain the mind of All-Wisdom, and*
> *Cross over the flow of birth and death, and*
> *Gain liberation from all their suffering.*

As I recited these lines in my mind, Heng Sure and I were engulfed in a sea of children. A school bus had pulled up across the road and about forty happy, pure-faced little Dharma protectors ran over. They completely surrounded us—some sitting, some on bikes, some standing. They made offerings from their lunch pails and piggy-banks. The strange men were confused and thwarted. They couldn't get near us. A couple of men came up and tried to pester Heng Sure, but the kids' innocence and good energy mellowed them right out. The evil men got very polite and quiet in a hurry.

"Are there really 10,000 Buddhas up there?" "Is it hard bowing all day?" "It's neat helping the world, huh?" "Do you take baths?" asked a little one. His sister kicked him gently and scolded him for getting too personal. "Of course, they take baths," she said quietly. "But how?" he persisted, "I want to get the inside scoop."

"What if bad people throw rocks?" asked a child.

"We only see good things," I answered.

"What if people come by and call you weirdos?" wondered another.

"We only hear good things," I said.

"What do you say when you pray? Does he (Heng Sure) talk to pray?"

"Real softly, huh? Shhh! Listen, maybe we can hear him." They all stand quietly there on busy Highway One listening to the sounds of "Hua Yen Hai Huei Fwo Pu Sa," as Heng Sure comes up from a bow.

The angry, dark men one by one drift away, muttering. The first to come and the last to go is the dark figure in the tall black hat. He is waiting on the other side of the intersection. But as we cross, the kids ride/escort us on their bikes and he slowly turns and leaves.

On the other side of the intersection is a little stretch of open country. The intersection marks the geographical end of Half Moon Bay. Scores of enthusiastic supporters load us up with offerings and kind words. They are happy and full of light. The kids slowly head for home.

"It's fascinating," says an older woman making an offering. "A wonderful idea. I wonder where all those kids came from back there all of a sudden... Did you see them?"

"Yeah. We saw them. We certainly did!" I said.

The sign says "25 miles to San Francisco." Ahead is Devil's Slide. Our map is the *Avatamsaka*. Everybody's a teacher. "Everything's okay. No problem."

Peace in the Way,

Disciple Kuo T'ing (Heng Ch'au)
bows in respect

San Francisco!

February 21, 1979

Dear Shr Fu,

When you reach the place of seeking nothing,
There are no worries.

Yesterday Heng Ch'au and I reached the top of the hill—looking south we saw Devil's Slide and the town of Pacifica, looking north, inconceivably, we saw the orange towers of the Golden Gate Bridge, Mt. Tamalpais, the Mt. Sutro T.V. spire—San Francisco! It seems only yesterday we were in Santa Monica contemplating Highway One and the mind-boggling journey ahead. Now in less time than a finger-snap we have bowed into the Bay Area and left Highway One for the trek through the City. Life is surely like a dream. As the Sutra says:

The past, present, and future are nothing but talk.

Yesterday could have been day one of the pilgrimage for this disciple. I learned a lesson in my heart that took twenty-one months of study and patient practice to fully grasp. Have I really got it now? I hope not, because each time I attach to a state, I'm ripe for another fall. What is the lesson? It's called "don't seek".

The Master has given these instructions dozens of times in a variety of expedient ways: "Don't seek anything. Don't seek Buddhahood, don't seek great wisdom, don't seek enlightenment. Seeking is putting a head on top of your head. It's nothing but greed. Simply cultivate with a single mind. That's enough. Cultivate without a thought of self-benefit. Cultivate just the way you eat, dress, and sleep. It's a necessity, that's all. And don't have that second thought. Be single-minded."

The *Avatamsaka Sutra* specifically instructs the Bodhisattva not to seek.

> *The Bodhisattva only wants to uphold the pure precepts. He does not seek great power, high class and status, abundant wealth, beauty and style, nor the throne of a king. His thoughts are attached to none of these.*
>
> Ten Practices Chapter

Again:

> *The Bodhisattva is a great master at giving. He can give away anything at all and his mind remains level and equal, without regret. He does not expect a reward, he does not seek reputation as a benefactor, nor is he greedy for benefit or gain.*
>
> Ten Practices Chapter

As clear as the message is, somehow it has not connected with my deepest heart. I thought I was in control of my greed. In fact, I am controlled by it.

We talked with Gold Mountain on the phone one day last week. Heng Ch'au gave our new route to the office and I translated a story that happened to us that morning. It was a thrill to be so close to home. But back on the street bowing, I suddenly felt upset and worried. Why? I thought, "Wow, I've been at this for nearly two years and what have I got to show in the way of any real accomplishment? Have I changed in any way?"

In short, I was seeking inside of the Dharma. But because the object of my search was enlightened wisdom and compassion, I allowed the thoughts to dwell, feeling that they were a "purified desire." The longer I reflected on myself, the deeper the afflictions grew.

Then I got my lesson. Three young boys walked by me on Monterey Road as we bowed up the hill in the rain. The boys were full of light and smiles as they passed. But at the first sight of my face all three lost their light immediately. Their smiles turned to sad and worried looks. I saw my forced effort, my seeking, mirrored in their eyes. I turned them off completely. What their faces silently said was "Hey, this guy is nothing special. He may be a monk, but he's as unhappy as anybody. He's got something that he's looking for and he has not found it. What a disappointment! What is he? A Buddhist? Phooey!"

Shame on me. By seeking for results from my cultivation I hurt those three boys and maybe turned them from the Dharma.

Seeking nothing there are no worries.

Doing holy work to get something out of it defiles the purest of Dharmas. If you seek enlightenment because it's the best of all good deals, it isn't going to happen. Wanting results prevents them. I realized this huge obstacle that I held on top of my head was just the ego, the self, seeking benefit. I gave it away on the spot and suddenly felt a great, black cloud lift off my shoulders. I'm not doing this work for myself, I'm going to relax and just take it as it comes. It's said,

When the effort is complete,
accomplishment happens naturally, all by itself.
Not for himself does he seek benefit,
He only wants peace and happiness for all beings.
Not for an instant does he give rise
to frivolous debate.
He only contemplates all dharmas
as empty and without a self.

Avatamsaka Sutra
Ten Transferences Chapter

Instead of false thinking about self-benefit, how much better it is to take the energy and use it in faith on the method of practice. What a simple truth and how long it's taken me to see it.

* * *

Dear Shr Fu,

The Bodhisattva thinks again, "Throughout the long night, I loved this body and was attached to it. I took food and drink because I desired to fill it up. Now I will use this food to give to other living beings. I vow to eternally sever all greedy attachment to my body."

Avatamsaka Sutra
Ten Inexhaustible Treasuries Chapter

Everyone has a favorite flavor. Until I began the bowing pilgrimage, I had a big sweet tooth. Things changed when bowing started to generate more *yang* energy. I found that sugar dispersed my concentration. Now I can't even look at sweets without feeling the flush rise in my face. It's my temporary state—others might have no trouble eating sweets. Ultimately any discrimination can obstruct one's view of the basic unity of the Dharma-nature body.

Two Garbage Poems:

The Sweet Tooth's Lament
or "Bitter is Better" (for me now)

Sugar is this bhikshu's bane.
Just one bite can fog my brain.
One sweet cookie melts my spine,
gets me drunk as quick as wine.
Turned by sugar that I ate,
I forget to cultivate.
Red of face and short of breath,
I'm unconcerned for birth and death.
Sugar makes me want to rap,
makes my tongue begin to flap,
Makes me want to laugh and play
and wander from the Buddha's Way.
Sugar makes my mouth run on,
'til all samadhi's lost and gone.
This monk's eaten his last dose of
dextrose, syrup, and sucrose.
Sugar's fine for one sweet lick
but greed for pleasure makes me sick.
Sugar used to taste just great,
now I would rather concentrate.
Sugar is the lover's friend,
sweet and sticky to the end.
Sugar is the family glue,
sticks him to me and me to you.
Of all the flavors, I confess
I'm attached to bitterness.
So when it comes to sugar treats,
forgive me if I pass the sweets.
One day, to be really true,
I must put down sugar, too.

Until then I would rather be,
   bitter-sweet and sugar-free.

Food is One of the Five Desires

Food is neat; I like to eat.
   But greed is really common.
Overeating pleases me,
   but only for a moment.
Knees on fire, hot desire
   spoils my meditation.
Just a touch too much at lunch
   obstructs my cultivation.
Not too little, guard the Middle.
   Just don't crave sensation.
What a shame if greed for food
   kept me from liberation.
When my belly's full,
   my mind for Bodhi is retreating.
Food is nice, but what a price
   I pay for overeating.

* * *

The five desires are dharmas that obstruct the Path, even to the point of preventing one from realizing Unsurpassed Bodhi. For this reason I will not permit myself to have even one thought of desire. My mind will be as pure as the Buddhas'.

Avatamsaka Sutra
Ten Practices Chapter

Disciple Kuo Chen (Heng Sure)
bows in respect

Any truth would have to be a simple one

February, 1979
Daly City, California

Dear Shr Fu,

Yesterday morning, while waiting for our clothes to dry in a laundromat, I realized something very clearly: all my problems and all the problems in the world come from false thinking. In less than a second, this simple truth lit up and cut through aeons of confusion. I could never put it into words, but right after seeing this, I had the thought, "Almost two years of bowing, Heng Ch'au, and you still are false thinking! What are you false thinking about? About *me*. About 'the self and all that pertains to self.'" Then I went on with this self-talk and asked, "But why is a thought of self false? I mean, here you are right here in the laundromat. If that's not a self, then what's true? Isn't this me?"

Who is me?
I am who?
You ask me,
I ask, "who?"

This verse keeps answering my question. There is no me. That's why self is a false thought. The self does not exist. So the *Avatamsaka Sutra* says:

Discriminate and contemplate within yourself in this way:

"Who am I inside?" If you can understand it in this way, then you will realize that the self does not exist.

This body is falsely set up. It's dwelling place has no fixed position. When one truly understands this body, then within there is nothing at all to attach to.

Contemplate the body well
    and see it all clearly.
Be aware that its dharmas
    are empty and false.
Do not use mental effort
    to discriminate them.
Who is it that gives rise to your life?
Who is it that takes it away?
It's just like a twisting ring of fire—
No one knows its beginning or end.

Avatamsaka Sutra
Bodhisattva Enquires Chapter

This is such right-on, straight talk! It's so simple and yet I still haven't even understood the very simplest truths. I get so caught up with being smart and putting on clever words and phony faces that I can't even see the obvious. Last week a jogger showed up to help me wake up from this dream.

We were standing outside the car in the early a.m., getting dressed for bowing after exercising. Like a wind, this jogger suddenly ran up. He was strong and muscular, clean and straight-forward, maybe 45 years old. There was something unusual about him. He came right up without a pause, almost aggressive. Around his eyes and head we both could see an energy—like dancing flames. It was hard to look at him, because his glance was so penetrating, and hard not to look because he commanded a certain respect. He wasn't the least polite or respectful.

He asked Heng Sure if he talked at all and Heng Sure indicated to talk with me. "Oh, so you talk, huh?" he challenged and came right up to me.

"Are you the guys who are trying to get rid of greed, anger, jealousy, arrogance, and all those other bad things, and find the truth?" His tone was teasing and almost mocking, like he didn't believe a word of what we said we were trying to do. I felt defensive and couldn't answer. He pressed closer until he was just inches way from my face. This guy was making me nervous.

"Well, ah, yes, we are..." I finally squeaked out.

"Well, it occurred to me that any truth you find would have to be a simple one," he said. He was looking right through me without even blinking, waiting for an answer. I felt that anything I could say would be stupid and phony, a pretense at being wise and at ease. The fact was I was squirming and feeling like a fool.

"Don't you think?" he pressed, holding a stare that cut through all my defenses and false coverings. Then he smiled and said, "Well, good luck!" and jogged away.

After he left I realized why he made me so nervous. I was still hiding behind my words and thoughts. I was using the "path of words and language" to hold on to a view of self. With my tongue and pen and false thoughts I was creating an artificial reality to avoid facing the simple truth: "the truth of no-self."

At the most intense points of the pilgrimage, especially in Big Sur, the emptiness of all my words and ideas stared me in the face just like the jogger did. I was ready to put down clocks, calendar, and tongue and just bow and sit until:

> *The path of words and language is cut off.*
> *The place of the minds' workings is extinguished.*
> *Right in thought, one is apart from thought.*
> *One thinks, and yet has no thoughts.*

But I hadn't been able to put it down. The good knowing jogger reminded me that "the truth" is very simple: there is no self. If I had really understood the fundamental teaching of the Buddha, then "even one word would be too many." I still haven't seen through the emptiness of self. If I had really understood this principle, then how could I feel nervous in front of the jogger? "Who" was squirming and feeling cornered?

People ask what is the biggest obstacle or hassle we've met on the pilgrimage. My own mind is the biggest obstacle. I am my worst enemy. My mind wants to keep going in its mad circles and make something out of nothing. Where there is no problem I make problems; where there's no business, I make business. Selfishness is the root of all evil.

After the jogger left, I felt resolved. "He's right!" I thought. "Don't pretend and hide behind anything, not even one word or a single thought for self. Go for the real and true. Don't be so smart."

> *When one attends to the here and now,*
> *The false returns to the true.*
> *With one thought unproduced,*
> *The entire substance manifests.*

What time is it? What day, month, year? How many miles this way or that way? When will we arrive? What will we do when we get there? What did we do before? What will we do tomorrow?

These are all false thoughts. "Who" needs to know? It's time to be a big dummy, and to bow with a single heart, to shut my mouth and open my mind.

Peace in the Way,

Disciple Kuo T'ing (Heng Ch'au)
bows in respect

Don't pick up germs off the street

March 12, 1979
Sausalito, California

Venerable Master,

It seems like we've covered miles in the space of a single thought. Bow down and beneath my feet is the wind-swept sand of Pacifica. Stand up and behind me the orange towers of the Bay Bridge disappear below the hills of Marin. We've nearly reached the foot of Mt. Tamalpais. Once across the ridge, we'll be on Highway One all the way north until we turn east to the City of Ten Thousand Buddhas. Truly as the Sutra says, "The three periods of time are level and equal."

As we have often heard,

When you can concentrate,
then it is magical.
When you are scattered,
then there is nothing.

I realized today on Bridgeway Drive in Sausalito that of all the different kinds of work that people do, cultivating the Buddha's Way is the job that requires more concentration than any other. To really concentrate takes everything I've got and then some. Bowing on the highway helps concentration tremendously because we get instant response to our false thoughts these days. It's uncanny.

For instance, the mystery of the car horns is still at work. Since the trip began, every time my mind wanders into thoughts of self, what I've done, or plan to do—every time I get involved in my surroundings—it seems that I'll hear a car horn on the instant of the thought. It's spooky. When I really concentrate on the bowing method and don't scatter my thoughts, the road is completely silent and still. It works this way every day. It can't be coincidence.

It gets even more specific. In San Francisco last month I put on my glasses for the afternoon's bowing up Point Lobos Avenue outside the Seal Rock Inn. I had this false thought: "It will be fun to see people's expressions for a change." Not recognizing this as a step down the road of scattered concentration, I let it dwell in my mind.

Two bows later an unusual-looking woman walked by. Nothing about her appearance fit together. She could have been put together in a hurry by a committee. She looked like a rush-job at the people plant. From lopsided beehive hairdo to her yellow tennis shoes, she was very strange.

She said in a mechanical voice, "Watch your eyes. Be careful you don't pick up lots of germs off the street," and she walked on by towards the Cliff House.

I understood immediately that it was not okay for me to leak light out my eyes, chasing forms and shapes. I took off my glasses and went back to work at concentrating on the method.

> *So that my mind does not dote*
> *on the pleasures of the world,*
> *Nor is it stained by attachment to what is practiced,*
> *I want to concentrate my mind to receive and uphold*
> *The Dharma taught by all the Buddhas.*
>
> *Avatamsaka*

A cultivator must concentrate like a diamond cutter: the mind is that hard and that bright. It shines light from every polished facet. Concentrate like a hockey goalie: desire and bad habits fly from all directions like a hard rubber puck. Concentrate like a bomb-defusing expert: let an angry or selfish thought dwell and you can lose your nose to a speeding can of Pepsi, as I nearly did in Pacifica.

Concentrate like a lion-tamer: don't allow fear or doubt to impede your moves or tarnish your will. Concentrate like a harbor pilot: you know where the shallows and the rocks are in your nature. Guide your Prajna boat safely through the channel.

Concentrate like a mountain climber: follow the pitons and footprints of climbers who have made the safe ascent before you. Concentrate like a brain surgeon: get right in to the stuff of the mind, pull out the diseased parts without harming the healthy parts.

Concentrate like a soldier behind the lines: the self doesn't like being told to drop dead. You've got to trick it and subdue it without a direct confrontation. Fighting with the mind makes everyone lose.

Concentrate like a Buddha: relaxed, patient, courageous, unsurpassed in strength and kindness. Concentrate like a cultivator:

> *One who takes the Buddha's state as his own*
> *And concentrates his mind without rest—*
> *That person will get to see Buddhas*
> *Equal in number to his thoughts.*

Avatamsaka

Disciple Kuo Chen (Heng Sure)
bows in respect

The "Ego" sutra

March, 1979

Mt. Tamalpais, California

Dear Shr Fu,

I've had a big change of heart. In the last few weeks I've begun to see my deepest false thoughts and oldest flaws. I clearly saw the "Ego Sutra" of "me and mine" that I have been reciting inside day after day, life after life. I call it the "Emperor's Sutra." All month, bits and pieces of this truth have been coming to me. When I stopped talking and began reading nothing but the *Avatamsaka*, the light increased. The *Avatamsaka* opened up and came alive, and so did my old sickness—my mind for being #1.

Then, one night, right at the last bow of the day, everything stood still and in that space of stopping, I saw myself like never before. I saw the heart of my false mind, unfiltered and clear through. It wasn't pretty. I saw how I am always looking to be #1; how I'm always looking for others' faults and shortcomings so that I can feel I'm #1—always competing and contending, jealous and obstructive. Thought after thought, like beads of a necklace, are strung together by "how great I am." "I alone am #1." It was like the whole world was silent and the only sound was the sound of my little mad mind reciting the "Emperor's Sutra." It was as loud as thunder. There it was, just hanging in empty space. It was just a small ball of bad noise, like a small child wailing in the void.

I wanted to cry for shame. It was so ugly and unkind. How small and selfish, my little "song for myself" that was running my life! I sat down to meditate in an empty lot next to a big Howard Johnson's Motor Lodge. I thought, "Okay, so now you know. Now you see what a crummy person you are. Now you know your Sutra. What are you going to do about it?" *CHANGE.* I knew I could change. My heart was truly sick of being so arrogant and self-inflated. How? I didn't have to think about it. I knew. Just single-mindedly concentrate with no other thought until all the false thoughts are crossed over to wholesome thoughts. Hold precepts purely and return the light. Walk the Way of nowhere dwelling and don't neglect it for an instant. Don't allow yourself to follow after one thought for self. Don't schlep through the garbage of name and fame and the five desires any more. "Be one of the Way with no mind" by bowing with a single heart. Let it all go.

With no false thinking, everything's okay. With a single mind there are no worries. Pure and happy, things are naturally done as they come and left behind as they go. With no time to false think, how can I fault others? Clean up my own junk, mind my own business.

I was happy and ashamed, humbled and new. It's really hard. I have so many false thoughts and bad habits! But it feels so right and basic to put down all the false coverings and just be real, just be a sincere person.

That night we read from the *Avatamsaka Sutra* about how the Bodhisattva "in one thought is able to know all thoughts." Why? Because everything is made from the discriminating mind. From the one thought of self, everything else is born. Knowing your own true mind is to know the Dharma Realm. But I only just now saw all my false thoughts. I knew them. I know who I wasn't. But I didn't know who I was. I felt empty, like a baby, but incomplete.

A few days later, the Master stopped with Dharma Master Heng Lai and some lay people on their way to the City of Ten Thousand Buddhas. It was the day before Gwan Yin's Birthday. I told the Master, "Shr Fu, I've been really seeing my false thoughts and flaws these last few weeks. I'm really ashamed."

Shr Fu: "So you've had a big change of heart, eh?" The Master turned to the lay people. "This is Kuo Wu's sister, do you recognize her? Do you recognize Kuo Wu? Surely you recognize these two! Do you recognize him? Do you recognize me? Do you recognize yourself?"

I was speechless.

Shr Fu: "So you've had a lot of false thoughts?"

Me: "Lot's of them. So many…"

Shr Fu: "That's for sure. You've been emperor for so many kalpas since beginningless time, it's for certain you would have false thoughts. Well, if you recognize your faults, then you can change them." The Master's tone was encouraging and positive. Then he spoke this verse:

> The living beings of my self-nature are boundless;
>   I vow to take them across.
> The afflictions of my self-nature are limitless;
>   I vow to cut them all off.
> The Dharma-doors of my self-nature are numberless;
>   I vow to learn them all.
> The Buddha-Way of my self-nature is unsurpassed;
>   I vow to accomplish it.

and asked, "Do you understand?"

Me: "Yes, Shr Fu." The words went right to my heart and hit the empty spot. Tears of understanding welled up in my eyes.

The next morning, while bowing, the Master's words came back to me and began to grow in my heart. It was as if my teacher was saying, "Do you recognize that all is one? We all share the original True Suchness Nature. Within it, there is not a single dharma that can be obtained, much less is there a self or an emperor. Do you see now? There is no you, there is no me. No self, no others. Do you recognize the self-nature?"

My body shook, and I got a run of shivers up and down my spine. In a small way, I was beginning to understand. Finally, these

verses from the *Avatamsaka Sutra* that I'd been puzzling over for
weeks untangled.

> *The Tathagata's Dharma body,*
>   *all karma which is created, and*
> *Everything in the world has this appearance:*
> *We say that the mark of all dharmas has no mark,*
> *To know appearances like this is to know dharmas.*
>
> *All disciples of the Buddha in this way know:*
> *The nature of all dharmas is always empty and still.*
> *There is not a single dharma which can be created,*
> *And just like all Buddhas, they enlighten to no self.*
>
> *They understand and know*
>   *that everything in the world*
> *Is identical in appearance*
>   *with the nature of True Suchness...*
>
> *He vows that all beings skillfully*
>   *enter the level equality of all dharmas*
> *And understands that the Dharma Realm*
>   *and self-nature are not two.*
>
> *Avatamsaka*

But, my ego is strong, Shr Fu, and my false thoughts are like a
blizzard. How to change and really expand the measure of my heart
naturally to where the "self-nature and the Dharma Realm are non-
dual"? Compassion. Compassion crosses over arrogance. Being
one with everyone transforms the mind of #1. Probably for the first
time since leaving home, I got a clue to my name, Heng Ch'au. It
doesn't mean, "always the Emperor." It means "always bowing
away the Emperor." Be humble and compassionate. Bow your
"self" away. Bow with a single heart to all beings. Be a good person
with a humble heart and don't give anyone afflictions.

Peace in the Way,

Disciple Kuo T'ing (Heng Ch'au)
bows in respect

* * *

P.S.: Shr Fu, the $120 is from a man who just came up and said,
"I'd like to help support your work." He emptied his pockets, and
then very sincerely said, "and thank you" and left.

Just watch how it grows

March 18, 1979

Mt. Tamalpais

Dear Shr Fu,

> *We're holding a Gwan Yin Session this week. I'll bet*
> *you have thoughts of greed, wanting to run up to the*
> *City of Ten Thousand Buddhas and join in, don't you?*
> *Well, don't worry. For you two bowing once every*
> *three steps, every day is Gwan Yin's Birthday and*
> *every day you're at the City of Ten Thousand*
> *Buddhas...*

...said the Venerable Abbot when he visited this Friday. How right
he is. Gwan Shr Yin Sessions are special occasions. The
Bodhisattva of Great Compassion bestows happiness and plucks
out suffering in miraculous ways. Single-mindedly reciting Gwan
Yin's name turns anywhere into the City of Ten Thousand
Buddhas.

Everyday, cultivators experience a rich treasury of learning that is the study and practice of Buddhism. In the heart of it, the big lesson is learning to be a good person.

> *Disciples of the Buddha, the Bodhisattvas take great compassion as foremost... through increasing their faith... through becoming sympathetic... through accomplishing great kindness... through adornment with repentance and reform...*
>
> *Avatamsaka Sutra*

Although the Buddhadharma contains supreme, subtle, profound, wonderful perfection of wisdom, its highest application is in the realm of living beings. By going towards the good in everyday life, by using kindness to make beings happy and compassion to end suffering, every day becomes a Gwan Yin Session.

The same day of the Master's visit we were bowing on the rain-slick Shoreline Highway in Tamalpais Valley. An old woman came walking down the road, bareheaded and alone. She wore scruffy slippers and hunched her shoulders against the cold drizzle. Cars passed going much too fast on the narrow road, missing her by inches. She made a purchase at the local "convenience" food store and then shuffled by us again on her lonely way back home. My heart went out to this old lady. Why did she have to risk her life and her health on this treacherous road just to get food to eat? Where was her family? I knew that she could have been my own kin.

There are millions of old people in the world in her situation or in worse straits. I reflected that establishing the Buddhadharma here in the West will certainly have a great deal to do with changing our attitudes towards old people. This old lady needed caring for. She needed the basics of food and shelter against the elements. By making homes for our elders and providing care for the lonely old people of the world, we will be doing good and repaying a part of our debt of kindness to the Buddhas, our parents, our teachers, and elders. This is the work of Gwan Shr Yin Bodhisattva. This is the promise of the City of Ten Thousand Buddhas.

I recalled the Hyatt family of Cambria, a young couple who made space in their home for old Pappa Joe, their invalid father. The Hyatts came to visit us and brought old Joe along, bundled in blankets and full of smiles. He was a happy man, despite his infirmities and failing health. The Hyatt's model of compassion shines a light of goodness. It made that day very special. Every day was Gwan Yin's day for the Hyatt family.

As I saw the old lady on the road, I thought how good it will be to bring all our lonely old folks together and teach them about the Pure Land, to share with them the peace and joy of reciting the names of Amitabha and Gwan Shr Yin. By doing this work, Buddhists will make a great contribution to the world.

This morning I had a dream. It was like a T.V. commercial in style, like a message from the United Nations. A man and a young boy stood together. The boy's eyes were wide and full of wonder. The man said, as if to a teacher on the first day of school, "Here is my son. Please train him well. Take good care of him in your school and show him how to be a good person."

Following him were four more men, each with his son and they repeated the same message, one in English, one in Chinese, one in Japanese, one in French.

The Master has always stressed the importance of education and making schools into places to provide wholesome training in the basics of growing into good people. This is the path to Buddhahood.

> The Bodhisattvas... have vast, great intent and inclinations which cannot be destroyed. They intensely and diligently cultivate all roots of goodness which become accomplished... through seeking learning without satiation...
>
> Avatamsaka Sutra

Instilling Virtue School, Dharma Realm Buddhist University, and the middle schools and high schools that will be established at the City of Ten Thousand Buddhas are really important to the world. The children we have met on the bowing pilgrimage still have pure light and great trust. If these children can grow into adults with the guidance of True Principles in their education, if they can pass the difficult years of adolescence in a community of people who believe in and practice kindness, righteousness, propriety, wisdom and faith, then the world will naturally turn into a better place. By following the light of Gwan Yin Bodhisattva and cultivating the Dharmas of Great Compassion, we can make education the total transformation of the heart and spirit that it should be.

With the elders happy and praying for peace and with the youngsters excited by their discovery of the world, of great ideas, and of true principles, and with the middle-aged people busy as Bodhisattvas cultivating the Way and transferring the roots of goodness to the Dharma Realm, then every day is a Gwan Yin Session and everywhere is the City of Ten Thousand Buddhas.

This is not just a dream. It's as real as the next thought in our minds. Before many years pass, the world will know the Proper Dharma has found it's new home in the West. People like the Iowa farmer we met on the Great Highway near the San Francisco Zoo will no longer say, "Buddhism? I thought that was in Asia. But you're Americans? Ever been through Iowa?" I wanted to say, "Yes, I have, Pop. I grew up in Ohio. And before long you're going to be proud to tell your neighbors in River City that your sons and granddaughters have taken refuge with the Triple Jewel, or even left the home life to study the Way. Soon your friends will be investigating vegetarianism and Ch'an meditation. You may be reciting Gwan Yin's name yourself before you know it. Just watch how it grows."

Conversation We'd Like to Hear: 1984

"Buddhists? Oh, yeah, they're the ones with the big hearts, right? Educators aren't they? They take care of the old folks, I understand. They're the ones who don't fight, right? Yeah, I've heard of them. In fact, I've been thinking of subscribing to that magazine that they put out and looking into it for myself. What's it called? 'Yankee Buddha Sea,' or something like that. I heard about it on their radio show that comes on every week. Real decent listening, I'll say. I like best the sing-along part when they chant that Homage to the Bodhisattva tune. Yes, I used to think the Buddha was an Oriental God, but kindness and compassion, happiness and giving, why that's as American as cornflakes, yes, indeed."

The Bodhisattva gives rise to happiness because he is mindful of the ability to benefit living beings.

Avatamsaka Sutra

Signs We like to See: (Posted on the fence outside Pigeon Point Lighthouse)

Notice: No hunting, fishing, killing, trapping, or disturbing of any creatures allowed.

by order of the Commandant
U.S. Coast Guard

* * *

Dear Shr Fu,

I had my mind blown three times today by the *Avatamsaka Sutra* and by "Vajra Bodhi Sea." Each time I picked one of them up for a quote to add to my writing, I turned to lines that read my mind and mirrored my thoughts exactly! It was just as if the words on the page were speaking to me, using my own thoughts. It felt totally uncanny. We disciples are used to the inconceivable way that a Good Advisor can know our thoughts even before we think them, but when magazines start to mirror our minds it's something else again!

Flower Garland Round

Everything is made from our minds alone.
Everything exists within the Dharma Realm.
The Dharma Realm is contained
    within the Flower Garland Sutra.
The Sutra came from the mouth of the Buddha.
The Buddha lives in the hearts of all beings.
All beings live within the Ten Dharma Realms.
The Ten Dharma Realms are fathomed
    in a single thought.
Everything is made from our minds alone.

(repeat until the mind falls silent)

From compassion and kindness
    and the power of vows
Appear and enter the practices of the ground;
Gradually there is perfection of the mind.
Wisdom's practices are not reflections' realm.

Avatamsaka Sutra

We have learned that nothing we have thought, or written, or said matters as much as a single, silent, sincere bow. The visions, the insights, the dreams, and the revelations all bear on the actual practice of the Dharma in the same way a match reflects on the sun. It's the doing, the effort, the faith in following instructions, and the giving that tell the story, wordlessly. What a discovery. Reality is totally empty, real and true. But it's also totally the Dharma, the truth of reality like it really is, a gift from the Buddha's great kind heart.

I return and rely in reverence to the Triple Jewel of all time and space. May all beings remember their original home within the

Proper Dharma. May all beings return to their roots and go back to the source of original purity.

Disciple Kuo Chen (Heng Sure)
bows in respect

You're only kids, of course you didn't believe

Early Spring, 1979
Muir Beach

Dear Shr Fu,

Back on Devil's Slide I made a vow to never again seek private relationships or anything that excludes or rejects others. That night I had a dream about the Master dying and I saw a powerful dragon. When Shr Fu visited us back in Pacifica he asked, "Any dreams?" I related the dream and the Master said, "Oh, so you want me to die, huh?"

"No, Shr Fu, that's not it at all!" I protested.

"I'll die for you," said Shr Fu.

"I have to die by myself," I replied.

"Then I'll live for you."

"I have to do that on my own, too."

"Well, then, what use am I as a teacher?" Then the Master recited a verse:

Eat your own food to get full;
Resolve your own birth and death.

Later, I thought to myself, "Is it really the case that I wanted Shr Fu to die?" I didn't really feel settled about it at all. But I let it go, or so I thought. (The "dying" has to do with my "mind for desire" dying. This is the dying the Master was referring to in saying he hoped I would die soon, that is, "hurry up and kill off your view of self; your mind of selfish desire.")

When the Master visited the next time we were on Mt. Tamalpais. A lot had changed inside. I saw my faults and bad habits like never before. I felt after two years of bowing I was only just beginning to face up to my deepest faults and big view of self. I was humbled and ashamed. Moreover, it was due to the Master's timely instructions and help that I was able to see this—not my *own* insight. Specifically, Shr Fu advised me to close my mouth. And in closing my mouth my eyes opened a little.

Right after the Pacifica visit as the Master was preparing to leave and I was all set to "stand on my own," two hostile men came up. I felt confident I could turn their attitude. I started rapping and verbally sparring with them. Shr Fu leaned out the car window and yelled. "No need to talk. Don't talk so much!" I had felt my energy draining in talking with the men but didn't know why. The two "men" turned white as sheets at the Master's words and ran down the road. They were not people at all. Shr Fu smiled and said, "See, I chased the demons away from you. Ha, ha. See you later." It was a lesson I'll never forget.

Now, on Mt. Tamalpais, I saw the foolishness of my assertion "I can stand on my own." (To really stand on my own I need to truly be able to recognize myself and have no self to stand on.) During that visit the Master looked me right in the eyes and said with a smile, "So now you can stand on your own, huh?" The next day while bowing I understood the dying dream. I did, in fact, wish Shr Fu would "die." Unconsciously my ego wanted to live and so I dreamed of Shr Fu dying. When I first saw the *Diamond Sutra*, I ran away and avoided it. Why? Because I knew it was about the truth of no-self. When I first met Shr Fu I couldn't and wouldn't bow. I was too proud. The "emperor" doesn't bow to anyone. Now after two years of bowing and seeing the emptiness of my big self, I still resist "dying" and instead dream of my teacher dying. "If your teacher dies, no one will be around to subdue you. No one will call your trip and stay on your case," was the unconscious false thought behind it. Basically, I didn't want to face this. I didn't want to admit that I could have such a shameful thought about my teacher. I wanted to hide my faults and cover over the bad parts. But I've been that way, sneaky and not straight, and it only brings suffering to everyone. I know I have big faults, but I am not going to add to them by being a phony ever again.

Too late to apologize to the Master. He had already left. By not being right out front, I miss opportunities. I'm always behind myself, which is why I need a "Good and Wise Advisor" who is always ahead of me.

This week Shr Fu stopped by again.

Shr Fu: "Anything to say?"

Heng Ch'au: "There's been lots of changes. Shr Fu, since your last visit I know now my dream of the Master dying was my ego not wanting to die."

Shr Fu: "Sure, then no one would be able to control you."

Heng Ch'au: "I'm ashamed, Shr Fu, I'll change."

We then sat down to talk. The Master sat on the car bumper. It had just been raining prior to Shr Fu's arrival. Now it was sunny, but the ground was mud. My hat was lying on the ground next to the Master's feet. Shr Fu casually put his foot out, stepped on my hat, and began grinding it into the mud and wiping the dirt off his shoes all over it. I wanted to say, "Hey, Shr Fu, don't! That's *my* hat!"

But then the thought came into my mind. "That should be my *head* the Master is stepping on. I deserve it." I figured the Master thought it was just an old hat on the side of the road. Then the Master picked up my hat, carefully brushed off the mud and dirt, folded it neatly and handed it to me. "Heh!" I thought, "The Master *knew* all along that was my hat. What's up?"

After Shr Fu left, I understood the wordless teaching with the hat. When I first came to Gold Mountain I felt I was pretty good. I felt at home, except for the bowing, especially the practice of bowing. Then one night the Master said in the Sutra commentary, "It's just like someone always wanting to be number one. They're always looking for a high hat to wear... wanting everyone to give them a high hat so people will say, 'He's really great. He's number one.' Isn't that how it is?" The words went right to my heart. That was exactly my attitude and the Master saw it, read my very thoughts. I bowed to the Master that night. But my high hat didn't fall off with one bow.

By rubbing my hat in the mud, I felt the Master was saying, "So now you recognize a little. All is forgiven if you can change for the good. Here, put your hat on, but remember it's not a crown. Don't run out and be emperor again."

Push over Mt. Sumeru
The mind ground is flat.
Jealousy, arrogance
Ultimately are invisible.

Cultivation! How could there be
Anything more esoteric or wonderful?
Put down the three minds and four marks
And Buddhahood accomplishes itself!

Master Hua

A dirty hat and a lesson in the level equality of all things. No one is number one. The nature is flat like the ground. Be humble. Keep your mind contrite and compassionate. Put it all down, and Buddhahood takes care of itself. The verse says:

Offenses arise from the mind,
*   yet the mind is used to repent.*
When the mind is forgotten,
*   offenses are no more.*

When both mind and offenses
are eradicated, both are empty.
This is called true repentance
and reform.

Shr Fu, I am deeply ashamed of my arrogance and for the trouble I've caused. I'll change. I don't ever want to "go back to the palace" and be emperor again. My home is the eternally dwelling Buddhas, Dharma, and Sangha of the ten directions. I'm going to turn my back on the dust and unite with enlightenment. I'll try my best, bowing in repentance and reform.

Peace in the Way,

Disciple Kuo T'ing (Heng Ch'au)
bows in respect

* * *

"…standing on my own."

There was a time I thought I could prance off by myself to the mountains and get enlightened. "Who needs a teacher?!" I thought. But somewhere inside I knew I needed a wise advisor. The ego's tricks and all the states of mind that arise with cultivation are hard to recognize on your own. The biggest demon is one's own self and it's the hardest to break through. It's like a knife trying to cut its own handle. But having a good knowing advisor doesn't guarantee success. You have got to follow instructions.

This month the Master paid us a visit. Before leaving he cautioned us on accepting offerings. "Just be really careful." We weren't careful and got food poisoning. At the peak of our illness the Master returned. "Anything special happen?" he asked.

"Yes, Shr Fu, we've been sick for three days. Bad food," I said.

"Oh? See?" replied the Master with a knowing smile and a look of "I warned you, didn't I?"

During the roadside visit we talked about food, sex and cultivation. I said, "Shr Fu, two years ago in Los Angeles, you told us that cultivators who ate good food can obstruct their Way-karma from too much fuel. I didn't believe it then, but now I know it's really true."

Shr Fu: "You're only kids. Of course you didn't believe," answered the Master.

"Well, never again will I not believe and I will always follow instructions," I thought to myself.

The Master said, "Holding that extra essence and being patient when it wants to run out—just that is cultivation. Otherwise... (here the Master pantomimed like a nervous, puffed-up balloon that sees something attractive and instantly deflates.) You get turned by what you see and suddenly you deflate. Then there's no more problem, no more pressure. If you cannot deflate, that's cultivation. It's right 'here'."

The very next day, the pressure inside was fierce and pulsing. We took a break to meditate. I grabbed the wash basin to clean up. When I turned around from the door there was a pretty woman standing right in front of me, smiling and staring, blocking my way. "Hi, what are you doing?" she asked softly. I caught her eyes and lost mindfulness for a split second. Just like the full balloon... "suddenly there is no more problem, no pressure." Try again, and this time follow instructions.

> *He vows that all living beings constantly meet good wise advisors, concentrate on, carry out, and not oppose their instructions.*
>
> *Avatamsaka Sutra*

I couldn't believe it! How could I be so slow and stupid? Even when I get such a remarkable teaching the day before, I can't "concentrate and carry out" the teaching. The Master's timely instructions and true words go in one ear and out the other and each time I take a fall.

"I can stand on my own" wasn't an assertion of true strength. It came from the false mind. It wasn't from self-control, but, rather from a self that didn't want to be controlled. My independence was premature and unnatural—an act of ego rebellion, not true liberation. I was just attaching to a state and being turned by a false thought. The ego resists dying in ways that are hard to believe and see through. Right here is the importance of a Good and Wise Advisor: no matter what age you are in years, your wisdom age is a child's. It's said one can't trust one's thoughts until the fourth stage of Arhatship… how much the less as a first stage novice?! As soon as you think you've got something, you're ripe for a loss. Hard to ascend, easy to fall. A good guide makes all the difference.

Disciple Kuo T'ing
bows in respect

Don't think

March 28, 1979

Dear Shr Fu,

> *Truly recognize your own faults and don't discuss the faults of others. Other's faults are just my own. Being of one substance with everything is called Great Compassion.*
>
> Master Hua

Shr Fu, it's funny that I can't criticize anyone anymore. Every time I see something to criticize these days, I get an immediate feedback in my mind that says, "Wait a minute, don't you recall when you did the very same thing yourself? How can you stand apart from anyone and judge them? Return the light. Those are your own faults you are looking at and disapproving of." For example, I'll see a sports car driver speeding around a curve and think, "How can he put himself and others in danger like that, just for thrills?" Then I remember how I used to drive fast cars—no difference. Return the light. Don't fight.

I'll see tourists hop out of cars, run up and photograph the Golden Gate Bridge or the scenic coastline and then jump back in their vehicles and zoom away without ever actually looking at the sights, without ever being there. It seems like such an empty exercise. Then I get my warning buzzer: "Don't criticize! Return the light. I used to live far away from the present. Stuck in worries, dreams, and future fantasies, my feet rarely touched the ground. Who am I to criticize anyone else? It's only my own bad habits that I'm seeing and rejecting." What's going on here? It's called "attaching to appearances" and being confused by false thoughts. The Sutra explains it like this:

> *All worlds in all directions are completely created by the distinctions made in their thoughts. As for both thoughts and non-thoughts, there is nothing that can be obtained. In this way the Bodhisattva understands thought.*
>
> *Avatamsaka Sutra*

I spent so many years being pushed around by my false thoughts! I felt there had to be a plan in advance for every action. I made lists of projects and nailed down details before I made a move. Of course, I was never very happy. I was too bound up by the chatter of my mind. At every hand I sought self-benefit. I knew the score before I played the game. Take a loss? Never.

Why did I always feel tired and burdened down? Because discriminating right and wrong, chasing benefit and running from the fear of loss takes a lot of energy. And ultimately it's in vain.

There is never an end to rights and wrongs. Only by giving up the chase for self-benefit does the mind find peace.

On *san bu yi bai*, the Master's basic instruction to us has been "Don't do any false thinking." "Don't think." Why? Because the Ego, the Self that seeks advantage is a phantom, an illusion that lives only in our thoughts. The Ego is the boss that pushes us into the ridiculous pursuit of benefit and fame. When thoughts stop and the Ego disappears, everywhere is peaceful. All dharmas suddenly look flat and empty. All appearances and rights and wrongs vanish because the mind no longer needs to separate and name the world, there's no more Self to defend. The demons are subdued and every day is happy.

To serve the Buddhadharma

March 30, 1979

Above Stinson Beach

Dear Shr Fu,

We are constantly astonished by the magic of the *Avatamsaka*. When we read from it each night after the ceremony, unmistakable changes happen. If we are tight and nervous from our false-thoughts and *mau bing*'s the Sutra relaxes us and gives us courage to continue. If we are irritable or feeling off center, the Sutra cools the fire and brings us back home. If we are happy, the Sutra celebrates with light.

One night several weeks ago, I was feeling pressure in my head, my body ached in every joint. I was ready for a fight, anything to let off the steam. But when I opened the Sutra to translate from the Eighth Transference section, all my heat transformed into a feeling of crystal clarity and kindness. I recognized my state and pulled back on the light that I was ready to shoot out. After the reading was finished I was reaching for an incense stick to begin our Shurangama Mantra recitation, when suddenly I had an instant's vision of the age and the importance of our Sutra. Time seemed to stand still as the vision flashed by. Here's what I saw. It was like a movie, as if Hollywood had filmed a story to illustrate the rare treasure that is the Buddhadharma.

The supreme, profound, subtle and wonderful
Dharma is difficult to encounter in billions of aeons...

A band of people of all ages and races are travelling through deep and dangerous caves. The trail is long, narrow and filled with hazards. Their journey requires courage and stamina and faith. There are many trials and setbacks, but they do not weary of the walking. They are guided by a pure golden light that leads them forward through all the peril. On the walls of the caves are the traces of ancient civilizations. The company passes through levels of measureless time. Layers of entire worlds pass by with the stories of their coming into being and dying away recorded on the stones.

Finally, the travellers reach the source of the golden light. It is a secret fortress that conceals a library. It is made of vajra and locked with a magic power. Only beings with blessings and good roots may enter. Gods, dragons, and uncanny creatures guard the door.

Once inside, the company walks by the book racks in the outer chambers. They contain texts of ancient knowledge: the planets, the herbs, mathematics, music, languages, literature, and encyclope- dias of practical arts and ritual. The group walks past this worldly lore, it is valuable and worth preserving, but the light leads them on to another locked gate in the heart of the library. Awesome warriors, tall and pure, guard this crypt. They pay their respect to it with deep reverence. Within the crypt is a treasure chest which gleams with dazzling, jewelled light. This is the ultimate adorned place, the sanctuary of the Holy of Holies, the pinnacle of ageless wisdom.

The lid of the chest creaks open and a pure light blazes forth. The company breathlessly inspect the contents: crumbling scrolls and cobwebbed parchment. The printing is faint, the punctuation is missing, the meanings are hard to understand. No one has studied this wisdom for a very long time, very few practice it. But there is a feeling surrounding the chest. The group recognizes that this is a jewel beyond price, a treasure to be preserved and protected at all costs. It must be cherished and made known everywhere. Its truths must be practiced.

The group sits at the feet of their leader, one with wisdom and experience. He shows the group how to correctly venerate the treasure. He explains it for them. He calls it Dharma, the ultimate principles, the road to the end of suffering, the methods for gaining lasting and genuine peace and joy.

> *...I now get to hear it, see it, and hold it in my hands, and I vow that I will understand the Tathagata's true, actual meaning.*

The company of travellers are very happy. They recognize the value of their discovery and they marvel at their good fortune. Together they make great vows to give their lives to the Dharma, to protect it, to translate it, to practice it and make it known in all future times and places. As they make these vows the light radiating from the chest doubles in brilliance. A change takes place in the texts themselves: the words on the ancient pages grow more distinct. The books take on a new life and a new strength. The Bodhisattva guardians, the gods and dragons and all the protectors are delighted. The vows made by the company revive the holy Dharma and keep it in the world.

The light from the crypt in the secret library beams out and cuts through the cave walls. It illuminates all worlds, all civilizations throughout measureless time. Suddenly the company of walkers find themselves no longer underground. They now stand on a pure, magnificent mountain peak.

They have in their possession countless expedient means and tools for giving the Dharma to all beings in their great big family. The leader of the group explains that the secret library was in their hearts all along. But it required the journey through the caves and braving the dangers and the toil to discover it. The company is overjoyed and with great vigor they set off down the mountain to do the work of filling their vows. They know they will meet again.

That was the vision and as I looked at the Sutra rack in our Plymouth which holds our neatly bound and clearly printed Dharma books in English and Chinese, I realize that we must not take our good fortune for granted.

Disciples of the Buddha are steeped in the purest of the Proper Dharma. It is our highest responsibility to keep alive and fresh our vision of the precious treasure we possess. The presence here among us of the Proper Dharma, the real road to Buddhahood, is the rarest of jewels. It is nothing short of miraculous.

Like the members of the company in the vision, my happiness at being able to serve the Buddhadharma and to give my life to the Triple Jewel is measureless and boundless.

Disciple of the Buddha,

Heng Sure
bows in respect

Heng Chau writes: "Surprise! The Master rode all the way from Los Angeles with some disciples to pick us up and take us to Gold Wheel Monastery. Seeing the Master with his bright robe and sash and wise and awesome deportment at the gas station we just bowed past a few days ago is a mind blower!...

"…That's the way it is in the presence of the Master: whatever happens happens deep and is not soon forgotten. And always expect the unexpected!"

Kindness is supreme

April 2, 1979
Shoreline Highway, Stinson Beach

Dear Shr Fu,

This is an experience I had during the holiday season last year. I only now have found time to write it up.

> *I should rescue and save all beings and set them in the place of ultimate peace and joy! Therefore, the Bodhisattva immediately brings forth the bright wisdom of great kindness.*
>
> *Avatamsaka Sutra*

Kindness is supreme. Kindness can make us happy all the time, because kindness comes from giving and making others happy. Giving makes everyone happy. To be truly kind you have to have given yourself way, given your afflictions away, given everything away, let it all go.

> *Being brittle and hard is easy*
> *It takes courage to be kind.*
> *Being stingy and selfish comes*
> *   naturally to the weak, but*
> *It takes strength to be compassionate.*
> *Holding on to the self is not wisdom,*
> *But it takes faith to let go.*
> *Doubts and fears are greed for benefit.*
> *It takes giving to be happy.*

As I bowed in the icy shadows of the rocks on Christmas Day last year the voice of a wise, kind teacher in my ear gave me faith and courage. He said, "C'mon, let it all go. I'll catch you if you slip." In my heart I stepped over a chasm with eyes closed and found myself on another shore. Without thoughts in my mind, the peace and light was pure joy. Everything was okay. My heart wanted to give the happiness I felt to all beings. Every hard and selfish atom in my body felt permeated with the light of kindness.

> *Dwelling peacefully in an attitude of giving, all his faculties are happy, his merit and virtue increase. Producing a wholesome joy and desire, he ever enjoys the practices of vast, great giving.*
>
> Avatamsaka Sutra

Just then I bowed into the sunlight, out of the shadows, and took a good look at the selfish, fearful heart that I have lived in all these years. When I seek benefit from others, when I seek their approval, I cannot be kind. When I hold on to a self and project my fears on to others, I cannot be kind. Seeking approval and fearing hurt *by themselves* are the cause of my unhappiness. I make it all up by myself, in my own mind. Fear itself is the poison and the pain, it's not the object of fear that causes hurt. Give up the fear habit projection, stop seeking self, return the light and happiness fills the world.

> *Faith in my teacher's voice gave me strength.*
> *Strength gave me courage to act.*
> *Courage helped me give up my fears.*
> *Giving up the fear itself brought happiness.*

I rested in the heart of happiness that day. I felt clouds of black ch'i disperse from my body. Kindness came naturally with the practice of giving. The more giving, the more kindness; the more kindness, the happier the heart. To maintain happiness is easy when one gives to make others happy. With kind thoughts one is happy and wants to share it to make others happy, too. This refills the original happiness without exhaustion.

Giving the Dharma is the highest giving and it makes for the highest happiness in return.

To leave the home-life and cultivate the Way is the highest kindness, because it makes one able to give the Dharma without rest.

As I bowed on that rocky road, I realized how deeply good it is to practice the Dharma. Reciting the name of the Buddha is great kindness and great goodness. As we bow, we recite the name of the *Avatamsaka Sutra* and the Avatamsaka Assembly of Buddhas and Bodhisattvas. We say the word "Buddha" twice and Bodhisattva once with each bow. Just this alone is a happy deed, a way to give to others. It is a kind act. It is enough to fill the world and the heart (no difference) with light, joy and peace. All the happiness begins with giving, giving up the self, contemplating freedom. How fine it feels to be content and seeking nothing, unbound by all the afflictions we make for ourselves, on account of our Self.

At the place of seeking nothing there are no worries.

Be content, give up all afflictions, doubts, fears.

If you know contentment,
  you will always be happy.
If you can be patient,
  then you naturally are at peace.

Give all thoughts of Self away. Stop thinking and get happy. Then be kind and make others happy. How? Give Dharma by cultivating the Way.

He vows that all beings will perfect the speaking of
the Buddha's road to Bodhi, and constantly take
delight in the supreme giving of Dharma.

Avatamsaka Sutra

A family of Dharma-friends joined the bowing that morning and "manifested bodies to speak the Dharma." Passers-by saw seven disciples of the Buddha praying on the highway, cultivating the Buddha's road to Bodhi with happy hearts.

When the Bodhisattva cultivates the practice of
giving, he makes all beings happy and delighted.

Avatamsaka Sutra

Cultivation gives;
Giving makes happy;
Happiness wants to be kind and give;
Kindness wants to cultivate.

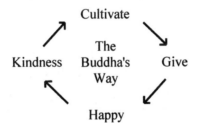

Did the state last? No. It was a state, and states come from the mind, they change like the weather. It was a natural thing. I didn't seek it, it came by itself. I didn't attach to it, it left by itself. I admit it was the happiest I've been in my 29 years of living. Until my Self has been completely given away I will still turn and flow in attachments and false thoughts. Now happy, now afflicted. I don't want it this way, and I don't want it any different. I just want to cultivate the Way with a single mind and really learn to give. I want to unite my light with the light of the Sutra.

*In thought after thought the Bodhisattva makes
increasing advance into the Perfection of Giving.*

Avatamsaka Sutra

**Disciple Kuo Chen (Heng Sure)
bows in respect**

Bodhimanda in a wilderness

April, 1979
Near Stinson Beach, California

Dear Shr Fu,

Daily our resolve deepens. Each obstacle and demon we face
leaves us stronger and happier in the Way. Yesterday I wrestled
with a doubt demon all day. The demon was my own false thoughts,
not outside. I borrowed strength from my vows and light from my
teacher to subdue this demon. Today the world looks different. The
world didn't change, my mind did.

The weight and dust of all the doubts and false thoughts lifted
like the dark clouds at the end of a coastal storm. What I saw was
very simple. For endless miles everything was clear and calm,
empty and still. For two years I've been a monk but the only
monastery I've lived in is my own mind.

"The straight mind is the Bodhimanda." The Master said this in
Hong Kong as we climbed the steep hill to visit the simple Way-
place, Western Bliss Gardens. It stuck with me. Today I found
myself returning there like home. Western Bliss Gardens made a
strong impression. Rough wood and stone, quiet, sunlight coming
through the trees and open windows. Nothing in excess or

decorative. It was like a simple shelter in the wilderness meant only to keep out the elements and to realize the Way within.

My own monastery, my mind, should be this unadorned and basic. What really matters? Just being a real person and getting rid of all coverings of jealousy, arrogance, stinginess, and affliction is my work. The greatest good I could do right now is to clean up my Way-place—and truly purify my mind. Leave behind all false thinking and be "one of the Way with no mind." No thought for the past, present or the future. No mark of a self or others, of living beings or a lifespan. I should work hard, live simply and close to nature and give no one hassles or obstruction. Just be "pure, peaceful and happy" was the Buddha's instruction. "Do good. Do no evil. Offer up your conduct according to the teaching, and purify your mind."

I feel like I'm starting from scratch: building a pure Bodhimanda in a wilderness. Trying in each step to be true within the true. In every thought subduing my greed, anger and stupidity, and returning to principle. Sweeping out all marks and throwing away all dharmas. "Constantly brush it clean and let no dust alight."

The foundation work is the bowing with a single mind. Bowing levels the gilded palace I've caged myself in. Living close to nature is holding pure precepts and guarding my mind from error. It's so clear that there is nothing outside; it's all made from the mind.

If one wishes to know all Buddhas of
the three periods of time,
Contemplate the nature of the Dharma Realm:
Everything is made from the mind alone.

We read some lines from the *Avatamsaka* the night before, that really went to my heart. I thought, "This is so good and true. I should be this way. But I am not like this. Where do I begin?" The next day I had this vision and realized that all Buddhas of the past, present and future are just made from the mind alone. I should begin right where I am: purify my own ground of enlightenment, rectify my own mind. This is the Bodhimanda, nowhere else.

These were the verses we read from the *Avatamsaka Sutra*:

> *He fulfills the level equality*
> *of all Buddhas of the past*
> *He accomplishes the level equality*
> *of all Buddhas of the future.*
> *He peacefully dwells in the level equality*
> *of all Buddhas of the present.*
>
> *He practices the states of all Buddhas of the past.*
> *He lives in the states of all Buddhas of the future.*
> *He is the same with the states*
> *of all Buddhas of the present.*
>
> *He obtains the good roots*
> *of all Buddhas of the past, present and future.*
> *He perfects the seed-nature*
> *of the Buddhas of the three periods of time.*
> *He dwells in what is practiced by all Buddhas*
> *of the past, present, and future.*
> *He accords with the states of all Buddhas*
> *of the three periods of time.*

Peace in the Way,

Disciple Kuo T'ing (Heng Ch'au)
bows in respect

* * *

P.S.: When the Master visited us last month he said, "Tomorrow is Gwan Yin's day. We're holding a session. We'll be tying up the boundaries tonight (big smile). You've got greedy thoughts about attending, don't you? Well, don't worry. For you, here doing Three Steps, One Bow, every day is a Gwan Yin Session; every day you're at the City of Ten Thousand Buddhas."

A straight mind is the City of Ten Thousand Buddhas. When the mind is straight no matter where you are, you're at the City. When the mind is crooked, then even if you were at the City of Ten Thousand Buddhas, it would only be the Old State Hospital.

> *Bodhisattvas are made from people.*
> *Buddhas come from what people cultivate.*
>
> *A straight mind is the Bodhimanda,*
>   *practice understands;*
> *A straight mind is the Buddha City,*
>   *every Buddha is made by hand.*

It's all made from the mind alone

April, 1979

Near Pt. Reyes National Seashore

Dear Shr Fu,

> *He leads all living beings through the wilderness of*
> *birth and death with its places of danger until they*
> *safely arrive at the City of Sarvajna. He and all living*
> *beings do not experience disasters. Therefore, the*
> *Bodhisattva should never be lax.*
>
> *Avatamsaka Sutra*

Every day, I eat, sleep, and wear clothes. I'm not the least bit lax about this. Why do I eat, sleep and wear clothes? So I can cultivate, not so I can eat, sleep and wear clothes again tomorrow. The focus of my effort and thoughts should be cultivation. I should be vigorous and hurry up, cross myself over so I can lead others "through the wilderness of birth and death."

Last night, I thought to myself, "Here you are in the middle of the ultimate path and you still drag your heels and cheat. All your instructions are pearls, hard to meet with in a million kalpas, and you don't truly cherish them. Cross over and truly realize your heart's resolve to end suffering for all beings. Don't be lax! Start with the bowing and meditation," I told myself.

"Don't do any false thinking. Whatever you feel you can't put down, put it down the hardest. Purify the mind, this mind. It's all within your own mind, not outside. The absence of false thoughts and defiling attachments is enlightenment. Concentrate to the extreme while walking, standing, sitting and lying down. Single-minded concentration crosses all over to the other shore," instructed the Good Knowing Advisor within. Simple instructions often hold the deepest truth.

Last night, during meditation, I was struggling with the pain and nervous-ninny mind that wants to always quit and do something else. Out of the blue, this verse from the *Avatamsaka Sutra* appeared:

> *His mind does not falsely grasp at*
> *   dharmas which have passed by.*
> *Nor does he greedily attach to*
> *   things which have not yet come.*
> *He does not dwell any place*
> *   in the present,*
> *He understands the three periods of*
> *   time are completely empty and still.*

All my false thoughts are rooted in the three periods of time. With a single mind, there is no time and there is no not-time. There's just nothing at all. Everything is "completely empty and still." "In bowing and meditation, from now on, you should look at it this way. Just be with 'no mind'. Don't worry or get nervous. Don't get all hung up. Let all your doubts and false thoughts go," I exhorted myself.

What about attachments? I think about things I like and things I fear, things I want and things I don't want. Things, things, all these things. Things I long for from the past, things I hold on to in the present. Things that are coming in the future. "How are you going to get free of all these things that tie up your mind?" I thought. Then, just like before, the *Avatamsaka* appeared from empty space in my mind, with a passage we have just translated.

> *If the Bodhisattva is able to not be attached to all*
> *dharmas, then he is also not liberated from all*
> *dharmas. Why? There is not the slightest dharma*

which exists, whether presently produced, already produced, or about to be produced. There is not the slightest dharma which can be grasped. There are no dharmas which can be attached to. The true appearance of all dharmas is this way; it has no self-nature.

Bang! How could it be more clear? Within these two passages is all I need to quiet my worried, rambling mind. I have no more excuses to go on like I have in the past: cultivating some, false thinking some; cultivating some, attaching some.

Somehow, last night, a door was opened in my mind by the *Avatamsaka*. Its wisdom gave me the boost needed to get on with being "right on." Only the practice of uninterrupted "pure mind, continue, continue" remains. If I don't finally put to rest all my doubts and mind's stupid clatter, then who will do it? There's no place outside on which to rely, there's no place inside to hide. I know now clearly that my false thoughts are not okay, my attachments are not the real thing. Almost two years and only now am I truly ready to start bowing with a single mind to the City of Ten Thousand Buddhas.

It's spring. The whole world is speaking the Dharma. The *Avatamsaka* is everywhere and everything keeps saying, "It's all made from the mind alone. It's all made from mind."

Grateful and happy in the Way.

Disciple Kuo T'ing (Heng Ch'au)
bows in respect

The Bodhisattva Path is home

April 1979
Near Pt. Reyes, California

Dear Shr Fu,

Some people say, "Get a job! What a waste of talent." Others say, "Yes, but why do you give up all of the good things in life? You could be really comfortable... a good job and all."

Why aren't we "successful"? When I was in graduate school there were more students than jobs. Everybody was uptight, nervous, and worried. There was intense competition to the point of cheating and nervous breakdowns. Some people were literally "worried sick."

It wasn't just that way in the teaching field, but the whole job market was glutted and good positions were hard to get. Many of my fellow students were married and had families to support. Making ends meet was not easy.

I also saw that many good paying jobs involved a lot of compromise. Personal integrity and freedom seemed to take second place to not rocking the boat and keeping in good standing. This made people even more nervous and confused. They worried they wouldn't get a good job, and then they worried about losing it if they got a job.

I looked for jobs nobody else much wanted. Partly I felt there would be one less person to worry about getting ahead of or losing out to for a job, grant, or scholarship. It felt honest and not a big thing. It eased the pinch a little for others and I liked living marginally. It gave me time to look into things—like yoga, t'ai chi, hiking and meditation—that didn't pay off but were really interesting.

When I started to teach, I saw students were under a lot of stress and not at all sure about their lives. They had questions "who am I, where am I going, there's a lot of injustice and poverty in the world, what am I doing that matters?" The material I was supposed to teach didn't deal with their real needs. It was irrelevant. They studied to get a grade and I taught to get a paycheck. How could something that made my colleagues so worried and didn't help my students be worth pursuing as a career just to pull in $15-20,000 a year?

Fellow students had hundreds of rejection letters from all over the country pinned to their office doors. During the doctoral exams the fellow in the test room next to me froze in panic. He just stared at the wall for eight hours. It was his last chance to pass or be kicked out and lose his fellowship to Europe. He just couldn't take the pressure. When I shared my feelings with a senior faculty professor, he matter-of-factly said, "That's why I chose this field… you can avoid these matters." Things never felt right after that.

Whenever I went after a good job or a name and fame position, I felt burdened and not honest. In my mind I knew I was climbing, cheating, and turning my back on the path with heart. At that time, government and business were rife with corruption and scandal. Almost any of the good jobs implicated you in this bad energy and added more suffering to the world. The way of the world was: "your loss is my gain; every man for himself." I couldn't participate knowing this. I couldn't put it down either. Why? Because I wanted to be #1 at everything. The desire to be the best, to be #1 kept me from being real and true to my heart and tied me in knots for a long time.

Even the marginal jobs entailed "eating crow" (as a teacher once called backing down on your moral principles to "make it" in the world). I ended up working the night shift at the hospital's psychiatric unit because I couldn't go along with electric shock treatments, drug "lobotomies", pretending not to know what I was doing. "Eating crow" is everyone's loss. No man is an island.

I didn't have the guts or the vision to do more. I straddled the fence between trying to "make it" and doing what was right. Not until I came to Gold Mt. Monastery did I get off the fence and take a stand. The Bodhisattva Path is home.

He (Bodhisattva) can take himself across and cause others to cross over. He can liberate himself and cause others to gain liberation; subdue himself and cause others to be subdued; gain still tranquility for himself and cause others to obtain still tranquility. He can gain peace and security for himself and cause others to gain peace and security. He can leave defilement and cause others to leave defilement. He can purify himself and cause others to be purified. He can enter Nirvana and cause others to enter Nirvana. He is happy and he makes others happy.

Disciples of the Buddha, the Bodhisattva has this thought: "I should follow all Tathagatas and leave all practices of the mundane world. I should perfect all the Buddha's Dharmas, dwell in the supreme place of even equality, with a level mind contemplate all beings. I should clearly penetrate through all states and leave behind all mistakes; cut off all discriminations and forsake all attachments. I should use clever skill to make my escape with my mind constantly dwelling in peace, in supreme, inexpressible non-relying, unmoving, measureless, boundless, inexhaustible, formless, deep, profound wisdom."

Disciples of the Buddha, this is the Bodhisattvas Mahasattva's second practice, that of benefitting.

Avatamsaka Sutra

Now we have a "good job." It's called, benefitting. Trying to be
#1 is a waste. Selfishness wastes blessings and the jewel within.
Seeking self benefit leaves the whole world poorer. We work for
the Buddha. It's the best job in any world. "He gives (to all beings)
the doing of the Buddha's work." (*Avatamsaka*)

Disciple Kuo T'ing (Heng Ch'au)
bows in respect

* * *

P.S. We are in a parking lot of a laundromat. As I finish this letter,
two men look over into our car. "What are you reading, dude?" asks
one, looking at the *Avatamsaka* sitting on my lap. He shakes his
head and says, "Get a job!" I was looking up this quote:

> *He does not defile the Buddha's household*
> *nor abandon Bodhisattva precepts.*
> *Taking no delight in worldly matters,*
> *he constantly benefits the world.*

I thought, "We have a job. It's 'taking no delight in worldly
matters.'"

* * *

Dear Shr Fu,

This is the verse the Master gave me in Pacifica:

> *Your words are false and your excuses many.*
> *(When you) value your energy,*
> *you can become a Buddha.*
> *Still dreaming? Stop talking and*
> *do no more false thinking.*
> *Awakened? Originally there were*
> *no words in it at all.*

My name is Kuo Chen, Fruit of the Truth, because I have been a liar. My mouth karma is extremely heavy. Only after practicing "returning the light to shine within" and "seeking the completion of oneself" have I begun to recognize the depth of my bad habit of false speech. It permeates my bones.

> *The Bodhisattva accomplishes the foremost honest and true speech... he obtains the non-dual speech of all Buddhas in the three periods of time.*
>
> *Avatamsaka Sutra*

I wrote a half-dozen notes to Heng Ch'au over the past two weeks and each one was misunderstood. Each note back-fired and required more writing to clarify the meaning.

I realized that my *hu fa*[3] doesn't believe what I say! It's my karma as a liar. I vowed to stop writing altogether, using the principle "originally there are no words."

Then, by continuing to return the light, I understood more. The answer is not to cut off the tongue, but to cut off the self and its defensive habit of lying.

"Master, why would someone tell a lie?" I asked.

"Because he wants to cover over his ugliness. He only wants others to see his long points and he hides his faults by telling lies," the Master replied. "Don't you think that's how it is?"

I realized that the answer is not to lie to myself. I don't believe what I say either. I am not true within my mind.

"Your words are false and your excuses many."

All day I do things with an eye open for self-benefit, for a way to slip around the true principles. Words fly by in my head without any charge of sincerity. I made excuses for myself endlessly and allow cheating behavior without shame. I don't hold myself to the principles I know to be true. Nothing that I write seems to count, it

---

[3.] Dharma Protector

comes and goes like the wind on the Bolinas Lagoon that we're bowing beside.

The road to the purification of liar's karma is to have faith in myself, to choose principle and value it over selfish greed for advantage and benefit. Practice principle and do not tolerate the slightest deviation. No excuse for selfish thoughts. Give away the good behavior as an offering to the Buddhas and transfer the merit to all beings everywhere. Send the defiled self and its bad habits back to emptiness where they came from.

No wonder my Ego is still in charge of my life; I don't have any virtuous practice that can transform it. I don't have any "inner power" of virtue to move the beings of my self-nature to change for the good.

When my faith in my true self is not dual, then my words will be believed. How to achieve it? "Value your energy and you can become a Buddha. Still dreaming? Stop talking and no more false thinking…" In other words, cultivate! Don't try to figure it out in words, it's the words that are the sickness. Concentrate instead on the real treasures, the wordless tools of the practices: the vajra sword, the bowing method, the pure, non-retreating Dharma Wheel. Return the light, in every thought sincerely repent. Hold faith that the powerful *yang* energy of the Dharma can transform my liar's tongue into "the non-dual speech of the Buddhas of the three periods of time."

And remember cultivation is about growing healthy, new, natural wisdom-sprouts in the place of old, diseased habits. Guide the growth gently, with kindness, don't smash it. Use wisdom. Let it expand and contract naturally like the heart, like the tides. Force kills and distorts. It stops the Dharma.

> *Although he does not rely on the path of language,*
> *nor does he attach to not speaking…*
>
> Avatamsaka Sutra

The "Fly" invades planet Earth

January 2, 1979

South of Half Moon Bay, California

Dear Shr Fu,

I had a dream last month that really moved me to work harder:

Dream: It came silently gliding in from outer space, passing galaxies and covering incredible distances in seconds. It was huge, black and a totally evil thing. Attracted by a foul, amber smog, it was honing in on our galaxy. The smog was a color, a smell, a texture and vibes of a bad energy that permeated our whole universe. This "fly" was drawn to it like a bee to honey.

Everyone thinks the smog is beautiful—like looking at a colorful sunset through layers of air pollution. No one notices the fly as it quietly zeros in on our galaxy, then our solar system, and finally Earth itself. The Earth is center of the bad *ch'i* the fly is attracted to. The fly is diamond-hard concentrated evil and destruction. There is no goodness whatsoever to it.

It banked around the moon. You could see the footprints of the astronauts on its surface. The astronauts were jumping and playing around like kids digging in a sand-box. They never noticed the fly. It could change shape from the size of the Milky Way down to an atom particle faster than a thought.

At the top of a tiered flight of stairs, in an awesome, idyllic place, lived an absent-minded professor-type. I asked who he was, "Oh that's God," someone said. "God the Father." It blew my mind! "I'm going back to work!" I thought, "to fight the fly." The force of the fly was way beyond God's power of influence. He was having a party, and, like the carefree child, waiting for the next surprise delight. He knew only bliss.

In a weird, *yin* mortuary-temple, devotees dressed in long, white Greco-Roman robes were engaged in bizarre rites about death and the dead. It was like a deviant Forest Lawn. They were pouring oils and wines over a corpse, laughing and merrymaking. The fly was there, unemotional and very at home.

A radio station in a big city: it looks on the up-and-up out front, but inside it's a nerve center for the fly. It may have even beamed the fly in with its broadcasts.

An urbane, young, unmarried "people's politician" is at the radio station. It's his campaign headquarters. His aides excitedly tell him there's a major revolution going on in the High Schools and Junior Highs. The station is broadcasting the take-overs of the schools and fomenting the violence: "Orange Jr. High has been occupied by… Glendale High School has been taken over by… The east wing of…" The politician is cool and calculating. He is going to ride the revolution to political power. There is a bloodbath—children are killing their parents and teachers.

People were in heavy trances, as if under a spell. Their hearts and minds were numb and beyond the reach of reasoning or pity.

On an airport runway all ready to go like a 707 was fighter jet plane with an ominous rocket/missile mounted on its nose. The rocket could not be stopped. It could penetrate anything and be shot anywhere. The missile was like a silver metal sliver and it could kill a single person by entering the eye, or wipe out an entire country. There were lots of them.

The Sangha was working day and night in groups and teams. They were not under the spell and could see the deviant energy of the fly in all its manifestations. We travelled everywhere fighting it and planting good seeds, neutralizing noxious vapors. Our method was the Great Compassion and other mantras. Wherever the Great Compassion Mantra was recited a circle of pure, bright light was produced. The light was sunny and correct, like the colors on the coast after a rainstorm when the sun comes out. The color of the fly-smog was the dense, choking amber of an old photograph, a stuffy attic without windows.

> *I should be a light for all living beings, and cause them to attain the light of wisdom which eradicates the gloom of stupidity. I should be a torch for all living beings which breaks through the gloom of ignorance. I should be a lamp for all living beings and cause them to dwell in the place of ultimate purity.*
>
> *Avatamsaka Sutra*

The Sangha was pure light travelling to all places, afraid of nothing. We told people just to sincerely recite the Mantra and "light up their minds, see the nature." The Mantra helped all invisibly. Lots of people had responses to the Great Compassion Mantra. "Lighting up your heart"—these words registered deep inside and cut through the smog. Wherever it was recited, a clear and wholesome goodness broke through the gloom. All who saw it returned to the good.

We moved around on foot, on bikes and scooters, telling our friends and all with whom we had conditions and affinities. But the fly was huge and our efforts seemed like trying to stop a typhoon with an eyelash. And yet the power of the Mantra was indestructible and unsurpassed.

An electrician teamed-up with us and was able to cross some wires in a panel in the bowels of the radio station. The station looked like an ordinary public service company, but with the electrician's skill we were able to see that inside were the fly, the deviant death rites, the politician and a constant wave of broadcasted evil.

Everyone knew about the fly. But they saw it as auspicious. They were blind to its true nature because they were immersed in the smog. People said, "Oh, groovy, far out—just like science fiction!" They were merging their minds with it like in the mortuary cult. Even though the fly was eating them up and sucking up their lives, they were in a trance and getting off on it. No one could tell right from wrong, true from deviant—they didn't have "true eyes" anymore. The collective blindness was chilling and horrible.

It was all tied together: the fly, the jet-rocket, the radio station, the revolution in the schools, the strange religions and the slick politician. The fly was going into underground missile silos to spawn its eggs. The radio station and mortuary were its nest. Much of what went on was behind the scene. It took the mysterious electrician to penetrate the radio station.

God was like the card-playing fire chief who doesn't notice he's about to be burned by a forest fire. Right below his happy heaven were all these destructive missiles in silos, ready to be shot off. The missile silos looked like organ pipes or art sculpture and no one could see the fly go in and lay its eggs.

The electrician let us listen to the radio announcer say in a polished, sonorous voice, "And remember friends... kill, kill, kill..." There was a fade-in to a popular folk singer masking the evil message with a simple song, "This land is your land..." It made it palatable.

There were lots of people engaged in a colorful ceremony hanging themselves. It was a religious group. They were killing themselves in order to obtain some kind of spiritual state and salvation. Death and ignorance were feeding each other. They were in a trance, too, and had no light of wisdom.

When I awoke, my resolve was deepened. Heavy demonic forces and darkness created from bad karma could only be stopped by cultivation. What really counts is the Forty-Two Hands and Eyes, the Great Compassion Mantra and the Shurangama Mantra. And most of all, a *pure heart*—a vast, unselfish, kind and pure heart. That's where the light was coming from in the dream, pure, peaceful, happy people reciting mantras and transferring the benefit to all living beings. The politician had color but no light. It was the color of good food and cosmetics, not the light of wisdom and compassion. The people of goodness in the dream were like little suns of kindness, compassion, joy and giving. Even though our efforts seemed small in the face of big darkness, they were pure and done with big hearts for everyone.

> *I should be like the sun which shines universally on everything without seeking repayment for its kindness. No matter what kind of evil comes from living beings, I can handle it. I would never give up my vows on account of it...*
>
> *Rather, I vigorously cultivate the transference of good roots to universally cause living beings to obtain peace and happiness.*
>
> *Even though my good roots may be few, I gather in all living beings and using a mind of great happiness, I transfer it on a vast scale.*
>
> *If there were good roots and I did not desire to benefit living beings, this could not be called transference.*
>
> Avatamsaka Sutra

Unselfishness and great compassion is where it's at.

Peace in the Dharma,

Disciple Kuo T'ing (Heng Ch'au)
bows in respect

Final bows at sunset, along the Pacific Ocea

ear San Gregorio, Pescadero coast. 1978.

The Big Play

May 1979

Stinson Beach, Olema, Pt. Reyes Station
and points north

Dear Shr Fu,

> *As for the place of language of all beings, ultimately
> there is nothing within it to obtain. If you understand
> that the labels are all discriminations, you clearly see
> that all dharmas are totally without a self.*
>
> *Avatamsaka Sutra*

Bowing along a deserted stretch of highway—Mt. Tamalpais National Forest to the right, Pacific Ocean to the left—crisp, blue morning air, silent and pure. Inside my mind, just the opposite: a regular circus of sophistry, foolish debate about what to cultivate in order to cut off discriminating thought and reach the place of self-lessness.

Walking under a great burden of instructions, all misunderstood. Checking every move, every step with principles, got to do it just right. Right? *Wrong!* Why? Because thinking is not the cure for false thoughts. Every time I think I've got myself and cultivation all figured out, I haven't. It's the figuring out that is false. To discriminate with words about words is an endless maze, a trap of afflictions, a dead-end and a big drag.

What's wrong here? It's attaching to the greedy notion that within the realm of words and thoughts there is something to get. It's seeking, and as the Sutra says, "Ultimately there is nothing to obtain."

I applied this verse to my mental block, and bingo! The whole circus-tent fell silent. My mind felt suddenly light as a breeze.

> *At the place of seeking nothing,*
> *there are no worries.*

It's all a play! None of it is real. Ha! I get so uptight seeking this or that small advantage and then catch myself in the act. Affliction is Bodhi, but it takes work to flip it over.

The Bodhisattva knows it's all a big play. He doesn't get hung up in the props, he doesn't get attached to the sets of the scenery, he doesn't take his lines seriously. He wants to let everyone else in on the secret: don't get attached to any dharmas, including the body. None of it lasts. As soon as you take any part of the world as real and true you're in for suffering.

The basic truth of the Buddhadharma: all existence is suffering because of the accumulation of ignorance and desires. It's based on the false view that "me" and "mine" exist, and it comes home to me every time I try to control the world with force in my thoughts, in my speech, in my actions. When I let it all go and just cultivate the Way with a happy, pure heart, everything works out just right.

> *The fruit of retribution comes from the karma that*
> *we create. But the creator does not exist. This is what*
> *all Buddhas tell us.*
>
> Avatamsaka Sutra

That's the secret. The Bodhisattva uses the Dharma which tells him that all states are level and equal, empty and selfless. And with this wisdom he is liberated from suffering. With no self, who worries? With no self, who feels pain? What is there to desire when the self no longer seeks advantages for "old #1"?

The average person, before he begins to cultivate, might hear this and say, "But how can this be so? Look at the stack of unpaid bills on my desk! Look at the newspapers full of endless evil and suffering! Look at those bags under my eyes. I've got to go run the

rat-race again today and I'm sick of it! Here's the Sutra telling me
it's a play. How can I believe it?"

> *It's like a pure bright mirror.*
> *Depending on the object that stands before it.*
> *The different images and the nature of karma*
>   *is the same…*

So, why not put down the false and cultivate the Way? Why
don't I realize the Buddhadharma's supreme place of pure, still,
level equality? Why not, indeed?! It's because from past lives since
beginningless time I have been trapped on stage, wandering
through the endless acts of the Big Play. Covered by doubts, pushed
by fears, I haven't believed in the road to escape. Cultivation is
totally up to the individual. As I plant the seeds, so do I harvest the
fruit.

> *It's like the seeds planted in a field.*
> *The seeds do not know of each other.*
> *Yet, they naturally grow forth by themselves.*
> *And the nature of karma is the same.*

Avatamsaka Sutra

The Buddhas and Bodhisattvas patiently tell us over and over
again, "Everything's okay. Basically there's no problem, but we
make all our troubles by ourselves. Stop the mind's chatter and all
things are done."

I can write of this very easily today. But, due to my heavy
karma of ignorance and seeking, I'm very likely to go out and start
forcing the Way in my thoughts again today. I did it yesterday, and
caught a cage-full of demons. I'll continue to do it until the seeds
I've planted in the past are exhausted. Meanwhile, I'm not going to
stop my practices and wail over bad luck and past stupidity. I want
to plant good seeds now. My faith in the Buddha's field of blessings
grows stronger each day.

We were bowing in gale winds this week, faces black with dust and grit, concentrating on our *dan tyan* "gyroscopes" in the center of the body so as not to be blown backwards each time we stood up. A man stopped his pickup truck and said, "Amazing. You just use your mind to overcome all obstacles and pain, eh?"

I thought, "Yeah, and isn't it funny how the mind is also the source of the obstacles of pain?" If you know it's all a play and don't let your mind attach to good or run from bad, just go out and cultivate pure practices to benefit others, then obstacles and pain don't stop you, and they don't make you unhappy. It's all level and equal. It doesn't hurt less, but it doesn't bother you anymore. Nothing is a problem, not even birth and death. It doesn't matter anymore. "If you can truly understand 'Everything's okay,' just that is wonderful beyond words," said the Master last month near Bolinas Lagoon.

The Sutra says,

> *If one can, while in the mundane world,*
> *Leave behind all attachments and be happy,*
> *With an unobstructed mind,*
> *Then one can get enlightened in the Dharma.*

Avatamsaka

The man asked, "You don't have any special gear that you use?" I thought, "In fact, we do." This precept sash makes the return possible. We have a Sutra that shows us the Way. We have a Good and Wise Advisor who protects us and gives us instruction. We have growing heart of faith in the Triple Jewel. We have a sense of shame for how long it has taken us to wake up and get to work cultivating for real. This is all gear. But it's available to everyone.

Disciple Kuo Chen (Heng Sure)
bows in respect

Everything's a test

16 May 1979
Marconi Cove

Dear Shr Fu,

Who am I? My body is borrowed and all too soon returns to the elements. No matter how hard I try, I can't keep it from falling apart. That's just how it is. Am I my thoughts? Maybe it's as the philosopher Descartes said, "I think, therefore I am (cogito ergo sum)." But, my thoughts are even less real than my body. They are like the morning fog that's gone by noon. The mind is a puff of wind.

This a.m. I woke up and stepped outside. It was dark and still. No cars or people—just the mist and fog from Tomales Bay and a few birds. I started to laugh at all the time and energy I've spent doting after the self and what belongs to the self! What a waste! In the vast, big picture there is no me. How stupid I've been! I chased after my false thoughts and clung to my attachments until I was stuck up to my neck in a muddy sea of suffering and affliction. I never knew.

Everything I did was upside down, "conjoined with inversion," as the *Avatamsaka* says. I didn't even know they were errors. Sometimes it feels like cultivation isn't bringing results. All I do is make mistakes. But, cultivation itself is a response. Recognizing one's mistakes is getting results.

Cultivating purely for a while and then taking another look at the world makes clear what is true and false. The contrast is loud. Cultivation brings everything into sharp focus. The phony coverings and fat get trimmed away, exposing the bare bones. Yet, right before my eyes, I turn my back on enlightenment and unite with the dust. In a single act of ignorance, the "sprouts of suffering" are produced, and in the space of a few hours I'm entangled in the causal links of conditioned existence. It's all very real, not abstract philosophy. "Ignorance produces action, action produces consciousness... all the way to suffering and death." You don't have to have psychic powers to understand how we pass through beginningless rounds of birth and death "covered by a film of ignorance."

In just a few seconds, as fast as a single thought, one can slip from all Buddhas' proper Dharmas and fall into deviant views. Right in front of my face is the whole story. In every single thought I know why I am not a Buddha and how I could be. So it says,

Everything's a test,
To see what you will do;
Mistaking what's before your eyes,
You'll have to start anew.

Last night, after a hard day of bowing, I was making some tea on the tailgate of the car. It was dark with no one around for miles. I relaxed a little and let my mind and eyes wander to the beautiful ocean sunset while waiting for the water to boil. I stopped reciting the Great Compassion Mantra and "gazed at beautiful forms with a mind in violation of the precepts" (*Brahma Net Sutra*).

Suddenly, a car pulled up right next to me. Out jumped two young women. "Hi there, do you need some food for tomorrow?" they asked. I felt I "recognized" one of the women, although I'm sure I've never seen her before. It was a different kind of recognition. My mind moved. Faster than it takes to turn your hand over, I felt the whole can of worms tumble and spill out on the ground.

...mistaking what's before your eyes, you'll have to
start anew.

I dropped my guard just for a second and fell a thousand feet. Going up is hard, sliding down is easy.

Was it a bummer? Yes and no. We try to just cultivate every day and not to worry about success or failure, highs and lows. If it's good, we don't jump for joy. If it's bad, we don't cry and say, "What a bummer!" Everything speaks the Dharma that nothing is real. So we try our best to listen and change towards the good and just take it as it comes. Nothing's a bummer unless you call it a bummer.

If I take a loss or fall, it's a lesson. If I make a gain and progress, it's a test. In cultivation, everything naturally works out for the best. You don't have to worry or make plans or calculate for this and that all day. Just "be pure, peaceful, and happy" was the Buddha's message. "Return the light and illumine within."

So, if we cultivate for awhile and then flunk a test, we don't fall back as far as when we didn't cultivate. Cultivation is forever.

I laughed at myself this a.m. because I saw how small and lopsided my view of "me and mine" has been. I laughed because I've been hanging up-side down and suffering, while all the time thinking I was really smart and doing okay.

I've been studying this section from the *Avatamsaka* for weeks. I couldn't penetrate it. And, yet I kept coming back to it like a piece of metal filing is drawn to a magnet. It felt true to something I knew naturally inside.

Disciples of the Buddha, this Bodhisattva further makes the following reflections: "All Buddhas' proper Dharmas are so profound, so quiet, so still and extinct, so empty, so markless, so wishless, so undefiled, so limitless, so vast and great, while ordinary beings in their minds fall into deviant views. They are covered by the film of ignorance. They erect the banner of pride and arrogance. They enter into the net of thirsty love, and course in the dense forest of flattery and deceit, unable to extricate themselves. Their minds are conjoined with stinginess and jealousy, which they never abandon. They constantly create the causal conditions for undergoing birth in the evil destinies. With greed, hatred, and stupidity, they accumulate all karma, which day and night increases and grows. With the wind of resentment they fan the fire of mind-consciousness, whose blaze never ceases. All the karma they create is conjoined with inversion. In the flow of desire, the flow of existence, the flow of ignorance, and the flow of views, the seeds of mind-consciousness continually arise. Within the field of the three realms the sprouts of suffering are repeatedly produced.

"That is, name and form arise together and do not separate. Because name and form increase, the assemblage of the six places arises. Amidst their junctures, contact arises. Grasping increases. Therefore, existence arises. Because existence arises, birth, old age, anxiety, sorrow, suffering, and vexation come to exist. Such living beings as those produce and increase the mass suffering. Within it, all is empty, devoid of knowing and awareness, with no doer and no receiver, like grass and wood, like rocks and walls, and also like reflections. Still, living beings are unaware and do not know." The Bodhisattva sees all living beings within this mass of suffering, unable to get out. Therefore, he immediately brings forth wisdom of great compassion and makes the following reflection, "All these living beings I should rescue and save, and set in a place of ultimate peace and joy." Therefore, he immediately brings forth bright wisdom of great kindness.

Avatamsaka Sutra
Ten Grounds Chapter

I opened the *Avatamsaka* this a.m. and read this passage again. Suddenly it started to make sense to me. It confirmed what I'm coming to see from my own errors and bowing on the road with my

Dharma companion. Once, I read this passage and it seemed confusing. Today, I read the same text and it was illuminating. I was confused, not the Sutra.

My heart is light. Slowly, bit-by-bit, I know I can get out of the prison of the world. And, if I can make good my escape, then for sure I'll be able to help others make their escape and "set them in a place of ultimate peace and joy." Cultivation is really hard and really happy. Changing toward the good is hard. Benefitting others is happy. Kindness lights up the world.

Disciple Kuo T'ing (Heng Ch'au)
bows in respect

* * *

Just as murky water clears when still, if we cultivate for real, then the waters of the mind will naturally turn pure.

Bhikshu Heng Ch'au

An old woman who spent her life in darkness

May 18, 1979
Marconi Cove

Dear Shr Fu,

Today was quiet and solitary. The sound of a ship's bell blowing in the wind from one of the small fishing boats anchored in the bay. A dead snake lying on the road. A four-day fog lifted. A resolve to work harder: bow more single-mindedly and really stop the false flow. To be one with a truly pure heart—how fine! Bowing with one heart is home. Leaving home is home.

> *I give rise to happiness because I have left all grounds of ordinary people far behind. I give rise to happiness because I draw near the Grounds of Wisdom.*
>
> *Avatamsaka*

Inside, a peaceful feeling from being right here where I'm supposed to be.

A bag of fruit and fresh flowers hanging on the car door at the end of the day. Inside is a note:

> *I'm a foolish old woman who has spent most of her life in darkness.*
>
> *Three years ago, I was given a peek at enlightenment, and at this point I'm trying to incorporate truth into my daily life. It's not easy. I ask for your prayers.*
>
> *signed, "Baraka Bashad"*

Peace in the Way,

Disciple Kuo T'ing (Heng Ch'au)
bows in respect

My self-nature contains all dharmas

13 May, 1979

Dear Shr Fu,

Flower Garland Features
presents
The Longest-Running Film in the Dharma Realm
The Bodhi-Drama
Starring, The Self-Nature!

* * *

Everything you meet is a manifestation of your own mind.

by Venerable Master Hua, February 1979

The mind of a cultivator does not allow for a thought of affliction. One selfish thought brings demons, like a bleeding fish draws sharks. One angry thought explodes like a bomb, showering my mind with painful fragments in all directions. One critical thought feels like I've stepped into a pit of spiders—all my thoughts turn in on me and trap me in a web. It's a horrible sensation. One thought of worry or doubt puts me all alone at the ends of the world without the sun. These states are as real as the weather outside. If I let them dwell inside, they manifest as flesh and blood demons before my eyes.

Just like a vision of the Guiding Master in his many forms and distinctions, according to what beings practice in their minds, their visions of Buddhalands follow suit.

Avatamsaka

But, all it takes is to return the light and swing the vajra jewelled sword, and all states return to spring. A positive thought of kindness, compassion, joy, and giving brings the Buddha's sunlight back to our hearts, just that quickly. The relief we feel is measureless and boundless.

My self-nature contains all dharmas. Originally it is pure and still, but I make discriminations in my mind. All dharmas are level and equal, but I go ahead and discriminate in my thoughts due to ignorance. Ignorance arises out of desire. Desire thoughts set up a self—someone exists who wants to move out of the center and get something. Desire creates selfishness, greed follows right behind. Greed is a poison; it has the power to ruin the entire world. But, yet, it still comes from nowhere but my own thoughts.

All retribution is born from karma.
It's like a dream, unreal, untrue.
Thought after thought is over and gone.
As was the former, the latter is the same.

Avatamsaka

All troubles and afflictions, and ultimately birth and death follow this same highway out of one's own unmoving, perfect self-nature. It happens in thought after thought.

It's like a movie that I watch all the time in my mind. When I take it as real and let it go out my senses, I project into the world. Then I've just bought a ticket to the melodramatic farce of suffering. No matter whether the movie is a comedy or a tragedy, it still falsely sets up a self that feels suffering or bliss and discriminates among dharmas.

> *The fruits of retribution come from the karma that*
> *you create. But, the creator does not exist. This is what*
> *all Buddhas tell us.*
>
> *Avatamsaka*

When I follow instructions and use the Buddhadharma to return thoughts to the screen before they run out the sense-gates, everything's okay. Cultivation is all about practicing a method to turn back these thoughts as they arise. Concentration is the ticket. My own thoughts are the whole movie. Pull them back and the film breaks. The Dharma Realm dissolves, because there's no self to perceive it. Desire is the glue that sticks the film together, scene after scene. End the desire and we step right out of the film, free to come and go. Not that thoughts stop, but they don't push us around any more. We direct the film, instead of being directed by it. Originally there is nothing that needs to be done. It all rolls on by very naturally, without a word, without a self, without a problem.

What kind of film is it that we contemplate? It depends on the seeds we plant. Buddhahood is nothing but a thought of perfect humanhood. The hells are made from afflicted and stupid thoughts.

Last night as I sat in the Plymouth during evening recitation, my mind fell into a snakes' den of doubts. The pressure and mental discomfort grew unbearable instantly. I checked and sure enough I had dropped my vajra-sword and stopped my concentration on the practice of returning the light. I was letting my thoughts drift. Like a ship without a rudder, I was heading for the reef. I thought, "I've been through this movie before, it's a horror story about greed, fear, and selfish desire. STOP IT!" Up went the sword. Snick! The energy behind the negative doubts came back to center and I laughed out loud. It was all my own ignorance after all, pushing me around again, making me dance like a puppet on strings.

How unexpected! The self-nature is originally complete in itself... How unexpected! The self-nature can produce the ten thousand dharmas...

The Sixth Patriarch's Sutra

What a funny film! Sometimes it's looney-tunes, sometimes it's a melodrama, sometimes it's a travelogue through the Three Paths of Suffering, sometimes it's a holy epic. It's all my film, but I can't find myself in it anywhere. When I've got the *kung fu* together, I can sit back and contemplate it reeling by. More often than not, however, I forget it's a movie, stop cultivating, pick out a scene I want, or run from one I dislike, and wham! The express train of false thoughts flattens another ignorant living being. Be still, Kuo Chen. Just be happy, cultivate, and watch the show!

You have to learn to see all things as "no affair". Observe the rise and fall of conditioned dharmas with complete detachment. Everything's okay.

by Master Hua November 1977

Disciple Kuo Chen (Heng Sure)
bows in respect

Some day, you'll know that Ch'an is the highest

May 24, 1979
Blakes Landing, California

Dear Shr Fu,

We meet a lot of different kinds of people on the road. But, it's clear that the happiest and healthiest ones are active and exercise. People stop to jog, bicycle, do t'ai chi or yoga or just walk. Some people work outside all day. They all have a spark of youth. It's just like moving water that's pure and clear, while stagnant water goes bad. Acupuncture has the same principle: energy that freely circulates is the key to health and long life.

This is the value of sleeping sitting up—it keeps the blood and energy freely moving, even while you sleep. Unless you lean against things. Last night while sleeping in meditation posture, I slouched back on some stuff sacks. This a.m. my body was stiff and sore. When I can sit upright and not lean or prop myself up with artificial supports, I wake up feeling like I've just taken a cool shower or done a set of t'ai chi. False thinking cuts off circulation in the same way. Attachments leave you stiff and sore. Our basic nature is nowhere dwelling and leaning on nothing.

Heng Sure has a sweater I had my eye on. I didn't need a sweater, it was just another false thought surfacing. The sweater was a desire surrogate (all desire is one desire). We had been bowing in a cold, stiff wind, and the pressure of cultivation was at a peak. No people, no talking, no towns—the mind was facing emptiness and squirming. On impulse, I pick up the sweater. Heng Sure, seeing my interest, gave it to me. I "stole" the sweater. I went for it under pressure. Immediately I felt a change. The air became heavy and close. I felt like I was suffocating in a small cave. My eyes grew dusty, and the sweater felt uncomfortable and confining. During meditation it got unbearable. So, I took off the sweater and returned it. Right away the world got big, cool and smooth again. The dust left my eyes, the heavy, hard-to-breathe state lifted. Ah, at home again! It was a good lesson: greed and too many possessions cuts off the circulation; seeking self-benefit is the source of suffering and unrest, personal and world-wide.

> *He makes no mistakes,*
> *His mind is vast, big, and pure;*
> *He is happy, blissful,*
>   *apart from all vexation and worry;*
> *His heart and will are soft and flexible;*
> *All his organs are clean and cool.*

Avatamsaka

Each false thought and attachment, all greed, anger, and stupidity cut off the circulation. Afflictions drain our energy. Worry, jealousy, arrogance, and fear cut off the light and make us old fast. Whatever we can't see through and put down blocks our natural wisdom. It's just like laughter makes you young and crying makes you old. The principle is the same. Holding precepts purely and concentrating with a single mind is the source of blessings, happiness, and the pure light of wisdom. When we can do this, we are like little children without a wrinkle or care—just full of the energy of spring. But, as soon as we get uptight or start false thinking, then trouble appears where there was none to begin with. This is the energy of winter.

Truly, the mind is boss. When we bow sincerely, if it's cold we get warm; if it's too hot, it cools off. Strong winds and heavy rain are no problem. No matter what happens, it always feels "just right". But, as soon as we strike up false thinking or get uptight, then if it's too hot, it gets hotter. If it's cold, it gets even colder. The wind and rain make us angry and we want to fight with them. If our thoughts are scattered, the bugs and insects give us trouble. The hotter we get under the collar, the more trouble they give us. It's all made from the mind. The ultimate source of all health and happiness is "an unattached, unbound, liberated mind." When thoughts are right, everything is right.

Exercising the body is good. But, no matter how good we treat the skin bag, it goes bad and falls apart. My t'ai chi teacher once remarked, "Some day you will know that Ch'an is the highest." Back in Pacifica as we did t'ai chi outside a laundromat in the early morning, I had an insight, "If I didn't false think and form attachments, I wouldn't need to do t'ai chi. Originally there are no obstacles or deficiencies. Naturally we are healthy and free. False thinking and attachments make all our problems—they make the world go bad, too. It's all the same." So it's said,

> The best power-spot (acupuncture point) is right in
> the square inch (the mind).

This is the big lesson of this pilgrimage: "Everything is made from the mind alone." The way of the world is to ruin your insides trying to look good on the outside. The way of cultivation is to return to the source and purify the mind and forget about the superficial. I am seeing how my false thinking to be #1 cuts off my circulation. My running out after forms (desire) wastes my energy. My bad habits and deviant views cut off others' circulation and block the energy in the world. The entire Dharma Realm is one body—perfectly fused and interpenetrating. Nothing exists in isolation. No one stands alone.

> The realm of living beings and
> the Dharma Realm are not two,
> The Dharma Realm and
> the self-nature are non-dual.

Avatamsaka

We cultivate and everyone benefits. If we don't cultivate, everyone loses. Everything created from body, mouth, and mind touches all living beings. If what I do is good, the world improves a bit. If what I do is selfish, then everyone suffers. It is becoming so clear to us that what counts is what we've got on our minds. It's easy to hide behind the covers and put on a good show, but sooner or later the truth comes out. Why not put it all down and go for broke?! What else besides cultivating a pure mind matters? All beings accomplishing Buddhahood together, what else is worth anything? There is something special about bowing outside in the stillness of nature that cuts through all the garbage and leaves cultivating the Way standing tall and strong, above all else,

> ...like Sumeru spreading across the seas,
> lowering retinues of peaks' high altitudes...
>
> *Avatamsaka Preface*

Each day the truth of cultivation grows brighter and our happiness grows with it. Like the song says, "I'm really lucky to study Buddhism." When we work on the mind ground, we work for everyone. The sounds of the world are the sounds of one's own heart.

Peace in the Way,

Disciple Kuo T'ing (Heng Ch'au)
bows in respect

I cultivated greed, hatred and stupidity

June 21, 1979

Duncan's Landing, California

Dear Shr Fu,

At the end of the day, a man in a van stopped. He said, "I've been watching you. I figure you're trying to make atonement for the sins of men. Why don't you join the Peace Corps or help the poor? Oh well... you're doing your thing, I guess."

On the surface, it might look like cultivation is just "doing your own thing," but it's really doing something for everybody. Why is there war and suffering in the world? Because of selfishness and the "always more" desire mind. Why is there poverty and injustice? It's also because of false thoughts of greed, anger, and ignorance. All the hassles and problems of the world begin in the mind. If I don't clean up my own mind and end the war inside my own heart, how can I possibly help the world? Reducing desire is getting rid of wars. Stopping false thinking inside is really helping the entire world outside. As it says,

> *Small worlds are just large worlds;*
> *Large worlds are nothing but small worlds.*
> *An inexpressible number of worlds enters into a*
> *   single world;*
> *Single world enters into*
> *   an inexpressible number of worlds.*

Avatamsaka Sutra

My small world of greed fattens the big greed in the world. My small anger and ignorance feed the larger worlds of hatred and stupidity. How is the large world going to change if I don't change my small world? It's all woven together. If I hold precepts purely, then there's a small world of good that can "enter into an inexpressible number of worlds." My small concentration adds to a larger stillness and universal peace. If I can cultivate wisdom, then the good in the world increases naturally. If I don't recognize and change my faults, this bad energy pollutes the world in the same way and touches everyone and everything without my directly wishing it or even knowing it.

Cultivation is for all living beings in all worlds to the limits of empty space.

I didn't always see it this way. But last week a young family near Tomales put me back in touch with parts of my life I hadn't seen clearly before.

The family lives on a small farm in a little valley. Their lives are wholesome and basic. With their four children, they raise most of their own food. They have gone "back to the earth," living naturally with traditional values and morality. Everything about their lives and home says, "With few desires, know contentment." They made an offering of food and water as we bowed by and said, "Thank you." Everyone was healthy, happy, and simple. Clear eyes, clear faces.

Their blessings were obvious and abundant. Blessing retribution like this comes from good roots planted in the past. People whose lives are happy and free of disasters and distress held the moral precepts in the past. Healthy, loyal children, the absence of enemies, and a peaceful mind come from having cultivated the Paramitas of Giving, Morality, Patience, Vigor, Concentration, and Wisdom. Like causes, like results. Everything that happens to you is the fruit of seeds planted in the past. Tomorrow is being set up today.

All retribution is born of karma.

Avatamsaka

This happy, "rich" family led me to reflect on my own roots and blessings. I came from a good family and had many blessings. For a few years in college, I took a wrong road and nearly exhausted my blessings. When good roots are deep and blessings rich, they can open the door to leaving the home-life and cultivating the Way. This is the highest field of blessings. It surpasses the best of worldly wealth and happiness. But enjoying those blessings cancels them. I turned away from chances to cultivate because I couldn't put down my mind for "more, always more." I straddled the fence until I nearly came apart at the seams. Clinging to greedy desire on one hand and trying to reach for wisdom with the other gave birth to a strange creature: a creature trying to end suffering with more suffering. He broke precepts, turned his back on his parents and teachers, drew near bad companions, and looked lightly on cause and effect like it was a game. Indulging in hedonism, he mocked and mooched from the world. He sat in between the true and false, the pure and defiled, and took the worst from both—like tea steeped in lukewarm water.

I couldn't see at the time that I was trying to get free by rebellion, license, and leisure. I cut off morality, concentration, and wisdom and cultivated greed, hatred, and stupidity day and night, without fatigue.

So, as we bowed down the road past this little farm, I thought of those few upside-down years and how I nearly wiped out my natural inheritance. I saw how wrong and selfish I had been. There was no one to blame but myself. And yet, here I was, happy and lucky, a Buddhist monk bowing with a good companion to the City of Ten Thousand Buddhas. How could this be!? I think it's because no matter how far from the true and proper you drift, a single act of goodness—a single thought of repentance and reform—can turn it all around and put you back in the Buddha's field of blessings. The Buddha's field of blessings levels all differences, voids all transgressions and eradicates all afflictions. It can cause everyone to be delighted and peaceful. With a single thought, one can turn around and go back home. The Buddha's field of blessings does not come or go, we just neglect it. It doesn't reject anyone, just like the great earth.

> *Just as the earth is all one, yet it puts forth sprouts each according to the seed, and it does not prefer or reject any of them, so it is with the Buddha's field of blessings.*
>
> *Avatamsaka Sutra*

Peace in the Way,

Disciple Kuo T'ing (Heng Ch'au)
bows in respect

P.S.: Just as murky water clears up when still, if we cultivate for real, then the waters of the mind will naturally turn pure. I shouldn't worry, pretend, or grab for self-benefit. Seeking more and running out for the biggest and the best just brings loss and trouble. I've always recited this "Sutra": "more, more, always more," and got no satisfaction. Now I'm learning to recite "Everything's okay, no problem. Whatever comes is enough." Things are getting better.

P.P.S.: I've been trying to curb my tongue in order to catch my wild mind. But not talking and trying to be *hu fa*[4] has its humorous moments. Last week George Miller from the Bay Ranch invited us to stop by when we got to his place. We don't accept invitations to visit with people, so we didn't plan on stopping. But, when we bowed past the ranch, a little boy came out and said,

"Hi. I'm Peter Miller. Can you come to our house?"

---

4. Dharma Protector

I figured he was old enough to read, so I wrote a note: "No. We don't visit." Peter looked at the note carefully and said, "Good! Are you coming right away?"

I wrote another note: "We can't visit because we made a promise not to."

He looked at this note and nodded like he understood and said, "Oh, good! What time do you think you'll be coming, then?" he said brightly.

Peter can't read. So I indicated, "Okay, we'll stop by at 7:00," pointing to the 7:00 on my watch. Peter nodded and was very pleased.

Peter can't tell time, either.

At 5:00 he returned and watched us meditate and sew our robes. He kept looking at a picture of Gwan Yin Bodhisattva hanging in the car window and said, "Are you coming now? We have lots of water. You can bring all your jugs and fill 'em up." We went.

The offering of water made it okay—it wasn't a visit and we didn't go up to the farmhouse and socialize. Peter was very happy. He showed us his goats and made an offering of matches and carrots. Somehow without words or clocks or any hurt feelings, everything worked out okay. Another lesson in getting along.

The five flavors dull the palate

June 23, 1979
Shell Beach, Sonoma County

Dear Shr Fu,

At the place of no seeking
There are no worries.

Yesterday I had a good laugh. My life fell apart before my eyes. My personality melted like an ice cube under the sun. I felt very foolish and very happy. I couldn't do anything but keep on bowing and keep on asking "Who am I?" I don't know who I am, but I can see my ghost, and he's a phony. Kuo Chen, "the Fruit of Truth" is an actor. Everything I do is a put-on. It's all done for show. Somewhere way back aeons ago I got the idea that I am special, an exceptional person, a unique star. Really big and important. #1!

So everything I say and do and think, I do to fit this false image. I tell lies to keep the show going. I wear masks and pose and act in order to be #1, the Fastest Gun in Town. What a huge amount of energy goes into this comic opera that I play out. I run on through the days out here in the midst of seagulls and empty highway, seeking and sweating, fighting and frowning, worrying over this petty advantage and that little bargain. It's insane and I've done it all my life. No one forces me to be false. No one else writes my script. I'm the author, the actor, the audience, and the critic all at once.

Why not make life a good show with proper knowledge and views, kindness, giving and happiness? The world is full of pain and there's no reason to add to the quantity of suffering.

Where does my confusion come from? From greed, hatred, stupidity and a huge view of self. My worst fault, besides being false, is seeking benefit for myself. Because I feel I'm #1, a special character, I make a lot of bad karma by acting out greedy desires. I seek fame in all that I do. I don't return the light. Instead I let my energy flow out seeking little bargains. I make waves on the still waters of my originally pure mind. Now that I recognize my mistakes, I'm still paying the price. Originally there is no purity or defilement, but the water of afflictions will splash me until the waves I've made calm down.

In the past, all I've known was how to take. I am stingy and see the world as a place built to satisfy my greed, a place to compete and vent my anger, a stage where I parade my stupidity. I've felt that because my job is to be #1, the only rule of the stingy world is that I am free to take as much as I can get and not let any of it go. The more the better. This was success, this was being smart. This was being famous.

From women I've taken food, shelter, and affection. From men I've taken knowledge and "light". The ones who were better, I fought with and cheated, lied to and slandered. The men not as good, I've stepped on or ignored. I feel great shame for the harm I've done by my selfish seeking to be the best. Most of all, I'm sorry for all the giving I've failed to do. This has been my life—no wonder I've felt lonely and frightened for so long; it's exactly the karma that I've created.

Truly recognize your faults.
Don't discuss the faults of others.
Others' faults are just my own.
Being of one substance with everyone
    is called Great Compassion.

Master Hua

But that's not the verse I learned. I've always recited it this way:

Quickly cover up your own faults.
And point out all the faults of others.
Others' shortcomings are to my advantage.
Feeling superior to everyone
*   is called Great Selfishness.*

Kuo Chen

As I learned the game of life growing up in the stingy world, I was supposed to be big and strong, brawny and virile. So I've always eaten too much, and posed as being clever and smart, widely learned, in touch, aware, an expert. I have to know everything. So I still read the license plates on the passing cars.

I was supposed to be inside the circle, part of the in-crowd, the best group. So I still try to relate and make connections with people. Since I don't talk, this has led to some comical scenes.

I was supposed to be pleasant, attractive, charming, and handsome. So I still wear an automatic phony smile. I was supposed to be an authority. So I force myself on the world and never yield.

I was supposed to be responsible and serious. So I never take life lightly. I was supposed to be competent, capable, cool and mellow, tough and slick, a good athlete, a winner. No matter what, I may not be a loser. I must win!

The Bodhisattva vows that all beings forever pluck
out the host of sufferings and that they be mutually kind
and loving and have no thoughts of harming.

Avatamsaka Sutra

Since I've learned that I must be famous, I still compete with Heng Ch'au at every turn of the road. What's the name of the game? Eating less? Okay, however much he eats, I'll eat less.

Bowing more? I'll hold my thirst until I'm dry as a bone, but I won't reach for the water until after he does. Sitting longer? I won't move my legs until he goes to sleep. Hah! What an evil, stupid notion is this seeking to be First. No wonder I can't realize Great Compassion! I don't practice it! I practice Great Contention. When we got a beer bottle thrown through the window last Friday, I woke up to this state of mind. The bottle hit right behind our picture of Gwan Yin Bodhisattva. It was my own angry thoughts manifesting before me. By turning my back on Great Compassion, I turn away from Gwan Shr Yin Bodhisattva.

This is exactly where wars begin. I put bad energy, black vibrations, into the atmosphere with my desire to be #1. It turns me into a phony, a liar. And it never ends. I've known men who have reached the top of the heap in terms of material success, power, and prestige. Most of them still have to shoot it out with the young guns who come to challenge for the top spot. The big guns were still hungry, still looking for more, always more.

I've tried hard to be a star. I've worked hard at the show. I've worn the right masks, displayed the right feathers in the right seasons, told the right lies I needed to score points and be a big winner. And I'm sick of it. Kuo Chen the liar has left the stage. I'm dropping out of the fight. I don't want to be #1. The game has brought me unhappiness and bad karma. With my selfishness I've caused trouble for everyone I've known. Why do we fight? I fight because I'm afraid to stand alone. I know in my heart that I'm going to die and it scares me. So I grab at the world looking for proof that I won't have to suffer pain and die. I've always felt that if I could make my life different and exciting, big and spicy, that it would hurt less and I could forget about death. It doesn't work. Everything in the world is false and unreal, even the "best" parts that living beings desire. Wealth gets stolen. Sex is a snake's nest of trouble and grief. Fame is empty, like a wind that stirs the ocean waves. Food fuels the body like gasoline does a car. And sleep wastes precious time. What is there that is lasting or true in any of it? It's all impermanent, like a dream.

The Buddha was a crown prince. He had all of the best the world could offer in wealth, power, luxury, and fame. But he woke up to the fact that despite his good life, he was bound to die. He saw it all as empty in the face of death. Gold heaped high as a mountain cannot buy off the Ghost of Impermanence when it's time for us to die. The Buddha recognized it and set out to resolve the matter of birth and death. He succeeded. He became the real #1 in the world. He left instructions and encouragement that we might also cultivate our way off of the turning wheel of suffering. What stands in the way? The Five Desires and attachments to Self. The false view of self is rooted in desire. Desire is the cause of birth and death.

> *As soon as you have desire,*
> *   then you have selfishness.*
> *Once you have selfishness,*
> *   then greed arises.*
> *Once you have greed,*
> *   then all the troubles begin.*

Master Hua, 1979

For example, I never knew that I have a big desire for food and flavors until just this week. Heng Ch'au told me that everyday for the entire two years of the bowing pilgrimage he has watched me at mid-meal slip into a glassy-eyed trance. My cheeks flush, my back slumps, my face takes on a contented smile like a baby after a meal, like a drunk in his cups. It happens after I swallow enough well-seasoned, nourishing food. I was surprised to hear it. I had no idea I entered this trance. All I knew was that my mindfulness and concentration always came to an end at lunch time and resumed hours later when the food was digested.

I watched my hungry ghosts rise up all week. Sure enough, as soon as I added the sesame salt, soy sauce, and oil to the vegetables, my cheeks got hot and my eyes turned up. Then I discovered that it wasn't any specific food that sent me into my blissful space-out; it was my mind. One day I really wanted some green vegetables. Cabbage was on the menu and I dived into it. Same results: flush, trance, slump. The next day I went for a tofu dish and entered tongue-samadhi. Eureka! I've been eating for flavor all along!

The five desires are dharmas that obstruct the Way. They can even keep one from reaching Supreme Bodhi. Therefore, I will not produce even one thought of desire. My mind will be as pure as the Buddha's...

Avatamsaka Sutra

This gold-plated American kid feels that because I'm a special character, everything I eat must be flavored, spiced, and good. It's the same old #1, the big ego seeking self-benefit. No wonder my cultivation ends in my food bowl each day. Because I've always been groomed to be uncommon and superior, I've expected to get more, and always the best of everything. Like many Americans, I really go for bargains, for good deals, discounts, extras, for the personal touch, for novelty, for the free lunch. If something is on sale, if I can save, if it's easy or new, I fall for it every time. What is this but greed for self-benefit? It's ego-food, it's the self on top, looking out for old #1. And it's never, never satisfied.

Dessert was always the best part of any meal. The cherry on the sundae, the filling in the cream-puff, the gravy on the potatoes—these always turned me. In everything I do I look for the bonus, for the pay-off, the good part, the reward. And I never seem to find it. What do I avoid? Hard work, taking a loss, taking the blame, I like the headlines, I like action, I like sensational, exciting, fast-moving thrills. I've never done anything that was slow or hard, dull or quiet, ordinary in any way. And I've never known peace.

This is purely desire for fame and desire for flavor. I seek it in everything I eat and everything I say. I am a liar because I feel that I can't have any faults. I cover over my ugly parts with fancy words and false poses. No one else is fooled. I'm the only one who believes my act.

To finish the story, I ate a very bland meal yesterday, no seasonings, no fancy mixtures. I ate without thoughts of getting a reward from the food. Nothing special. Nothing extra. Nothing in excess. I ate simple, straight, and true. I ate the way Kuo Chen, the Fruit of Truth, and Heng Sure, Always Real, should eat. What happened? My tongue went wild. My mind jumped like a rabbit looking for goodies. Desire flared up and made me shake. "What are you so nervous about?" asked Heng Ch'au. Ha! I found a gold-mine of desire. What a loss for the gold-plated star! I understood why I have had such a hard time being silent on this trip and why my words and letters are so false. I seek flavor. I must be special! I must win! I've got to be bigger than life. Why do I make this fuss now? Because I've met the Buddhadharma. I've seen the Buddha and I'm not him. I'm not pure, not true, not real. I've lost the Way, fallen from the Middle. But through cultivation of the Way, I'm slowly, step-by-step, working my way back to a place of balance and health.

When lunch was over, I realized I hadn't gone into a trance, my eyes were clear, no flush, no slump. As I bowed that afternoon, I saw my Self as never before. Always seeking, never satisfied; always taking, never happy; always faking, never true.

I recalled the summer I ate carte blanche in a gourmet restaurant. After a week of fancy delicacies and superb flavoring, my tongue went dead. I couldn't taste a thing! Truly, as the *Tao Te Ching* says:

> *The five flavors dull the palate.*

All I wanted was plain rice and clear tea. I forgot that lesson until yesterday. Plain food tastes fine. Slow, ordinary hard work is where it's at, because it satisfies.

> *When you are content,*
> *   you are always happy.*
> *Able to be patient,*
> *   you are naturally at peace.*

All along it's been desires pulling me off center, endlessly greedy, never knowing enough, that has brought me pain. Taking three steps and bowing to the Buddha looks simple and dull. It is enough. It is infinitely rich and truly rewarding. It's brought me happiness and satisfaction. Seeking to be #1 makes me miserable. Bowing my self away and giving the benefit to all beings makes me at peace and content. The couplet around the door at Western Bliss Gardens in Hong Kong reads:

> *With whom does the Greatly Compassionate Bodhisattva Gwan Shr Yin of the Southern Ocean compete to be #1? The Greatly Kind Buddha, Amitabha of the Western Paradise and I were originally never two.*

Disciple of the Buddha,

Kuo Chen (Heng Sure)
bows in respect

Guo Gao, faithful disciple of the Venerable Master, joins a mother and her two sons in paying respects to the monks, bringing them offerings, and joining them as they bow along the highway.

Youth from Gold Wheel Monastery hold the map while the monks check their route during a visit where the boys joined the three steps one bow pilgrimage for a few hours.

The modern world trains one to fight

July 1, 1979
Sonoma Coast

Dear Shr Fu,

A cultivator's powerful medicine of the *Avatamsaka Sutra* turns days and nights into an adventure of discovery. Cultivating the Way is constant learning. The teachers are everyone, the classroom is the world, the training rules are kindness, compassion, joy and giving. The courses include faith, vigor, single-mindedness, concentration, and wisdom. Patience is the proctor. Great Compassion is the constant aspiration, the Buddhas' Bodhi is the future graduation.

Every day I cultivate, I see more bad habits unfold. The light of cultivation shines into the dark corners of the mind. The harder I work, the happier and better I feel. Like opening the doors and windows of a musty attic, the fresh air of the Dharma makes useful space out of the parts of my life I've overlooked for too long. I want to be a Buddha. I've got a lot of changing to do first.

Growing up in the modern age, I learned how to fight for what was called "success and happiness". The teaching divided into struggles for power, pleasure, wealth, profit, and fame. When it got confused with politics, it was called the "struggle for freedom." In the end it is just a lot of fighting.

The modern world trains young men to fight for success. As I learned the rules of the fighting game, I was sold on the notion that more success brought more happiness, no matter what I had to do, no matter who I had to step on, cheat, or hurt in the process. The point of the game was to get more of everything. There was only one rule: win. No matter what: win big. We glorify our rule-breakers, outlaws, and clever crooks. It's upside down.

I tried hard to win at this crazy game of success. The better I got at it, the more unhappy I felt. "Oh, it's lonely at the top," says the popular song. And the part of the game no one told me about was that in the end, there are no free lunches. When you break the rules to win, you lose. You may not get the results back right away like in a horse race, but cause and effect is really true—not off by an eyelash.

The bowing pilgrimage has opened my mind to my past training. Only this month, after two years of bowing, have I seen how deeply I am programmed to fight. Leaving home and making vows set my feet on the right path. It takes a lot of pick and shovel work to uncover the roots of my bad habits. Because of the power of repentance and reform, I've gotten lots of help in returning to health.

As we bowed through the sleepy suburb of Daly City, we picked up a lot of hostile vibrations from young men. We heard shouts of "They're kissing the ground! What perverts!" "Get up from there. You kiss the sidewalk again and I'm going to shoot you!" "You can't do that here. Go somewhere else and kiss the ground!"

I thought, "Good grief! We've come nearly six hundred miles and not since the very beginning have people thought we were kissing the ground. What gives?"

> *Because he does not create bad karma, bad karma does not obstruct him. Because he does not give rise to afflictions, afflictions do not obstruct him. Because he does not slight dharmas, dharmas do not obstruct him. Because he does not slander the Proper Dharma, he is not obstructed by retribution.*
>
> Avatamsaka Sutra

Later that same day, two young men made it their job to instruct
me further about my fighting karma. They threw eggs, milk
cartons, copies of the rolled-up newspaper, and rocks. All of these
missed their target, but I got the message all the same. The boys
were vigorous in their efforts, however, and bold. I went down for
a bow and heard footsteps approach. Something soft and gooey
splattered my head from directly above. An entire cup of rancid
butter slid down my cap and covered my left ear. How did it feel?
Injury from empty space. How could I have used my mind to fight
and to hurt people in this way for so long?

This was the fruit of my search for success at any cost. How
does a Bodhisattva think?

*The Bodhisattva uses the Dharma to transform all
beings with a kind mind that never injures or harms.*

Avatamsaka Sutra

Bodhisattvas don't fight. They don't compete. They don't
discriminate among any beings. As I grew up, I learned to
discriminate social class at a glance, all based on competition to be
first. "Keeping up with the Jones's" was the name of the game. The
distinctions were based on surface externals, like the chrome trim
that makes one car look different from another. I wear gray, ragged
robes and have dirty hands most of the time. I see people react to
my appearance and I recognize how I used to size people up based
on false coverings and costumes. I was never satisfied. The people
with more style than I had made me feel jealous and inferior. Those
with no style made me feel superior, like a winner. What a trap I
made for myself with false discriminations. What a burden.

The joke is this: only this week did I recognize that I still
thought this way. After being a Buddhist for six years and a monk
for five, I still carry my habits of discriminating with me. My
seeking and desire to win are my deepest programming. Really hard
to shake!

How did I find out about it? We read these words of truth in the Sutra last week:

> *The offense of greed also causes one to fall into the realms of the hells, animals, and hungry ghosts. If born as a human, one obtains two kinds of retribution: the first is one's heart is never satisfied; the second is, having much desire without ever getting enough.*
>
> *Avatamsaka Sutra*
> *Ten Grounds Chapter*

The next day at lunch, I saw a car pull up, a Cadillac. A sun-tanned, well-dressed man got out and I pegged him right away as a success. Probably a professional man. Then, something changed in my eyes. I thought, "Hey, wait a minute. You don't know what's in his heart. Why do you do this act of competing with others? You do it so that your own ego can survive. Don't do it! Great Compassion does not fight. Say no to yourself. Leave him alone. Cultivate your own path. Return the light. Don't fight. That man is your father. He's your teacher. He's you! Vow to take him across no matter who he is. He will certainly become a Buddha sooner or later, so will you. Don't obstruct both of you with causes and conditions of fighting and killing. This is not a joke. Cultivate the Dharma, as much as you know."

That night, the Sutra spoke principle for me again:

> *The Bodhisattva further reflects, "All beings distinguish self and others and mutually harm each other. Fighting, conflict, anger and hatred blaze without cease. I should cause them all to dwell in unsurpassed, great kindness."*
>
> *Avatamsaka*

Disciple Kuo Chen (Heng Sure)
bows in respect

"Psst," just like a flat tire

June 27, 1979
Jenner, California

Dear Shr Fu,

Part One.

Everybody likes to hear about themselves. Who doesn't want to know who they are and where they came from, where they are going and the deeper reasons behind what they do? Even the most skeptical could sit for hours and listen enthralled to their own horoscope, palm or tarot card reading. The *I Ching* and geomancy, psychic readings and the Ouija board, and all the other occult forms of divination prosper because everyone knows there's more to life than the visible and tangible; there is more to each person than molecules, food, clothes, and sleep.

Last night we came to the section on the Ten Good Deeds in the "Ten Grounds Chapter" of the *Avatamsaka Sutra*. Ah, how wonderful! As Heng Sure translated I sat absorbed. I could have listened all night. It details the retribution one undergoes for committing each of the Ten Evil Deeds. This is the real thing! Unlike fortune telling, which is laced with half-wisdom and a lot of flattery, the *Avatamsaka* transcends the small and narrow and rises like the sun above all the worldly dust. Not only divination, but even the psychological sciences aren't very explicit on how to change your fate or personality. It's all touch and go, trial and error. The Buddhadharma is clear and complete. It covers all the paths of rebirth and how to get out.

The Sutra simply says that everything that happens to you comes from what you do. Good deeds bring good retribution, evil deeds bring suffering and obstacles. It's not off by a hair and has nothing to do with anyone else but yourself. Heng Sure and I got hit right between the eyes as we read the *Avatamsaka Sutra*. It's over three thousand years old, and yet it spoke right to our hearts as we sat in an old car on the California coast in the Space Age!

I read this passage and understood the core of my personality. What was once unclear now became clear. What I couldn't see about myself before was exposed, like ripping off an old band-aid.

> *The offense of greed also causes one to fall into the realms of the hells, animals, and hungry ghosts. If born as a human, one obtains two kinds of retribution: the first is one's heart is never satisfied; the second is, having much desire without ever getting enough.*
>
> Avatamsaka Sutra
> Ten Grounds Chapter

"Hey! That's me!" I thought. I've had all the fortune telling and readings and thought I understood myself. But last night, the *Avatamsaka Sutra* opened my eyes and heart like nothing I had ever experienced before. It was clear and straight-forward. Without frills or mystery, the message was the "sound of a hammer hitting steel". I knew beyond a doubt that what the *Flower Adornment Sutra* said was truth within truth. It deserves to be called "the ultimate understanding of the mind and all its states." It's the highest teaching and deepest wisdom of all living beings.

It wasn't a bummer or an ego-trip to hear who I really was. The Buddhadharma isn't like that. The truth is revealed without emotion and no punches held. The Sutras were spoken only to help all living beings end suffering and attain bliss. It was just like having a candid and kind doctor tell you right out exactly what sickness you have and what you need to do to get well.

I have never known sufficiency. "My" mind is never satisfied. Contentment was always around the corner—in the next job, the next town, the next year, but never right now in my own heart. No matter what it was—friends, education, food, even exploring my own body and mind—I had to have more, always more. I "gave up the near and went seeking for the far." I never knew when to stop or how to say, "enough". Too much is the same as too little.

Part Two.

A few weeks ago, the Venerable Abbot and a group of disciples stopped to share a meal offering. As we sat together under some trees outside of Valley Ford, I was feeling quite content and natural just being quiet. I had nothing to say, no questions to ask. Happy, seeking nothing. My good and wise advisor within said, "Okay, novice, you've had enough to eat. Remember, originally you have all you need inside. You don't need to seek outside after anything. All troubles, afflictions, and disasters come from seeking and desiring more. When you stop seeking, all worries vanish." Sufficiency.

But, then my bad knowing advisor counseled, "Hey, all this good food. A couple of more bites won't hurt. You can burn it up bowing. Take a little more of this and a little more of that, quick! before the meal's over!" So I did. Then, suddenly the emperor inside said, "Look at this. All these people and juicy conditions. You have not said a word. Now everyone's leaving. Let's climb on it, fast." And once again, I couldn't resist. I opened my mouth and asked the Master a stupid question just to make my mark. I made my mark and immediately lost my light—"psst" just like a flat tire.

> *The mind of greed is like a bottomless pit.*
> *Add some more, but it's hard to fill,*
>   *and soon anger appears.*
> *The five desires in confusion*
>   *turn thoughts upside down,*

And ignorant and unaware,
  the Dharma-vessel topples.

by Master Hua

The Master's reply was swift and direct, "Eat more, cultivate more, stoke the fires more. Go on like this forever. More, always more. Everything should be more." The Master voiced the worldly "sutra" that I've been reciting in my mind all my life. Because I was never content with what I had in the past, I am now undergoing the retribution of "having much desire without ever getting enough." Buddhism is not a head trip. The things the Sutras talk about contain the secrets to our own minds and the universe.

In a way, the whole pilgrimage is an effort to reduce our "greed for the flavors of desire." All disasters come from desire. Each inch of greed we are able to cut back brings that much understanding inside and an equal amount of peace in the world. All the troubles we have encountered stem from seeking. All the problems in the world—wars, famine, disasters, and calamities, families falling apart and individuals feeling lost and alienated—none don't begin with a single thought of greed and seeking more. This passage from the *Flower Adornment Sutra* has become the primary theme of the bowing. We take it like good medicine to cure our illness of greed.

> *I do not seek the unsurpassed path for myself, nor do I cultivate Bodhi practices to seek the states of the five desires or the many kinds of bliss in the three realms of existence. Why? Of all the happiness in the world, there is none which is not suffering, or which is not the realm of many demons; which is not what ignorant people are greedy for and which the Buddhas have not warned us about. All disasters that arise are caused by these (the five desires).*

> *The hells, animals, and hungry ghosts, King Yama's region of animosity, hatred, conflict, slander, insult— all of these evils are caused by greed and attachment to*

the five desires. The Bodhisattva contemplates the world in this way and reduces his greed for the flavors of desire.

Avatamsaka Sutra
Ten Transferences Chapter

We have just crossed a small bridge entering Sonoma County. Ahead is 125 miles of bowing and a chance to "reduce our greed for the flavors of desire." Who is this who's so greedy? Even though we don't watch television or listen to the news or read the newspapers, we still can feel the tension, wars, and disasters growing in the world. The whole world is contained within our self-nature. We know that now is the time to turn around, put it all down, and bow to the City of Ten Thousand Buddhas with a single heart.

Peace in the Way,

Disciple Kuo T'ing (Heng Ch'au)
bows in respect

* * *

As for the individual karma of living beings, there are worlds in measureless varieties; within them we grasp and cling to existence, and we each receive a different measure of suffering or bliss.

Avatamsaka Sutra

The Old Fool

July 1, 1979
Above Russian Creek, north of Jenner, California

Dear Shr Fu,

As your way progresses, the tests increase. As the saying goes,

The Way grows an inch,
*   the demons grow a foot.*
The Way grows a foot,
*   the demons are already on top.*

Venerable Abbot, May 1979, Olema, California

New territory and new tests. We have entered steep, winding mountain roads that rise up from the cliffs on the coast. It's a little like Big Sur. Yesterday a car-full of very strange men and women in long white robes stopped. "What group are you with?" one demanded. I gave them a hand-out. "Have you met Christ's family?" asked another in a hostile and aggressive voice.

Today another car pulled up while we bowed, "You ought to try Taoism… yes, or try drugs," said a man. Then he got really angry and screamed, "*You guys are losers!*" He tossed a rock. It missed.

At the end of the day, we were bowing on the top of a road that winds down a steep canyon, crosses Russian Gulch, and then turns into a series of switchbacks up a mountain on the other side of the canyon. It's very spacious and quiet—no towns or houses. I suddenly notice two men watching us from behind some bushes on the slope of the hill to our right. Way below on a deserted beach someone yells up to us. Heavy winds drown out the words. We bow and do transference and start back for camp.

From behind, a young man comes running up the road, "Hey, followers!" he shouts at us. He catches up and asks what we are doing. "Living off the land?" he asks. I indicate we don't talk and give him a handout. He doesn't read it. Something comes over him and he suddenly gets very angry and threatening.

"Lips sealed, huh?" he challenges. "You should be Christian. This isn't the way. You're wrong... all wrong." He's working himself into a frenzy of hate. We keep walking back to the car, as there is no reasoning with him.

"You're stupid, really stupid!" he screams. His whole face and body are out of control, like he's possessed. He starts throwing rocks with an intense violence. "You guys are on the wrong road. You're headed toward death." By now the rocks are coming fast and heavy—about the size of softballs. They're smashing all around us on the asphalt. Even though he's real close, the rocks keep missing us. He's not the least bit shy or holding back. He's throwing the biggest rocks he can find as hard as he can. What to do?

When we get to the car, the two men who appeared earlier in the bushes on the hill walk up. "Hey, our car broke down. Could you give us a ride to the nearest phone?" they ask. The young man who is heaving rocks has come back with his friends. They're loaded up with rocks and heading our way.

"Which way?" I ask the two men.

"That way," they say, pointing in the opposite direction of the charging young men.

"Okay. Hop in."

The car starts, then it dies. "Namo Gwan Shr Yin Bodhisattva." I try it again. It starts. We turn around and head toward Jenner. The rocks are crashing all around. Out of the rear mirror we see them throwing on the run, chasing the car as we pull away. The road is covered with broken rocks. No hits to us or the car.

"Hey, they were throwing rocks at you, huh?" laughs one of the men in the back seat. I nod. "They're only kids," he says in a kind and understanding voice.

I recall this verse we heard the Master recite as the way to be when facing adversity.

> *The Old Fool wears second-hand clothes*
> *And fills his belly with tasteless food,*
> *Mends holes to make a cover against the cold,*
> *And thus the myriad affairs of life,*
> *According to what comes, are done.*
> *Scolded, the Old Fool merely says, "Fine."*
> *Struck, the Old Fool falls down to sleep.*
> *"Spit in my face, I just let it dry;*
> *   I save my strength and energy*
> *   and give you no afflictions,"*
> *Paramita is his style.*
> *He gains the Jewel within the Wonderful.*
> *Know this news and then*
> *What worry is there of not perfecting the Way?*

Sing this song and you can't go wrong. But the Old Fool's song isn't what I've been singing. The way of the Old Fool is new to me. I was brought up in the culture of the "fighting Irish" and Manifest Destiny. I am so used to fighting and winning, it's really hard to sit back and take insult, suffering, slander, and loss. It's equally hard not to be pleased by praise, smiles, benefits, and success. One pleases me, the other I can't bear. Wanting the sweet and not being able to take the bitter are both a kind of suffering. Being free is: seeking nothing, fearing nothing. But it takes practice.

Out here we get lots of chances to practice. We drove a couple miles south of the rock assault to camp that night. But in the morning we would have to bow right through the gulch where the young men were camped. At our bowing pace of a mile a day we would be sitting ducks for them. There was no other road. I started to get uptight, feeling nervous and vulnerable. Why? Because I had just made a vow not to fight and contend anymore. No more fighting for self-benefit with body, mouth, and mind, with fists, debate, or thoughts. So tomorrow was mid-term exam, clearly a test of my resolve.

My adrenaline energy was up, squeezing my neck and shoulders into a dizzy knot. I turned and jumped at every car that passed. My heart doesn't want to fight anymore, but I've got the habit. I've put down my weapons but haven't learned how to put down my fears and "smash an army of demons" with strength of kindness, good karma, and a concentrated mind.

> He vows that all beings put down and leave behind all knives, swords, military weapons, and tools of evil and suffering and that they cultivate the many kinds of good karma... that they leave all their fears, and beneath the Bodhi-tree, subdue and smash the army of demons.
>
> Avatamsaka Sutra

I started looking for outs—thinking about food, alternate routes, of trying to reason with them—but it's no use, I can't relax and not try to control things. I feel like I'm going to battle blindfolded. I think, "This is like war. Where do wars come from?" Wars come from thoughts of greed, always trying to win and be number one. In my mind there's an "open 24 hours," non-stop junk-box record playing the "number one" song. Inside it plays the Super Bowl, the Top Ten, Hall of Fame, highest G.P.A., biggest G.N.P., the Miss America Contest, the Best Seller List and the Indy 500. My mind makes leagues, divisions, playoffs, semifinals and finals, out of everything from a to z. It keeps a running score on where I stand, my chances to come in first place, like the Wall Street Dow Jones tickertape. I compete with myself, my family, friends, strangers, the next country and empty space. "First on earth, first on the moon."

People all want to be number one. They all want to be leaders, to be the best in something. They fight for first place. All of the world's troubles begin right here. Do you believe it? It's true. All of our troubles come from greed and seeking. Originally there are no problems, but we people give ourselves all the hassles in the world.

Master Hua, Gold Wheel Temple,
Los Angeles, January 1979

Note: As a child in school, I never gave a second thought to the "number one song" we all sang. We studied and compared birth rates, death rates, crime rates, suicide and fertility; the strongest man, most beautiful woman, the smartest scientist, and the bravest soldier—everything from Olympic Gold Medals to fewer cavities taught us to compete to be the number-one winner. I did it with grades, sports, try-outs for this and that, so it seemed natural that countries did it, too. When the Russians launched Sputnik I into orbit, everybody flipped-out. The science programs in all the schools were accelerated. "The Russians are ahead of us! They're winning the 'Space Race,'" everyone said in near panic.

I turn everything into a contest and a game; everyone becomes an opponent and rival. Driving the freeway, getting the best deal, always racing and beating the clock, making a hit and score— bigger, better, higher performance... The Winner! It's said that breaking rules wins wars. But breaking rules causes wars, too. Always trying to win, "by hook or by crook" is waging war in my mind. Soon, it spills out and fills up the universe with conflict and destruction. Fighting inside brings wars outside.

The little war with the rock-throwers is just a scaled-down version of the bigger war going on in the world. It all starts right in my own upside-down heart. "Gotta make it big! Get to the top. Be a somebody. Be looked up to and admired." So I get back what I put out. I should take it and not complain and whimper. How stupid to fight back! When I stop competing and scrambling for name and fame, then people will stop fighting with me. If I play the game, I should take the bumps. How will the world get better if I don't change myself?

> *If I am unable to cultivate proper conduct myself, to get others to cultivate it would be impossible.*
>
> Avatamsaka Sutra

What should I cultivate? Not killing. Isn't fighting and putting down the other guy a kind of killing? When I strive to win, who loses? Do I care? There's lots of ways of killing and dying. Sometimes they are hard to see. When I was a boy, I went to the Super Bowl football game. During half-time, they brought out a "football squadron" of fighter pilots. They were soldiers who dropped the most bombs and flew the most missions (had the most "kills") in Southeast Asia. There they were lined up in T-formation on the field as a "Super Team." It pained my heart and opened my eyes to see that. How far we have strayed from the ancients who,

> *Even when he conquers does not regard weapons as lovely things. For to think them lovely means to delight in them, and to delight in weapons means to delight in the slaughter of mankind. He who delights in the slaughter of men will never get what he looks for out of those that dwell under heaven. A host that has slain men is received with grief and mourning; he that has conquered in battle is welcomed home with rites of mourning.*
>
> Lao Tze

Kids always ask us, "What would you do if someone hit you or tried to pick a fight and beat you up?" We tell them straight that if you treat people with kindness, compassion, joy, and giving, then no one will even bother you. "You'll have many good friends and never be afraid. Once you think to fight, then a fight will find you. And once you start fighting, it's hard to stop—there's grudges and 'getting even' and a 'score to settle.' If you push people around, even in your thoughts, people will push you around. Fear comes from doing the wrong things in the past."

So, I figure now if I'm afraid of tomorrow's "battle of Russian Gulch", it's because in the past I've done a lot of killing and fighting. My karma from trying to be number one and a winner is deep and heavy. Now I'm getting a taste of my own medicine. Heng Sure isn't the least bit afraid or nervous. Why? Because everyone's karma is different. There are measureless different worlds and realities mutually interlocking and yet none are confused or jumbled. So two people can be standing side-by-side in the same situation and one receives suffering, the other receives bliss.

> *As for the individual karma of each living being, there are worlds in measureless varieties; within them we grasp and cling to existence, and we each receive a different measure of suffering or bliss.*
>
> *Avatamsaka Sutra*

Note: We bowed through Russian Gulch the next day without incident. No rocks, no angry young men. It's all made from the mind!

Part Two.

Last week near Carmet, two boys kept hazing us, throwing water balloons, rocks, and curses. I saw clearly for the first time that this hassle was my karmic retribution earned from aeons of seeking and fighting to be the winner. When I stopped seeking, then troubles would stop seeking me. Now our only "weapons" are the vows of a Bodhisattva. Our only protection is bowing with a single mind in repentance and reform. This is the first base for getting straight and protecting others.

> *Using the adornments of repentance and reform, he diligently cultivates the path of benefitting self while benefitting others... He uses the shield and armor of*

the Bodhisattva's great vows to adorn himself. He
saves and protects living beings and never retreats.

Avatamsaka Sutra

In L.A., an outraged woman yelled, "Stop bowing! That's disgusting. This is America." And near Malibu a young boy asked, "Hey mister, aren't you 'un'barrassing yourself?"

Bowing came hard to me. Of all the doors of cultivation, bowing was last choice. It really makes you feel unimportant and humble. Bowing is the exact opposite of fighting for self and striving to be number one. Winners don't *kow tow*. That's for losers. Everybody wants to win. No one wants to lose. But winning is messing up the world. So we bow.

The more we bow, the more the ego hurts; the more the ego hurts, the better the bowing gets. My life started getting good when I began bowing. Yet it's not the kind of good and happiness you want to keep for yourself. There is no self, so how could anything be kept? We give the self away to end disasters and calamities in the world and so we may all become Buddhas together. When I'm bowing, I don't make so much trouble for everyone. That's how it helps the world. It's very patriotic! If I'm embarrassed, I should bow until there is nothing left to "un-embarrass."

As the young boys in Carmet were preparing for another water balloon pass at the monks, an older man walked over from his house. "Could I ask about your ritual and why you're bowing?" When he learned why we were doing prostrations, he got a big, soft smile and his eyes started to water. He proudly reached out to shake hands and patted me on the shoulder with the other. The boys, seeing this, left. All is quiet now. "This is good... yessir. I bet it would take all of two years," says the man.

I think to myself, "If I could treat all men like they were my father and brother then there wouldn't be any angry young men and no wars. If I could stop competing to be number one and treat all women as sisters, as my mother, then what a peaceful world this could be!"

A simple thought, but out here that's what it comes down to: putting down your own greed, anger, and stupidity with a straight mind and a lot of kindness and compassion. People who don't know much about Buddhism understand this: selfishness is ruining the world, dividing up countries; it splits up families and leaves us feeling lonely and empty. Those folks that take the time to check out what the bowing and Buddhism stand for understand right away. The Dharma speaks for itself.

"You're doing good work, keep it up," says a man in a VW. A woman with two teenage boys says, "Good luck. Good journey. More people should do that. We'd have a better world. Thank you."

A man near Duncan's Landing: "I want to give you some bread. I think it's beautiful, what you are doing. You don't have to say anything."

Buddhism is pure and simple: no more fighting to be number one. No more seeking name and fame. "Being one with everyone is called Great Compassion" (Master Hua).

> *The Bodhisattva always thinks of all living beings with kindness; with thoughts of benefitting, pity, happiness, harmony, and gathering in. He has forever left behind anger, hatred, animosity, and harm. He always thinks of acting in harmony with others, of being kind and humane, and of protecting and helping them.*
>
> *Avatamsaka Sutra*

Right on!

Peace in the Way,

Disciple Kuo T'ing (Heng Ch'au)
bows in respect

Buddhadharma Fair!

July 10, 1979
Fort Ross

Dear Shr Fu,

This letter is a rambling berry-patch of the thoughts I've had all week. The themes are: be happy, don't worry, Dharma-cultivation is good work. The harder the work, the happier we feel. Cultivation makes us happy for real.

The ancient immortal Sages had no other way.
They were vastly happy by night and day.

Part One.

A monk lights a stick of incense and bows respectfully to a statue of the Buddha. He sits down before the altar and crosses his legs. He picks up a dulcimer and strums a quiet, rhythmic tune. He begins to chant in English,

"At that time the Bodhisattva Forest of Merit and Virtue received the Buddha's spiritual might and entered the samadhi of the Bodhisattva's Good Thoughts. After entering that samadhi there were Buddhas in number like motes of dust in ten thousand Buddhalands who came from beyond worlds as many as motes of dust in ten thousand Buddhalands in each of the ten directions..."

and on he goes, singing/reciting the Ten Practices Chapter of the *Avatamsaka Sutra*. He does this everyday as his Dharma-door of devotion; it's an offering to the Sutra and to his own wisdom-nature. When he's through, he transfers the benefits to all beings everywhere with a wish that we all will work for the good and avoid all evil. He is always happy with his work.

Sometimes he sings his Sutra in public. The simple tune and the spell-binding stories of the Bodhisattva's conduct go right to the hearts of the listeners. He accompanies himself on banjo or autoharp, sometimes he just recites and lets the Sutra's words make their own rhythm in empty space:

> *My mind will dwell in peace in unsurpassed, unspoken, non-relying, unmoving, measureless, boundless, inexhaustible, formless, most profound wisdom.*
>
> *Avatamsaka Sutra.*

This is how it may happen as the practices of the Proper Dharma take root in Western soil.

> *When Bodhidharma set sail from India, fulfilling Shakyamuni Buddha's prediction that the Mahayana teaching would be transmitted to China during the time of the Twenty-eighth Patriarch, the Buddhadharma already existed in China, yet it was as if it were not there at all. Although there were men who studied, there were few who lectured or recited the sutras and repentance ceremonies were seldom practiced.*
>
> *Master Hua, commentary on Sixth Patriarch Sutra*

Sign posted on billboards and phone poles all over: Buddhadharma Fair! Come One, Come All! Come to the City of Ten Thousand Buddhas! Continuous Dharma-lectures! Free admission! Special Day-long Medicine Master Repentance Ceremony (reservations accepted at the City or by calling this number...) Vegetarian Food! No intoxicants or cigarettes, please. Art exhibit.

Booths: vegetarian cooking, natural health care, organic gardening. Dharma Realm Buddhist University Demonstrations: T'ai chi ch'uan, Acupuncture. Music: Buddhist choir, chanting, young people's concert. Plays: Instilling Virtue Players' original shows. Buddhist Schools Graduation ceremonies and awards for academic excellence. Meditation instruction. And fun for all.

This is how it could be as we expediently introduce the Buddhadharma to our family in the West.

Our generation has the inconceivable strength of good roots to have met our teacher in person. We are able to study and practice below his Dharma-seat day and night. The treasury of true principles that we receive is rich beyond counting. Decades from now our Dharma heirs will still be busy translating and gathering the wealth of Dharma that issues from our teaching-source like a never-ending spring.

Heng Ch'au and I are investigating the second of the Ten Grounds in the *Avatamsaka Sutra*. It is called "Leaving the Dirt." It's all about the basic rules for being a person, the Ten Good Deeds. It is like a medicine kit for the afflictions and suffering we all experience. In clear words it describes both the good and bad habits that beings practice in every move, all day long. The Ten Good Deeds are the real thing. The Sutra contains the ancient rules of proper conduct, the true Dharma.

I go out to bow feeling on top of my faults and in charge. A test will arise, I miss my cue, attach to a state and find myself really unhappy. That night, as I review the second ground, I see my mistake on the Sutra page. It always comes with a remedy attached, spoken in a kind, wise voice. It's a shocker every time to see my demons and ghosts revealed to my eye. The *Avatamsaka* is a holy scripture; ageless and as yet unknown to the West. It turns into a mirror, it turns into a good friend, it speaks to our deepest hearts the way no other printed words have done.

This is why we say how lucky we are and how happy we feel time after time. Who wouldn't want to share this magic with everyone? Who wouldn't feel a huge debt of gratitude to the Buddhas and Bodhisattvas and Wise Advisors? They have brought the wisdom and the goodness of the Great Vehicle to us and laid it in our hands. Our job is to recognize this priceless gift and to make it available to all people. Most important: to practice the teachings with pure faith and boundless energy.

> *What's spoken is Dharma;*
> > *What's practiced is the Way.*
> *Speak of it well,*
> > *Speak of it wonderfully.*
> *But if you don't cultivate,*
> > *It's still not the Way.*

Cultivation shouldn't sound burdensome, it's a light, a joyful way of life. Before we meet the Dharma, life is like standing in a pit of fire. The Buddha taps us on the shoulder and says calmly, "There's a sturdy ladder over here. You can climb out of the flames if you wish to. Oh, and let the others know about it on your way out, won't you?" You bet we will!

The work of the City of Ten Thousand Buddhas is to lay the foundations of the Proper Dharma here in the West. As the City is the body of the new, healthy, baby-Buddha, establishing the rules, bowing the repentance ceremonies, investigating the Sutras and translating them, participating in morning and evening devotions, holding the precepts, and daily practices will be the beating heart of the Dharma-body.

There is so much good work ahead, it's like hearing the Buddha say, "You're going to be working on this mountain of jewels for the rest of your lives, you should bring forth a great heart of vigor and boundless joys."

We have the world's best job: givers of the unsurpassed Dharma. Whether we translate it, recite it, meditate upon it, type it, lecture it, bow it on the highway, radiate it from happy thoughts, are mindful of it as we mow grass, answer the phone, and fertilize the crops, we are all practicing the giving of peace and happiness, good energy, and Buddha-light. What could be finer? When we cultivate the Bodhisattva Path by practicing a Dharma-method with the mind and holding the precepts with the body, then we are healing ourselves naturally. We are getting well! We all become Buddhas, perfect beings, when our practice is done well with energy and concentration, and that's the best news I've ever heard.

Monk: Master, some people try to convert us by saying, "The Buddha can't save you. He was only a man. You shouldn't try so hard. You can't be saved by works, either."

Ven. Abbot: So you tell them, "I have food to eat, clothes to wear, I can bow to the Buddhas, who needs to be saved? I save myself."

Monk: They say "You're in bondage!"

Ven. Abbot: You tell them, "Good, I like it. I'm happy."

> *The Bodhisattva always shows great happiness to all beings.*
>
> *Avatamsaka Sutra*

Sometimes when you return the light and look within it feels like a deep dive into a cesspool. There's a whole lot of filth and nastiness inside one. Before I began to cultivate I didn't recognize it. Cultivation is all about getting right in there and purging the poisons, slogging through the mud of self and greed, hatred, and stupidity. You have to shovel it out bucketful after bucketful. But the Buddhadharma is the great purifier, it's mind medicine, the heal-all herb for the poisons that afflict us.

> *Like the agada herb*
> *Which can purge all poisons,*

The Buddhadharma is the same;
It eradicates the disaster of afflictions.

Avatamsaka Sutra,
Praises in the Tushita Heaven Palace, Chapter 24

Universal Worthy Bodhisattva instructs us to "repent and reform of all karmic faults," and that's what repentance ceremonies are all about. Every time we sincerely call ourselves on our faults, recognize them and vow to change, the mind gets a little brighter inside. Those are *my* afflicted beings inside. I've vowed to save them all. No matter how much trouble I give myself due to my past greed, hatred, and stupidity, I'm going to keep on with this good work of cultivation until the mirror of my mind has no specks of dust remaining. Will it be tomorrow? Will it be nine aeons from now? Can't tell. Even if it takes forever, I believe that we will all become Buddhas and I make it my job to take my inner living beings across first.

At the same time, I don't have to wear my afflictions like a merit badge. This is seeking approval. I *caused* all my own troubles, I should bear the results in silence, not be such a weak crybaby and certainly not afflict others with the details of my daily ups and downs. How does a Bodhisattva do it?

He is universally a good and wise advisor for all beings. He speaks the Proper Dharma and causes them to cultivate. It's just like the great ocean: no amount of poison can change it or spoil it. And Bodhisattva is the same. All those he meets, be they without wisdom... all types of oppressive afflictions from these... beings cannot move or confuse him.

Avatamsaka Sutra

With faith in the Way,

Disciple Kuo Chen (Heng Sure)
bows in respect

A man's got to have gone through a lot of changing

July 16, 1979
Ocean Cove, California

Dear Shr Fu,

"Country Roads Cross Section."

It's Sunday afternoon. We are bowing through the Ocean Cove, a small hamlet on Highway 1. There is a gas pump, a country store, a weathered barn, and a few houses. In front of the store are the local young people sitting on tree stumps, old chairs, car fenders, and motorcycles. They're drinking beer, smoking, and rapping. Each is looking for something, waiting expectantly, but no one could say what it is they're waiting for. Even though there is a crowd, an empty loneliness hangs in the air like the dull fog that hasn't lifted today. They all have homes, but no one wants to go home. Their hearts have no place to rely. We know where they are at, and feel sympathy.

> *The Bodhisattva sees that all beings are lonely and without a place to rely on, and he feels sympathy.*
>
> *Avatamsaka Sutra*

As we round the corner and come into sight, a couple of the young men start testing us with taunts. The toughest-looking biker, wearing a black leather jacket and a beard, has pinned a handout explaining the bowing pilgrimage to the store's screen door for everyone to read. His name is Bobby. He says to the young men,

"You watch your mouth there, boys. Don't bother the fellows. They're doing hard work for a good cause, they're all right."

"Yeah, but they're weird, really serious. They won't even drink a beer... real party-poopers," replied one of the men.

"You'd be a little different if you'd been bowing on the road for two years. A man's got to have gone through a lot of changing doing that," answers the biker.

"Two years!? Like that?" says one of the young men.

"Yeah. They've got something going for them. It's for everybody. I figure I'm not going to let any young punks hassle them."

"Yeah, sure, okay, Bobby. Whatever you say," says the young man. They all sit down again and quietly watch. Then, a charter bus pulls us. Bobby hops off his bike and starts directing traffic so the bus can safely park. It's a narrow road and lots of traffic. The group of young people starts to hoot and holler at the bus—making things a little unpleasant. Bobby shouts, "You all be nice to these folks... be nice now." They quiet down again. Dharma Master Heng Kung hops out of the bus. He and a large group of people have driven down from the City of Ten Thousand Buddhas to see the bowing monks and make offerings.

So here we all are, measureless living beings from different worlds, yet all converge and come in touch today on a cross-section slice of country road. On the bus are happy, bright-eyed Buddhist disciples from all over the world. There are the two bowing monks. Outside, Mick Jagger and Rolling Stones' music blares in the air and irritates the spirit. The lonely kids are saying, to each other, "Don't go home yet. Stay a little longer. I'll buy everyone another beer." We people are all the same at heart. The suffering and bliss, the ordinary and the sagely, the pure and the defiled, the free and the hung-up are all mixed together in this little junction-stop town just as it is all mixed together inside each of us. Differences are illusions. We have one nature, the Buddha-nature and it is non-dual and perfectly fused. Yet this Dharma-nature has no face or appearance.

The Dharma-nature pervades all places,
  all beings and all countries,
It exists in all three periods of time
  with no remainder,
Without a shape or mark
  that can be obtained.

Avatamsaka Sutra

How strange the world seems sometimes! With houses and fences, with curtains and cars, we try to make a "you" and "me," and a "me and mine," but no matter how we try, we cannot divide our true nature. We are all deeply related. Ultimately, all differences are invisible. No one can stop the interrelatedness of all beings and all things any more than a barbed wire fence can obstruct the air, or a bridge can separate a river.

Today I got a glimpse of the level-equality of all beings. In this little town I saw that all our faces are just masks we wear. Bobby looked mean and tough, but he was soft inside. Behind the fierce front was kindness. Behind all our masks there is only one face. It has no color or shape, no size or place. It is without a mark of dimension. I thought, "Bowing once every three steps isn't two monks bowing, it is all living beings. This is the one heart. We never leave it; it never leaves us." The one face we all have is the Buddha's face. The Buddha's face is every place.

No body or mind inside,
No world outside...
No self or others, contemplating freedom,
Not form or emptiness, seeing the Thus Come One.

They are doing something and nothing

July 17, 1979

North of Ocean Cove, California

Dear Shr Fu,

In the early dark hours of the morning, I wake up outside, sleeping under a tree, to look around. For a minute or two I can't find me. Inside and outside, up or down, here or there don't exist. The jealousy and arrogance, desire and fear I carry around in my heart day after day, for a few seconds, seem like a dream. A smile comes to my face. "How can you possibly take yourself so seriously? Look!... See? Basically there's not one thing. Yet right within nothing the wonderful appears," says the Good Advisor inside.

Slowly, bit-by-bit, things are starting to come into focus. Bowing brings moments of clarity and stillness that tell us to let go of all false thinking and attachments. "With deep faith and courageous vigor, be 'one of the Way with no mind.' Everything that's supposed to happen, happens by itself," the bowing heart says. When I stop meddling and interfering, the Way naturally and effortlessly responds. When the heart is unobstructed, kindness, compassion, joy, and giving appear like the buds in spring. When the false mind stops and greed is put to rest, then by itself, the nobility and blessings of our original face appear. "One who can be like this benefits the whole world," the Abbot told us.

"What are they doing?" asks a bystander.

"Nothing. They aren't doing anything," answers a friend.

"Why don't they do something?" the bystander persists.

"They *are* doing something. They're doing *nothing*," answers his friend.

"I don't get it," says the bystander perplexed. But his friend understands. In doing nothing, everything is done. That is, by not giving rise to the karma created from greed, anger, and stupidity with body, mouth, and mind, the natural truth and goodness manifest. "Not doing" is being single-minded to the point of no mind, no thoughts, nowhere to attach. It's called "action that is actionless." This is what precepts, samadhi, and wisdom are all about. They make everything "neat". We haven't reached the point of doing nothing. Our simple instructions still remain: "No false thinking. Have no attachments. Try your best!" and this verse keeps lighting our path:

> *When the nature is in samadhi*
> *the demons are subdued and every day is happy.*
> *False thoughts not arising,*
> *everywhere is peaceful.*
> *When the mind stops and thoughts are cut off—*
> *that is true nobility.*
> *With selfish greed ended forever—*
> *that is the true field of blessings.*

> *Master Hua*

Peace in the Way,

Disciple Kuo T'ing (Heng Ch'au)
bows in respect

Don't kill

July 16, 1979
Ocean Cove, California

Dear Shr Fu,

Our bowing pilgrimage wants to stop wars, disasters, calamities, and suffering of all kinds. Our handout sheet that explains our work says, "If our bowing is sincere, then calamities and suffering will be reduced, and wars and destructive weapons will gradually disappear."

> *The Bodhisattva vows that all beings give up and leave behind all knives, swords, military weapons, and tools of evil and suffering, and that they cultivate many kinds of good karma.*

> *Avatamsaka Sutra*

Many Americans own guns. As a boy, I used to wear a quick-draw holster and practice shooting "bad guys" in the bedroom mirror. With the kids in the neighborhood, I played "guns" after school. It took various forms—cowboys and Indians, cops and robbers, Allies verses Nazis—but it all amounted to running around the block carrying toy weapons and shooting each other dead. At night, we learned how to do it by watching T.V. shows like Combat, Gunsmoke, Dragnet, the Lawman, Have Gun Will Travel... the television was our school for violence. I am deeply programmed to believe that when things don't go my way, it is perfectly okay to kill to resolve my conflicts. I'm not alone in this view. Social scientist, Herman Kahn, in addressing an ivy-league freshman class on violence and American way of life, as I recall, asked questions like these: How many of the students had ever lived with their grandparents? Very few had. He asked how many had owned BB guns by their early teens and .22 calibre weapons before entering college. Over half of the group raised their hands. (I'm quoting from memory—I read the article in a *Co-evolution Quarterly* three years ago, and the statistics may be inaccurate.)

Americans are not unique in the mental preparation for killing. Every society has respected the soldier caste: India's *Kshatriyas*, Japan's *Samurai*, Rome's centurions, the British Navy—all have maintained the sanction for bloodshed. Civilizations without armies are the exception. One can make a case that people are violent and savage by nature.

I came from a military background. My male relatives for the most part have all served in the armed forces. I took killing for granted until a few years ago, when I began to question it. "Where did all the disasters and misery of this world come from?" I wondered. "Is it our lot as people to kill?" I found my answer. My heart awoke to the Buddha's Way of kindness and compassion when I read these words written by Ch'an Master Hua:

> *There are so many wars! How sorrowful! How painful! Every single disaster comes from acts of killing... and acts of killing from the mind... What is the present time? It is the time of the imminent extinction of living beings. As we look around the Dharma Realm, we see that countries battle each other, families contend with each other, individuals struggle against one another, on and on until great wars between world systems arise... I hope that the leaders of all countries will embody the preference heaven and earth have for life, establish good government and dispense justice, banish quarreling and dispense with greed, ignore themselves and help others, benefit themselves by benefitting others, see the Universe as one family, and see all people as one person. An ancient*

Worthy said, "If anyone is killed, it is as if I killed him myself"...

Water-Mirror Reflecting Heaven, Preface

What a powerful statement against war! Here was the solid principle I sought. How clear-cut and simple: don't kill. See all people as kinfolk. It illumined our upside-down preference for death over life. The Bodhisattva's Precepts spell it out more clearly:

A Bodhisattva must not collect knives, clubs, bows and arrows, swords, axes, (guns), or any other weapons used in fighting or waging war, nor may he keep nets, traps, or other instruments of evil which may be used in killing beings...

Tenth Minor Precept

A disciple of the Buddha must not, for the sake of personal benefit or with evil intentions, act as a country's emissary in a capacity where his involvement may bring about the confrontation of military forces, the commencement of battle, and the subsequent slaughter of countless beings. A Bodhisattva must not even go among military troops or have dealings with them, much less deliberately act as a plundering brigand under the guise of serving his country.

Eleventh Minor Precept

This is the cornerstone of the Buddha's way of compassion: don't kill. A monk once asked our teacher if when confronted by hostile people could he defend himself with his fists. The answer: "Absolutely no fighting! If you fight with anyone for any reason, you may no longer consider yourself my disciple."

Fighting and anger are the source of killing and wars. As one man put it, "The Buddha taught compassion. That means, stop knocking the other guy around! I'm not your enemy, I'm your friend." And Buddhist disciples do not take life for this reason.

The Great Compassion of the Buddha embraces all living beings. We were instructed as we began our journey to "be really careful of the ants and mosquitoes." The Master said, "When you kill insects, they come to me and say, 'That disciple is no good. He breaks precepts!'"

Great Compassion sees all beings as one family. We all share the same basic substance. All men are my father and brothers, all women are my mother and sisters. Where is there space for a thought of killing or anger or fighting?

The second of the Ten Grounds describes a Bodhisattva's attitude towards killing in this way;

> A Bodhisattva by nature is apart from all killing of beings. He does not hold weapons. He does not harbor feelings of animosity. He knows shame and remorse. He is completely humane and merciful towards all that lives. His thoughts are always kind and helpful. He does not trouble living beings with an evil mind, much less think of other beings and then intentionally kill or harm them.
>
> *Avatamsaka Sutra*

Filiality is the basis of the Buddha's teachings of compassion. When the family is happy, then the cities can be peaceful and the nations of the world will come together. On Independence Day, as we bowed along the rocky blue Sonoma Coast, I came upon some new rallying cries for Americans. Not battle cries, but peace cries: It's time to turn myself around and to stop the killing habit.

> *We need filiality, not firepower!*
> *Drop your pistols, not your parents!*
> *Abandon your guns, not your grandparents!*

Why do we kill? It's because we have been killed in the past. Sickness and early death come from the same source: killing. Cause and effect—karma—is not off by a hair. As the Sutra explains:

> *The offense of killing can cause living beings to fall into the realms of the hells, the animals, or the hungry ghosts. If reborn as humans they obtain two kinds of retribution: the first is a short life, the second is much illness.*

> Avatamsaka Sutra

This is the Buddha's voice of Great Compassion speaking to us here and now:

> *If we do not wake up soon and renounce the causes, conditions, methods, and acts of killing, it will certainly be difficult to avert great disasters and difficult to obtain peace and happiness... Look at modern science: it is new every day and different every month. Military weapons are modernized every day and different every month. Although we call this progress, it is nothing more than progressive cruelty. Science takes human life as an experiment—as child's play. It fulfills its huge desires and aims through force..."*

> Water-Mirror Reflecting Heaven.

The beer bottle that broke our car window last month came from my thoughts of anger towards my partner. It might as well have been an atomic bomb. The source is the same, only the degree is different. Our bowing pilgrimage has opened my eyes to my responsibility to make a peaceful world by making my mind peaceful. Our thoughts make the world. As long as I still wear my childhood gun-belt and practice my quick draw and "make believe" killing "bad guys" when things don't go my way, then I am no different from the soldiers and scientists who kill outright. As long as I fight inside my mind or contend with the world to be #1, the

Fastest Gun, I am not fit to call myself a disciple of the Buddha. And this is, above all, my ultimate goal: to transform greed, hatred, and stupidity into morality, concentration, and wisdom, to be praised by the Honored Ones in all the worlds, and then to cause all beings to become Buddhas. There have never been more noble words written than these:

> *Why shouldn't we think instead of washing clean the body and mind, of brushing away accumulated dirt, of developing a sense of shame, of painfully changing our former wrongs to create a new life, of being unique and awesome persons full of great power, of doing beneficial deeds in the Dharma Realm, of taking the citizens of all nations as brothers and creating virtue, of establishing a model for all under heaven. Doing this is called representing heaven in teaching. For the sake of the country, teach the people with loyalty and filiality.*
>
> *Water-Mirror Reflecting Heaven*

Many people love their guns, but now that we have the Buddhadharma in our land, we will learn to love kindness and compassion more. Buddhism is the teaching of people, the teaching of all beings, the teaching of the heart. As the Master put it,

> *Buddhism changes the flat tire of the Universe by creating good energy in the world.*

Disciple Kuo Chen (Heng Sure)
bows in respect

How could you ever keep the lawns mowed?

July 19, 1979

Stewart's Point

Dear Shr Fu,

> *The Bodhisattva is a great master at giving. He can give away any material object whatsoever. His mind is level and equal, without regrets. He does not expect a reward. He is not greedy for reputation (as a bene-factor). He does not seek benefits. He only wants to save all beings, to benefit all beings, to gather in all beings.*

Avatamsaka Sutra

It was exactly five years ago that I was all ready to move out of my Berkeley boarding house and into Gold Mountain Monastery to live as a layman while I finished my degree at the University of California at Berkeley. First, there was a trip to Seattle for the World Peace Gathering. The Peace Gathering marked the end of the Gold Mountain Summer cultivation session for 1974 and was a big success. Bhikshu Heng Lai, who was known as Kuo Hui at the time, and Upasaka Kuo Sun Peterson and I made the trip in Kuo Fa Olson's pickup camper. We rode in the back, sipped cokes, and memorized the Great Compassion Mantra.

On the way home, we stopped in Ukiah to look at a piece of property that was for sale. It was the Mendocino State Hospital, closed by the Reagan Administration and standing vacant. The caretakers showed us around the grounds. It was an awesome place.

I had a feeling about the place. Kuo Fa was positive. Kuo Hui was doubtful, "Too big. How could you ever keep the lawns mowed?" Kuo Sun had a twinkle in his eye. None of us guessed that in two years almost to the day, Kuo Hui and I would receive the Bhikshu Precepts in the gymnasium there. I couldn't have imagined that within five years almost to the day, I would be sitting in a Plymouth station wagon below Stewart's Point on the California Coast after bowing eight hundred miles to this same magical city.

We returned to Gold Mountain Monastery and I went upstairs to wash my hands. There was the Venerable Abbot smiling and kind. I had never spoken to him face to face before.

"Well, how was it?" he asked.

"We saw the hospital, Shr Fu!" I blurted out.

"Oh? What about it?" he said with a grin.

"It's *big!*" I said.

"Do you like it?" he asked.

"Oh, it could be a great Bodhimanda! Just like Nalanda!" I answered breathlessly.

He laughed and said, "Oh, is that so? Good. You think we should buy it then?"

"That would be really wonderful."

Nalanda was the famous and huge monastery and university that pilgrim Hsuan Tsang visited on his journey to India in AD 640. It was the center of the study and practice of the Dharma for centuries. Nalanda is translated as "Giving without Weariness" or "Untiring Benefactor," and that's what the City of Ten Thousand Buddhas is all about: a place for the selfless giving of goodness and pure light to the entire world. What a wonderful gift!

> *"We are all here in a dream doing the work of the Buddha."*
>
> Master Hua, L.A., 1978

A good dream coming true.

Disciple Kuo Chen (Heng Sure)
bows in respect

Hiding in the closet, watching and waiting

July 21, 1979
Near Salt Point, California

Dear Shr Fu,

"Highway Reflections on the Dharma Ending Age."

The *Avatamsaka* says that all the periods of time are the same. Past, present, and future are false discriminations,

All the past, present, and future are nothing but talk.

Isn't the Dharma Ending Age, then, the same? Just the prattle of false words? "Everything is made from the mind alone," says the Sutra. However you look at it, that's the way it is. Cultivate the Dharma's ending and it becomes the Dharma Ending Age. Cultivate the Proper Dharma, and it becomes the Proper Dharma Age. Nothing is fixed. All the differences in the world arise from the minds of living beings. Level and equal, reaching to all places, the Dharma has no beginning and no end.

Yet, the idea of a Dharma Ending Age really cripples people's spirits and Bodhi resolve. It's a huge false thought, and a burned-out view of the world. Acquiescing to the Dharma's demise is being turned by external states. Like the demons we meet while bowing: think about them in advance and for sure they'll show up; worry and get afflicted with fear and they get worse. Ignore the demons and treat them as "no affair," and they vanish. Don't false think about them, and they don't come. Ugly men and beautiful women come to obstruct our work in the same way. We bring on all our troubles with our false thinking. When the false thinking stops, all our troubles vanish. So it says,

When one attends to the here and now,
The false returns to the true.

Gatha for Recitation Beads Hand & Eye #29

Isn't the idea of Dharma Ending Age the same? With an untiring, non-retreating thought of, "pure mind, continue, continue!"—the false returns to the true, and the Dharma's extinction becomes the Dharma's prosperity. The patriarchs and the ancients didn't follow states—they made states follow them.

Before coming to Gold Mountain Monastery, I heard some talk like this: "Oh, Gold Mountain? All those Buddhist disciples are just too strict and inflexible. They take the precepts too seriously—especially the prohibitions on meat, intoxicants, and sexual misconduct." I heard that others criticized, "This is the modern age! They're stupid. In the Dharma Ending Age this stuff doesn't hold. It's every man for himself. But they keep the bitter practices and build Way-places and now a big university… They don't know how to bend with the times. Why stick your neck out like that in the Dharma Ending Age?"

In the *Avatamsaka Sutra* it says that all is one; one is all. To the ends of empty space and the boundaries of the future, all is perfectly fused and interpenetrating without obstruction. There is no time, no coming or going, no place to rely or dwell. So where am I going to hide in the Dharma Ending Age? Under the bed? In a remote temple? Maybe on another planet? Wherever we go, we are not outside the Dharma Realm. Our self-nature and the Dharma Realm are one, not two. So where is there a place to hide?

In Cambria, California, there are some people who never heard of the Dharma Ending Age. For them it's the Proper Dharma Age, and things are starting to look up, not down. Don is an insurance salesman who used to be a school teacher. He and his family came out on Sunday, "just because bowing is so peaceful and nice to be around." They made offerings and watched quietly. Later Don came back and related that his job was in jeopardy, and "frankly, there's a whole lot about life that's pretty upside-down and meaningless," he said. He was very interested in Buddhism. He wanted to be a good father and husband and to help other people, but couldn't get an anchor down inside his own mind. Traditional religions left him cold. He started reciting the name of Gwan Yin Bodhisattva every night in a quiet corner of the house. A few weeks later he came back. He looked younger and centered, back on solid ground. He told us he got a new job and "all sorts of things have started to look better." Then he said, "You know, the other night while I was reciting Namo Gwan Shr Yin Pu Sa, a strange thing happened. The face of an old man with long white hair and a beard appeared. I felt very relieved and not the least bit afraid of him." The description he gave fit that of the Venerable Hsu Yun.

Tom and his wife and three children operate a motel near the ocean. They came out with an offering and said, "We envy you. This is what we should have done with our lives. But now it's too late. We got married young and have children." They thought the only way one could practice Buddhism was as a monk and nun in a monastery. They were happy and surprised to hear about all the levels of involvement and especially of the City of Ten Thousand Buddhas. "You mean, people can cultivate and bring their kids along, too?!" Tom later came back and told us he was really at loose ends. He had got involved with drugs and drinking, acquired a lot of debts, and felt hemmed-in by relatives and the responsibilities of being a parent. He was ready to despair. Then on an inspiration, he sent to Gold Mountain for a copy of the *Shramanera Vinaya and Rules of Deportment*. It's basic and solid teachings on how to base your practice on proper morality. Tom really identified with the principle that "everything that happens to you comes from what you do." He felt that the reason his life was a mess was because he didn't follow the rules. He wanted to change and begin all over again.

A year later, Tom and his family stopped on their way to a weekend outing. They were all real happy and obviously back together again. Tom was confident and relaxed. All his bitterness and pessimism were gone. The children now looked natural and bright, whereas before they were uptight and disrespectful. "You know," said Tom, "that book really changed my life... our lives... I can't tell you what a difference it has made!"

The McCauley family were devout Catholics all their lives. But they "left the Church" said Mrs. McCauley, "because it just didn't go far enough. This is the Space Age, and there's a new spirituality. Our children especially are asking questions and looking into things we never had the courage to when we were young. We are all really happy to see this pilgrimage and to hear about the City up north (CTTB). Buddhism seems to take everything in and still meet a person's quest for personal enlightenment. Our sons have followed you and are really hungry to go where our traditional religions never explored. It's healthy and I'm all for it. My husband and I will follow right along and learn. You know," she said quietly, "there's a *lot* of us peeking out from behind the bushes and hiding in the closet watching and waiting..."

A Bodhisattva makes four great vows and never retreats or takes vacation, even in the Dharma Ending Age,

> *Living beings are boundless,*
> *I vow to save them all;*
> *Afflictions are endless,*
> *I vow to sever them all;*
> *Dharma-doors are limitless,*
> *I vow to study them all;*
> *The Buddha Way is unsurpassed,*
> *I vow to attain it.*

Some people say, "World peace is impossible. Ending disasters and suffering is dream talk." So what? All the more reason to try. Or many say, "Society and the family are falling apart." That makes the Buddhas' teachings even more relevant and necessary. How are these reasons to roll over and belly up? It is just because of people's suffering that the Buddhas appear in the world.

> *Living beings from beginningless time,*
> *Have always flowed and turned in birth and death.*
> *And not understood the true, real Dharma.*
> *That is why the Buddhas appear in the world.*

Avatamsaka Sutra,
Verses in Praise in the Tushita Heaven Palace

If everyone were enlightened and free from all the sufferings and the evil destinies, then what use would the Dharma be? The Dharma is medicine. The more suffering and confusion there is, the more the medicine is needed. "But this is the Dharma Ending Age. It's useless. You're stupid to stick your neck out. No matter what you do, the Proper Dharma is going to go extinct," says someone. That's just the reason to do it. Because it's stupid. When the world is being driven to the brink of collapse by smart ones, it's a good sign that there are still "stupid" people who don't know how to look out for themselves, and just stick out their necks to benefit others like it didn't matter.

So I ask myself, "If you save your neck, monk, what are you saving it for? When you die and have to part with it, what good will you have done with it? The Ghost of Impermanence will just take it anyway. So big deal. Might as well put it out where it can do some good." The Bodhisattva not only sticks his neck out, but he gives away his arms and legs, eyes, ears, even his bone and marrow to benefit living beings. "No problem," he says, "I only want all beings to end suffering and attain bliss. I'm not the least bit concerned about saving 'me and mine' or anything that belongs to 'me and mine'. Being one with everyone is called Great Compassion. My body is the Dharma body."

The Dharma Ending Age is just another day to take as it comes, without weariness, without retreat.

> *He never retires from the vows of a Bodhisattva. Even though all kalpas might be exhausted, his heart never wearies. He does not grow weary of enduring all kinds of bitter suffering. None of the many demons can move him. He is protected and thought of by all Buddhas. He cultivates the bitter practices of all Bodhisattvas. In his cultivation of the Bodhisattva's practices he is earnest and vigorous, not careless or lax. He never retreats from his Great Vehicle Vows.*
>
> *Avatamsaka, Ten Practices*

Why? Because at some point it becomes clear that "every man for himself" isn't where it's at. The realm of all beings and the universe (Dharma Realm) are non-dual. All things are one. They don't increase or decrease. They aren't produced or destroyed. There's no self or others, nothing to attach to or rely on. Cultivation is forever, and because a Bodhisattva's work is inexhaustible, therefore the Dharma never dies.

> *It is like drilling wood to make a fire. What fire can do is inexhaustible, yet fire itself is never extinguished. The Bodhisattva is this way as well. His transforming of living beings is an inexhaustible matter, yet he always dwells in the world without cease.*
>
> *Avatamsaka, Ten Practices*

Peace in the Dharma

Disciple Kuo T'ing (Heng Ch'au)
bows in respect

I bet it was hard not being a monk

July 30, 1979

Sea Ranch, California

Dear Shr Fu,

Today: hot sun. Long hours of bowing in solitude down Highway 1 lined with tall pine trees. Your whole life passes in front of you while you keep a steady rhythm of three steps, one bow. You see where you went wrong and where you did right. Cultivating the Way stands above everything you've ever done like the midday sun. It's the center of brightness and all that's good and true in your life.

> *When the roots are deep, the fruit is flourishing.*
>
> *Avatamsaka, Prologue*

I want to repay my parents, teachers, and elders and be filial to them (the fruit blossoms because of the roots; the fruit in turn goes back to the roots). I want to see my friends free and happy. I feel like an old friend to all living beings. We meet again and again, looking for a way over to the other shore. People, animals, and all the beings we can't see, stop, watch and ask, "Have you done it yet? Are you for real and true doing it? Is the Buddha's Way really possible? Can we all become Buddhas?" Without words, we ask each other and look for a place to take refuge and something to believe in.

We are all one body, we are all one heart... A young person stops with an offering of fresh-picked berries. "I want to offer them. I picked them myself this morning at Pt. Reyes." This person is another old friend from somewhere long ago maybe, now travelling alone in an old V.W. bus with a bike strapped to the front. We have met hundreds of people of all ages and lifestyles that know they are just passing through a dream in this world. Each in his own way is making a spiritual quest, and in their hearts they feel a closeness with us. They hear "Buddhism" and "monks" and "enlightenment" and deep inside, a small door clicks open, a long forgotten seed sprouts a shoot. They stop, I think, not for us, but to look in a mirror. It is the Summer of 1979, but the Odyssey is timeless. We are all pilgrims.

After two years of bowing the roads, it's so clear to us that the only worthwhile and real thing in this whole world is cultivating the Way. The highest gift is the giving of Dharma. As this young person sat cross legged on the ground with berries in lap watching us bow, I saw as never before the truth of what we read last night from *Avatamsaka*,

> *Good man, of all the offerings, the gift of Dharma is the highest kind. That is to say: offering of cultivation according to the teachings, the offering of benefitting all beings, the offering of gathering in of all beings, the offering of standing in for living beings and receiving suffering in their place, the offering of diligently cultivating good roots, the offering of not forsaking the deeds of Bodhisattvas, and the offering of not abandoning the Bodhi Mind.*
>
> *Avatamsaka Sutra, Chapter 40*

To really put down all the greed, anger, and stupidity; to get rid of all the false coverings and phony masks; to cast out all thoughts of jealousy, arrogance, and doubt; to light up your mind and see your true nature and let shine your original face—that is a real gift. That gift is "the highest kind" and the most difficult to obtain.

Everyone is looking for a "true one". We look around outside, but the "true one" we really want to find is our own true self. Being a true one *is* giving the gift of Dharma. Pure, peaceful and happy and no false thinking. A clear, cool pool. An unlimited heart of kindness, compassion, joy and giving that is as pure and selfless as new-fallen snow, and a mind like empty space. It's said,

> *In all the world you may look,*
> *but a true one is hard to find.*

Below in a fenced-in private home development, people are playing tennis and swimming. The whole scene is identical to one we bowed past two years ago in a country club in L.A. The things of the world are empty and impermanent, and yet they never seem to change. Some people die and new ones appear, just like the changing of players on the tennis court. The game of suffering and searching goes on like tennis match after tennis match.

What a clean and fine feeling, right to the bones and marrow, to have met up with the Buddhadharma! Bit-by-bit I am slowly remembering how to be a real person. We know we are finally walking the right road. The giving of Dharma will come naturally, like the rain, as our steps become naturally true and without tracks.

At the end of a solid day of bowing, our lives feel so simple and genuine—so easy and natural—and yet nothing in the world can touch it. Three young men, out to see the world with packs on their backs, stop and ask us for some water. They have one small canteen between them. "Hey, who's that in the picture?" asks one looking at the Ven. Abbot's photo. "Hey, your hair's growing back," chides another in good humor. And then he asks honestly, "Was it hard becoming a monk?" His friend is reading our sign in the window and looking at the Buddha's picture next to it. He looks up. "No, I bet it was hard *not* being a monk," he says with conviction. He took the words right out of my heart. As they walk away, they say, "Hey, ya know, that's a really neat thing—doing it for everyone. I mean, so all beings will get peace and happiness. That's a neat way to be." I hear them and once again see that the principles of Buddhism are in everyone's heart—The Bodhisattva path is our natural mind. In their attitude, without knowing it maybe, they are speaking the Dharma,

> *People's minds are the Buddha;*
> *The Buddha is just people's minds.*

May we all accomplish the Buddha Way together, real soon. Peace in the Way to all beings everywhere.

Disciple Kuo T'ing (Heng Ch'au)
bows in respect

Those who gossip will fall into the Hells

August 1, 1979
Sea Ranch, California

Dear Shr Fu,

> *If you make great vows, you can't do any false thinking. If you make a big vow and then you have a few false thoughts, these can obscure the big vow. So don't have any false thoughts about killing, don't have false thoughts about stealing, don't think about saying false things...*
>
> Master Hua 1973

Shr Fu, this disciple is still trying to dig his way into hell with his tongue. Today I nearly succeeded and I only used my pen, not even my tongue.

This morning, Heng Ch'au and I were feeling really on top of the world, and we got careless. We were writing letters after morning recitation. The topic was the Vinaya. Heng Ch'au said "It would be really great to be a perfect Vinaya Master. One would be so good at keeping the rules that it would be perfectly natural-looking, effortless, and you'd never make a mistake."

I took this chance to break the rules and came out with a corking big error in cause and effect. I wrote this note: "Vinaya Master Hung Yi had one pair of shoes that he wore for years and years. The story goes that he walked like on eggshells, s-l-o-w-l-y, so as to avoid stepping on bugs."

I gave it to Heng Ch'au and watched his response. When he didn't say anything I did an imitation of a man shuffling along in terror of killing bugs and then made a slighting gesture with my hand to say "Baloney." I wrote, "You'd never notice the real one," meaning that one who walked like this could not be genuine. He would be attached to marks and the appearance of keeping the rules. I meant that true Vinaya Masters shouldn't be so forced and artificial. We finished writing with a discussion of the precept sash and agreed that keeping the rules purely is the single most important part of being a true Buddhist disciple.

As soon as I went out to bow, I realized that with my note and my gesture and my attitude behind it, I had just sent myself to Hell for slandering the Triple Jewel, slandering the Proper Dharma, committing the offense of false speech, breaking the Bodhisattva Precepts against: a) praising oneself and slighting others, b) disrespectful and rude behavior towards teachers and elders, c) baseless slander, d) treating Dharma teachers with contempt.

I repented on the spot, my mind dumb-struck that I could be careless. After lunch I wrote this note to Heng Ch'au: "My quick story on Ven. Master Hung Yi this a.m. is the causes and conditions of slander, false speech, duplicity, harsh speech, frivolous speech, and gossip. It is the source of boundless offenses and obstacles. I must not do it any more! I don't have the stature to talk about great monks in this way. How stupid to defame our own Virtuous Elders! It's like cutting off my hands just for laughs. First of all, I don't even know if the story is factual—it's just hearsay, idle gossip. I do know that any Ven. Master's purity in the Vinaya is totally admirable and deserving of great praise. This is shameful conduct on my part. It's my own funeral—a fast train ride to the Hells. With so few Sanghans in this age and fewer still of accomplishment in Vinaya practice, and I make it my business to casually slight one of the highest of them. Insane! If I don't cultivate control of my tongue, what Way am I cultivating?"

This afternoon as I bowed, I repented again, feeling greatly fortunate at being able to repent. The *Shami Lu* tells the story of a monk who slandered an Arhat by saying he sounded like a dog when he recited. The Arhat forgave the monk immediately and kindly advised him to repent. Because of the Arhat's compassion, the monk was saved from falling into the uninterrupted hells, which was his due. He was reborn as a dog, instead.

Just last week we read in the Third Ground Chapter of the *Avatamsaka Sutra* about the cultivator who has the Heavenly Eye spiritual penetration. It says,

> ...he can see how beings get reborn in good or evil destinies, depending on the karma they create. If a being accomplishes evil deeds with the body, or evil deeds with the mouth, or evil deeds with the mind, **if he slanders worthy sages**, if he is endowed with deviant views, as well as the karma of deviant views and their causes and conditions, then when his body decays and his life ends, he will certainly fall into the evil destinies and be reborn in the Hells.

How could I be so stupid as to try it out for myself? As I reflected, I felt really hot. I was miserable. I couldn't breathe, my inner beings were arguing, fighting, full of fear and doubts. My head was a little corner of Hell. I went to relieve myself and in the process stuck my hand with long sharp thorns.

I repented to the Triple Jewel and to my Teacher. I apologized to Ven. Master Hung Yi. I said, "Whatever I've got coming, I want to take on. I'm not afraid of suffering, knowing full well that I've planted an evil seed and will surely meet my retribution. I fear only that my vows will be obscured and that I won't be able to accomplish my Way-karma and be of benefit to all beings." I humbly requested that I be gathered in by the Triple Jewel, if I could be of any use in the future in propagating the Dharma, that I'd be forgiven and returned to purity.

Just as I made this request, a car came speeding out of nowhere. It made a deliberate pass at us, zooming over onto the road shoulder where we were bowing. The car door flew open as it passed, missing me by an inch as it roared by. This was nearly the end of the pilgrimage. I believe it was a compassionate rescue by the Triple Jewel from an "instant karma" payoff of my debt. I recite the Great Compassion Mantra and carry the Shurangama Mantra on my person at all times. These mantras have inconceivable power to overcome the karmic trespasses of sincere but ignorant living beings. I believe that I can still write this letter only due to the compassionate regard of the Triple Jewel and the power of repentance. I'm really lucky not to be roasting in the hells. Instead, I have another chance to cultivate the Way.

Why did I make the stupid statement in the first place? Three years ago the Ven. Abbot said to the assembly from the high seat, "Those of you who keep gossiping will fall into the Hells. I don't want you to, but cause and effect is really true. I'm powerless to prevent it. Be careful!" How come I haven't learned my lesson? Why does my mouth obstruct me, despite my best efforts to control it? It's because of the bad seeds I've planted in the past; it's the karma of anger.

Universal Worthy Bodhisattva explains it this way, "A Bodhisattva who has thoughts of anger or hatred towards other Bodhisattvas, will be obstructed by the following million gates of obstruction... (Among these is:) He will always give rise to the four kinds of mistakes of speech and thereby create the obstacles of bad speech karma."

It's the story of my life, and if I hadn't begun to cultivate the Dharma, I'd never have recognized it or had the chance to hear about it and change it. I would have carried my mountain of offenses through this life and the next one and the next, never reducing it, always adding to it, unaware of the source of my suffering. I never considered myself as having much anger. I came back to the car this afternoon and took a good look. The rear end was dented, the tail pipe broken off and the bumpers twisted. The same car that buzzed us, first had paid the Plymouth a call, Heng Ch'au informed me. When they couldn't break in, they rammed it from the rear, trying to push it into the ditch. Is this not an angry act? How can I deny that it's my retribution returning to me?

I recalled the beer bottle that broke the window behind the picture of Gwan Yin Bodhisattva. The bottle spoke Dharma for me then as the car spoke it today. It said, "Good Man, where in empty space is there a need for your fighting? Who told you that you have to be #1? Who makes you struggle to be special and different from everyone? You're not, you know. You're just like all beings, and that's good enough. Have compassion, brother. Everyone makes mistakes. Be more yielding. Let that anger go. See what it brings you when you do so much false-thinking?"

I thought of the Buddha as I saw my own sad reflection in the Plymouth's dusty window. The Buddha is a perfect person. He has eighteen qualities that are special to him. Among them are these: his body, mouth, and mind never make mistakes. He never sees anything or anyone in the world as different. His mind is never unconcentrated and never fails to renounce himself to benefit others. He arrived at these powers and this great compassion by cultivating for a long time. He certainly endured a lot of suffering, but he took it without fear and without anger. When he woke up to cause and effect, he stopped swallowing the poisons of greed, anger, and stupidity, and quite naturally he got better. One day, he reached perfect health: Buddhahood.

The whole experience today strengthened my resolve to work hard at cultivation and not do so much false-thinking. It deepened my faith in the power and purity of the Dharma of repentance. I felt like a father looking at this stubborn child who won't listen to reason. The child's face is all scratched and bruised, he's run his bike into the curb again and fallen off. The father picks him up and straightens the bike's handlebars. He points him back on to the street and reminds his son that as long as he rides on the level path, and in the middle, his way will be unimpeded. "It's true for you, son, and it's true for everyone else, too. Be careful and ride well."

The Buddhadharma is like that, it keeps us from smashing our lives on the curbs of karma while we head for the Buddha's City. We're all on this road, we all make it safely.

The repentance lifted a huge cloud of darkness from my shoulders. I recalled how three weeks ago a tiny bug caught my eye. It appeared on a rock below my nose as I bowed. As I watched, the bug, no bigger than a pinhead, defecated on the rock; a minute squirt of pee. It rubbed its little hands together, wiped its face and hopped away. I thought, "There I am. That's me. No different than a bug every time I forget to cultivate. Life is more than eating and defecating. Don't be so selfish, Kuo Chen. Go plant pure causes. Work hard! Don't be just another bug! Don't worry about yourself. Don't think! Cultivate the Way!"

I don't mean to slander insects. Bugs can be good advisors. I am truly of one and the same substance with insects. Their bodies transform and decay in an instant, mine takes just a little longer. But I don't want to be a *lazy* bug. Lazy bugs get dragged all over the universe by their karma. Vigorous cultivator bugs, one day, when their work has been done well, find themselves "in control of the thousand changes and ten thousand transformations, totally free to do anything you want to do" as the Master put it in December of 1977 at Gold Wheel Temple.

Disciple Kuo Chen (Heng Sure)
bows in respect

Beauty and health fades away

August 12, 1979
Near Anchor Bay, California

Dear Shr Fu,

We're taking our midday meal in the back of the Plymouth. Outside it's blowing cold and swirls of dust clouds. An old, feeble woman slowly staggers to her seat in the car parked behind us. She grips the car for support. Her gait is stiff and unsteady. Eyes and ears are failing. Her world, who could know it? She looks up slowly and fixes her gaze out to sea. A bowl of food sits in her lap. It doesn't interest her. As she shifts around in the car, the windshield glare makes it seem like she disappeared. All that can be seen is the reflection of overhead passing white clouds where once the old woman was.

Her daughter, and her daughter's daughter are with her. In their faces you can see how beauty and health fade and wither by themselves in a few short seasons. The three of them are like different steps in the life of the same person. Everything speaks the Dharma. I look at my own body and the food I'm eating. Then I look back at the reflection of shifting white clouds in the car window. "Thus it is." Everything is impermanent and temporary. What seems solid and secure today, tomorrow drifts away and disappears like the clouds. Everything speaks the Dharma: Hurry up and cultivate! How the temporary flies! There is so little time. Be swift and head for the true. Every night we end our day with,

> *This day had already passed,*
> *and life has thereby decreased.*

> *Like fish in evaporating water,*
> *what joy is there is this?*
> *Be diligent and vigorous*
> *as if rescuing your head.*
> *Be mindful of impermanence.*
> *Be careful not to be lax.*

Tonight, as we sing this verse I'll remember the old woman. I'll remember the pine cone that fell from a tree and the blackberries drying up on the vines alongside the road. I'll remember seeing that my own body is just like the reflection of passing clouds in a car window. I'll remember, too, everyone bowing together after the meal—even the old woman who stood tall and reverent in the cold wind with folded hands because her legs could no longer bend to bow.

Peace in the Way,

Disciple Kuo T'ing (Heng Ch'au)
bows in respect

To be a monk or a skunk

August 13, 1979
Anchor Bay

Dear Shr Fu,

This letter has a title:

Skunk or monk? Bathroom or Buddhahall?
Our thoughts and deeds decide it all.

The Janitor Reports:

Moreover, there are animals
In odious and repugnant shapes,
Which all come from their bad karma,
And they suffer an eternity of affliction.

Avatamsaka Sutra, Flower Store World,
Chapter Five, Part Three,
Verse spoken by Universal Worthy Bodhisattva

San bu yi bai has given us a great gift of faith in the Buddhadharma. It's hard to pinpoint what part we believe in most. It's like asking which drop of ocean water is wetter than the others, or which ray of sunshine is more bright and more pure than the next. The Buddhadharma is all true. Our faith increases the more we cultivate. And the more we cultivate, the more we find to believe in. It's like an ever-increasing bank account. For one who cultivates becomes fabulously wealthy in faith.

Probably the fundamental lesson I have learned on this trip is the truth of cause and effect: as you plant, so do you harvest. Why did the page-boy Wart pull the sword out of the stone when none of the noble knights could budge it? Because he had the causes and conditions from the past that allowed him to grow up and become King Arthur. Why did the poor wood-gatherer passing through the market place hear one sentence of the *Diamond Sutra* and become greatly enlightened on the spot? Because of past causes he became the Sixth Patriarch.

Why do the seals gather on the rocks outside Anchor Bay to bark and speak the Dharma of seals? Because in past lives they behaved like seals and now they live in seal bodies. Abe Lincoln became President and was shot in the head by a stranger, perhaps because in the past he killed the killer and it was time for his retribution.

All things in creation have their reasons for being. It's said,

If you see things and understand them,
  You transcend the world.
If you see things and are confused by them,
  You fall onto the turning wheel of rebirth.

One morning last week I rounded a curve in the fog, just in time to find a dead skunk on the black top. He had been hit only minutes before. He was still warm, a five-pound adult male with sharp, curving, meat-eating fangs. I removed him from the traffic lane, gingerly holding his sad corpse by the tip of his white-striped tail. The skunk spoke Dharma for me. He said, "In the past I was greedy and killed out of anger and stupidity. Now I've got my due. It's not enough that my body stinks so no one likes to get near me. Today I lost even this flesh bag. All because when I was a person, I didn't do a good job of keeping the rules. I killed myself by swallowing the poisons of greed, hatred, and stupidity. It's all my fault. There's no one else to blame."

I said the Pure Land mantra over the dead skunk and thanked him for the lesson. I thought, "How glad I am to have the chance to cultivate the Way. Being a skunk is a lot of suffering. You can't sit in full lotus, you can't bow to the Buddhas, you can't make offerings. Good thing I'm a person."

Then, at lunch, I behaved just like a skunk. I found myself watching Heng Ch'au's food bowl, criticizing his every move and thinking harsh thought of greed and anger towards him. In my mind I competed with him as I have done in the past. This time I remembered the Master's instructions:

> *Purge the false and keep the true.*
> *The straight mind is the Way-place.*
> *The everyday mind is the Way.*
> *Don't blame anyone and don't criticize others.*
> *Be a good person.*
> *Don't seek benefit.*
> *Don't be selfish.*
> *A great person starts in the small, subtle places.*
> *Real Buddhadharma is right before your eyes.*
>
> *Master Hua,*
> *Malaysia, August 8th, 1978*

Here I was, planting the seeds of skunkhood and going along with it! When I recognized what I was doing, suddenly the cause and effect became as clear as night and day. I couldn't turn around fast enough. Who wants to swallow poison? Monks think pure, lofty monk-thoughts. From this small place, they eventually become Buddhas. Skunks think smelly thoughts and eventually wind up like the dead polecat I mantra'd last week.

All along I've been running through the Dharma Realm looking outside for dharmas to blame, to criticize and find fault with. All this time, dharmas are not at fault. My own body, mouth and mind are the source of all my suffering and all my joy. No one can make me do anything. I choose to be a monk or a skunk in every new thought.

The Buddhadharma gives us the rules. What we practice in our minds creates Buddhalands or bathrooms out of our every waking minute. As the Master said to Heng Ch'au in his visit last week at Sea Ranch,

> *If you don't want to be emperor, first you have to flush the toilet. Once the toilet is flushed, you can go and be a Buddha. First you must do your own work and clean out the bathroom. Don't be greedy for Buddhahood, don't think about it. Just go cultivate.*

By bequeathing the Dharma, the Buddhas and Bodhisattvas have given us a gift of compassion. I have another chance to try my best today to be a good janitor, to use every second to flush my own clogged toilet in my mind. I can turn my bathroom into a Buddhahall. Why do it? Because it makes possible the highest giving of all. Using the Great King of Vows of Universal Worthy Bodhisattva while I bow and make transference, I clean out a corner of the universe as well. I truly believe that cultivation of these vows is the ultimate work, the best thing anyone can do in a lifetime. No matter how stinky a skunk I've been in the past, *anybody* who can keep the precepts and not false think, can fully complete Universal Worthy's practices and vows, and become a Buddha. The vows are "the road in Heaven," I believe, and the Supreme rules of the Dharma Realm. I bow to them in deep faith and respect in every thought and to the Sutra that contains them. How inconceivable is the *Avatamsaka*! That we have the causes and conditions to meet with it here and now is great good fortune. As National Master Ch'ing Liang says:

> *Moreover, when one meets a Sagely Ruler,*
> *Obtaining it on Magic Mountain,*

Exhaustively reflecting on its esoteric meaning,
How can one but jump for joy?

Avatamsaka, Preface

We bowed before the Anchor Bay Campground entrance. Inside, packed like sardines, were campers and mobile homes with names like "Wilderness," "Open Road," "Southwind," "Explorer". The smoke of the cooking fires and the hubbub of the jammed-in vacationers felt like the crowded marketplaces in downtown Kuala Lumpur. Why would people come to the middle of the deserted coast in expensive get-away cars to stand elbow to tailbone just like in any big city? Because of past affinities with each other. Someone died right here this afternoon. The rescue vehicles roared by. Don't know who it was or why. The Dharma of Impermanence is saying for us all, "Try your best. Keep the rules. Go towards the good! And flush the toilet." The ambulance rolled away, we bowed up the hill, the smoke of grilled hamburgers filled the air, and out on the harbor rocks, the seals bathed and barked.

Disciple Kuo Chen (Heng Sure)
bows in respect

* * *

Dear Shr Fu,

The Bodhisattva vows that all beings will be able to perfect the speaking of the Buddhas' road to Bodhi and constantly be happy to cultivate the giving of the unsurpassed Dharma.

Avatamsaka Sutra

On *san bu yi bai*, Heng Ch'au and I have learned respect for the rules. Following the rules makes us happy. When we subdue our thoughts about how things should be and quietly, sincerely return to true principle, everything works out just right. No thoughts needed, no effort wasted. It's true every time.

So what are these rules? Why are they true for us the same way they were true for the ancients? Why will they be true in the future?

You can sum it up in a few words. The rules are called the Buddhadharma, the Middle Way. When it's too little, add to it. When it's too big, reduce it.

Or you can speak of them infinitely and never finish, e.g., the Five Precepts; the Ten Good Acts; the Five Constants; filiality; the Ten Vows of Universal Worthy Bodhisattva; the Three-fold Non-outflow Study of Precepts, Samadhi, and Wisdom; the Six Paramitas; repentance; giving; faith; the Ten Thousand Practices, and so on. All of them are true principles. All of them lead back to the unchanging, perfectly balanced Middle.

Everything speaks the Dharma all the time if only we are receptive to it. For example, last night it was late and I hadn't studied my *Avatamsaka* memory-project, as I try to do each night. A little bit each day helps me keep balanced, on the ground, and in touch with the rules. When I miss it, I feel as if my mind hasn't eaten that day. My wisdom goes hungry. When people hear the Sutras tell of filiality, repaying the kindness of the Buddha, our parents, teachers, and elders, it never fails to touch the heart. Putting our seniors into rest-homes and breaking up families is unnatural. It weakens the country. It wastes a priceless natural resource: the wisdom of age and maturity. When people hear that Buddhism takes filiality as its basis and repaying kindness as its first duty, they want to hear more right away. It's like adding water to thirsty, dried plants. Filiality is a rule. It is the same with the others of the Five Constants.

The first of the Five Constants is Humaneness. To be humane means to be kind and compassionate to all lives. It's a fundamental truth: when we don't kill, the world finds the natural Middle. Of all the vehicles that pass us on the highway, there is one kind that we can identify with eyes, ears, and nose all closed. The death-trucks are unmistakable. This is a ranch land and the trucks that carry the cattle, sheep, and horses to the slaughterhouses drive by in a dark cloud of evil energy. Add to it the smell of the fearful animals jammed inside, the sound of their bleating, and it's a heavy moment each time. They know they are off to meet the butcher and their fear is a tangible, horrible presence on the country highways. Animals that die in fear produce toxic chemicals in their bodies. Doctors now recognize this "poisoned meat" as the source of many currently incurable diseases. The cure? Be humane. Don't take life, don't eat the flesh of living creatures.

The Second of the Five Constants is Righteousness. Whatever is righteous feels right on. It's natural, balanced and in harmony.

Another way to say it is don't steal. Theft is out of harmony. It makes waves and causes trouble. We've learned that our thoughts are like radio-beams. What goes on in the mind is broadcast to the world, there are no boundaries. When we have thoughts of greedy desire and seeking, we steal from the Dharma Realm, just as if we reached out a hand to swipe an apple from a fruit-stand. This lesson has been thoroughly taught to us.

One day, by the Half-Moon Bay Airport, we bowed through a big wind-storm. I have trouble concentrating in the wind, and my mind was full of thoughts of "Oh, pity me!" I was cold and hungry and had false thoughts of food and the shelter of the car. We returned at the end of the bowing day. Stacked by the car were over ten bags of groceries, all stolen by my greedy thoughts from kind-hearted people of the area who picked up on my broadcast. The food-blizzard continued for two days.

Stealing is not righteous. We barely had room to sit in the car. Over a hundred bananas! This ain't the Tao! No false thinking is the rule. It keeps the natural Middle in perfect harmony.

Disciple Kuo Chen (Heng Sure)
bows in respect

282

There's no place to run or hide

September 3, 1979

In the Mountains on the road to Booneville, California

Dear Shr Fu,

At the end of the bowing day, we did transference and drove into Pt. Arena to dump garbage. As we pulled into a closed gas station, suddenly we are surrounded by about ten men. They are tough-looking and full of whiskey. They start knocking on the car windows.

"Hey, what's happening, man? You guys is the ones that's bowing on the highway, right? What gives?" asks one in a mocking voice.

"Yeah, hey, there they are!" shouts some others spotting us. "Let's go check them out, c'mon!" And some more men run over from a motel across the street.

"Oh, you don't talk, eh? How about him?" he says pointing to Heng Sure sitting in the back seat. "He talk? Neither of you talk!? How we supposed to talk back to you, huh? Maybe write all over your car with paint, huh?" Everybody laughs, but they are not joking.

Another man steps up. He's got a big scar across his neck and is clutching an open whiskey bottle in one hand. He grabs the handout away from the other man and starts to read it saying, "What's their gig?" He looks at me and says roughly, "Your vocal chords shot or something?"

"No, it's their penance," shouts someone. More laughs.

"Hey, don't hassle 'em. They're doing their thing," he says and finishes reading the handout about the pilgrimage. He shoves the whiskey bottle in my face, "Here. Have a drink with me, or can't you? Your religion forbid it?" I nod. "How about him?" he asks, pointing the bottle to Heng Sure, "Can he drink?"

"Lookie, he's prayin!" someone yells and they all break out in a mocking laugh at the meditating monk.

"Ya see, his wife just had a baby. That's why he's so rude and obnoxious," says a tall man with scraggly beard and one eye missing.

"Yeah, usually I just go around and beat the hell out of people, but today I'm celebrating, so you're lucky, maybe," comes back the man standing by the open car window.

"Man! They've been at this since L.A.! Over two years!" exclaims the man reading the paper.

"That's a lot of miles. Many people hassle you?" asks one. I nod "No."

"Really! How about your car? Holding up okay? I know where you can get it wrecked real fast and cheap," he says. More laughs. Tension eases a little now.

Another truck pulls up behind us and more men jump out. The whole scene is touch and go. It could turn into violence or dissolve into "no affair" in a second. Heng Sure and I can feel the spotlight on us. Each move has to be true and proper or the scene will explode. They have crowbars, sledge hammers, lumberjack axes, and chains in their trucks. They could wipe us and the car out in a few minutes if provoked. We don't dare try to roll up the car window and pull out the log. There's too many of them, and they have us boxed in. Besides, it would only postpone a showdown for a day or two, when we bow through the town. They've been watching and waiting for us for weeks, they told us. We move at one mile a day. There's no place to run or hide. We've had to learn to get along with people. Pilgrims are on their own. Kindness, compassion, joy and giving are all we need to survive. These four unlimited minds cover *all* situation and leave everyone feeling good. We try to treat everyone the same. No matter what happens, we have vowed not to show anger.

> *The Bodhisattvas have entered into the level and equal nature of all dharmas. They have no thoughts of any living being as not being family or friends. If there is a living being who has a thought of hostility towards the Bodhisattva, the Bodhisattva views him with kind eyes, as well. To the very end, they have not the slightest anger.*

Avatamsaka,
Ten Transferences Chapter (First Transference)

There is something special about bowing outdoors, slowly going from town to town. It's hard to describe, but after a while, everything seems the same and everyone feels like family and friends—"level and equal". All the men look like brothers or our fathers. All the women look like sisters and our mothers. From L.A., through Asia, and back up the coast to where we are today, Pt. Arena, California, all the different cities and villages blend into one big neighborhood. We are hardly aware of leaving one place and entering another. The bowing naturally levels all the skin-deep differences somehow, and "being one with everyone" kind of sneaks into your heart before you know it.

As tough and threatening as these drunken men were, Heng Sure and I didn't feel uptight or angry. There was no hostility or rejection in the air. We all felt this and slowly things cooled off by themselves. The men relaxed.

"Well, ya' gotta get haircuts sometime. Or do you do that yourselves, too?" jokes one man. Some are huddled together reading the handout. Others are peeking in the car windows at the altar and pictures of Gwan Yin and the Master, while passing around an open whiskey bottle and taking swigs.

We slowly back the car off, smiling and waving good-bye.

"Hey!" shouts a short man with a mustache, "you know karate?"

"Yeah," chime in a couple more as they head for the car with renewed interest in the prospects of a fight. "You know... *kung fu*, martial arts?" They pose in T.V. kung fu stances. With beer bottles in their hand and dressed in dirty bib overalls and construction hats, it's kind of comic looking.

I nod "no" and fold my hands and bow, indicating "That's our kung fu." They like that, and everything softens again. Smiles come to some tough faces as if to say, "Yeah. The whole world could use a little more of that kind of kung fu. Who wants to fight, anyhow?"

As we drive away, the man whose wife just had a baby shouts, "Well, all I got to say is you better be careful, you two cosmics. Don't float away and disappear into the cosmos. Don't let the cosmos eat you up." More laughs and every one waves good-bye. It was a lesson in kindness and according.

> *When one's mind is level and equal towards all beings, one can accomplish perfect, full, great compassion. When one uses the heart of great compassion to accord with all beings, then one can accomplish making offerings to the Thus Come One. This is how Bodhisattvas accord with all living beings.*
>
> Avatamsaka Sutra,
> Universal Worthy's Conduct and Vows Chapter

The next day, we bowed past a large, wooded front yard and house on the edge of town. The local kids were "playing guns." "Bang, bang... got ya. Did not!... Did So!... Blast 'im Tony, kapow, kapow!" They see us bowing, and everything stops in silence. Then a rock comes flying at us from behind some bushes. It hits on the pavement next to us. We keep bowing. The kids keep watching.

In a few minutes, the braver ones inch closer. "What ya' doin, man?" they ask. I write a note and give it to them:

We are praying to help the world get better and to be good to our parents. We don't talk.

"I'll give it to my brother, John, he can read," says a little boy. John reads it for everyone. They smile. We keep bowing into town. The children stop playing guns and quietly sit in the shade and watch us bow. A car squeals by and someone yells at us. The kids stand up and defend us, "Hey, you better leave them alone; they're good," says the older boy. Two children run up with fresh-picked red flowers and offer them. The older ones ride ahead on their bikes scouting out the route ahead. "Better watch out for that dog up there, he might bite. The other one's okay," says Tony, pointing to a tail-wagging mongrel.

We are all changing together—the drunks, the monks, the children. Changing from guns to flowers, from anger to compassion, from confusion to understanding. We are all bowing together with one heart to the City of Ten Thousand Buddhas.

Peace in the Way,

Disciple Kuo T'ing (Heng Ch'au)
bows in respect

Basically, there's not even one Buddha

September 10, 1979

Mt. View Road, on the way to Boonville, California

Dear Shr Fu,

In a single day, how many living beings see me? How many do I see? In a month, how many living beings have I crossed paths with and affected? How many have influenced and touched me? Not just human living beings, but those with two feet, four feet, many feet and no feet. Those beings with form and without form; those with thought and without thought, and those with neither thought nor no-thought. There are beings born from eggs, from wombs, from moisture and from transformation. Some beings inhabit the earth. Some live in the water, fire, or air. There are beings who live in space or who are born and dwell in forests, underground, and inside other beings. There is a measureless ocean of living beings in all ten directions of the universe (Dharma Realm), and to the ends of empty space. Everything is "alive". Even rocks have lifespan. We just go so fast we fail to see it. In a lifetime, the number of living beings we have encountered is incalculable.

> "All these many kinds (of living beings) I will accord with and attend to, serving them and making gifts to them, just as if I were respecting my own parents. I will treat them as I treat my teachers and elders, as well as Arhats, even as I attend to the Thus Come Ones, without any difference in my attitude.

> "For those who suffer illness, I will be a good doctor. For those who have lost their way, I will show

them the right road. I will be a bright light for those who are in the darkness of night. I will cover and shelter those who are in poverty." The Bodhisattva, in this way, benefits all beings levelly and equally.

Universal Worthy's Conduct
Chapter 36

If I am good to all beings, then they learn goodness and are good, in turn, to others. If I am bad to beings, they harbor hatred and resentment and pass it on in turn. So, if the world isn't good, it's because I'm not good. But this is still holding to a view of self and others. If I can expand the measure of my mind to contain the whole world, then all is one. All beings in all the paths of rebirth are my parents. All earth and water has served as the substance of one of my bodies. All elemental air and fire has previously sustained the life of one of my bodies. Great Compassion is being one with everyone. Being one with everyone is the substance of all Buddhas.

All Buddhas, Thus Come Ones, take the heart of Great Compassion as their substance.

Avatamsaka Sutra
Universal Worthy's Conduct and Vows
Chapter 40

So, taking care of and being good to all living beings is the same as taking good care of myself. And when I respect and serve and make offerings to all beings, I'm doing it to all Buddhas. It's the same. All beings are the body of all Buddhas. It's said, "All living beings are contained within a hair-pore of the Buddha's body." And, yet what is big and small? Because it's also said,

Each and every minute speck of dust contains Buddhas equal in number to the total number of tiny dust motes in all world.

Avatamsaka Sutra
Chapter 40

The heart of Great Compassion is just simple kindness and goodness shown to all beings. And, yet this simple attitude embraces and goes beyond the ultimate understanding of the mind. The Buddhadharma is like that. Modern physics is straining and making revolutionary breakthroughs now and coming to the same conclusions that sages have known in their hearts since aeons ago.

July 24, 1979.

We are sitting in meditation on the side of the road under a Cypress tree. The air is clean out here. The only fragrance is a burning stick of incense. As the sun sets, the wind relaxes. Living outside, one is constantly brought face-to-face with birth and death. It says,

> *Within each variety of kshetras*
> *   are inconceivable worlds.*
> *Some are being created,*
> *   some are being destroyed,*
> *While some, having once existed,*
> *   are now extinct.*
> *Just like the leaves of a forest,*
> *   some hang and some fall down.*
> *So, too, within the kinds of kshetras,*
> *   worlds are created, worlds are destroyed.*
>
> *Avatamsaka Sutra,*
> *Chapter 5, Part 3*

When we bow through the tall grass and weeds, we enter an ocean of worlds of plants, bugs, and microscopic organisms. Some are young and green, some are old and sun-bleached. They are all changing—coming into being, dwelling, going bad and destroyed (extinct). The animals, the sea creatures, the people in the small towns and passing cars—we all share this reality. Everything changes, nothing stays. Look at the empty shell of a grasshopper, a falling star, my teeth cavities—they all speak the same Dharma: impermanence.

As the tea water comes to a boil, the rays of the setting sun hit the steam clouds. The cloud of steam is made up of billions of tiny swirling particles. They rise up in a mist and then vanish into empty space. I never saw this before. All the countless tiny particles! I turn and look at the incense smoke. It's the same, but made up of even smaller particles. "Now you see it, now you don't." In physics, this is basic: everything is made up of the same atoms. Matter and energy are not really created or destroyed. It all simply changes shape and appearance. In the *Prajna Paramita Sutra* it says,

> *Whatever is form is emptiness;*
> *Whatever is emptiness is form.*

A couple stops and asks, "What's a Buddha?" and "do you believe in God, or do you have your own God?" I can't find words to answer. I'd like to be able to say, "Well, it's this way, or that way," but I know so little about how it really is. A year ago, I would have piped right up with an answer. Now, we just bow in silence and learn from everybody and everything.

Our minds are coming apart at their one-dimensional seams. I want to grab and hold on to something. We are used to figuring things out and putting them into nice words. But now it's all becoming like the tea steam, incense smoke, and the grass and weeds: they can't be got at and yet they still exist.

> *All dharmas are non-dual and there are none which*
> *are non-dual. It's just like empty space. If you try to*
> *find it in any of the ten directions, in the past, present,*
> *or future, you will fail to get at it. However, it's not the*
> *case that empty space does not exist.*

The Bodhisattva contemplates all dharmas in this way: they are totally unobtainable. But it is not the case that all dharmas do not exist.

Avatamsaka Sutra,
Ten Practices, Chapter 21, Practice #8

And God? God cannot be got at, either. Even among people of the same faith, they can't agree on what God is. Everybody has their own God, because everything is made from the mind alone. That is why the ultimate state in Buddhism is non-attachment. It's in letting go of all views and attachments, emptying even emptiness, that we discover the ultimate.

People ask us, "Well, isn't Buddha your God?"

The answer is no. Because where most religions believe in "My God alone is true," and take to know, love and serve that God as the ultimate state, Buddhism says all beings have the Buddha-nature and all can become Buddhas. The ultimate state in Buddhism is non-attachment, an "unattached, unbound, liberated mind," as the *Avatamsaka* says.

I remember overhearing a conversation between the Ven. Abbot and a disciple while riding in a car in Kuala Lumpur:

Disciple: "Master, some people say there's only one Buddha and others say there are many Buddhas. How is it? Are there many Buddhas or only one?"

Master: "Basically, there's not even one Buddha. There is just great wisdom."

Sometimes, at the end of a long, good day of bowing, when the body is soft and quiet and the mind doesn't know whether my nostrils are pointing up or down, I get a little glimpse of the way the Sutras say it is. It must be so.

Peace in the Way,

Disciple Kuo T'ing (Heng Ch'au)
bows in respect

How come I got a water balloon?

September 3, 1979
Mountain View Road, Mendocino County

Dear Shr Fu,

> *The Bodhisattva never uses the causes, conditions,*
> *methods, or karma of desire to trouble any being.*
>
> *Avatamsaka Sutra*
> *Ten Practices Chapter*

Yesterday afternoon, as I bowed, I contemplated Universal Worthy Bodhisattva's fourth vow, "to repent of karmic obstacles." I repented of the heavy offenses I have created by talking frivolously. Frivolous, misleading speech disturbs people. It is born of emotion and comes from the desire to be famous and special, #1, and unique. It's the same as the desire for flavor in food. Plain, simple, food has never been good enough for me. I've always sought flavor and tasty, exotic combinations, sensational seasonings. It's a desire and it obstructs my cultivation. Truly:

> *All desires are one desire.*

My desires for fame and flavor have caused others to bring forth emotion, to move their minds, to lose mindfulness, to break off pure practices and to seek flavor and desire. Today, I repented of my desire-born offenses of frivolous speech. The repentance verse says,

> *I have defiled the Sangha's pure dwelling and*
> *broken up the pure practices of others.*

And I realized suddenly that the beings I have troubled by my frivolous speech live both outside and inside my mind. The reason I can't concentrate and lose mindfulness is right here! I speak misleading, loose and emotional talk inside my mind! I still allow myself to feel excessively happy, angry, sorrowful, and fearful. I still attach to love and hate and desire. These seven emotions confuse me and stir up the waters of my originally still, pure mind. I trouble the living beings of my own nature. All along I've assumed that merely holding my tongue and not talking on *san bu yi bai* would reform my bad-speech karma. But I still have not put down emotion and false speech inside. The Master spoke it for me back in Los Angeles twenty-six months ago:

> *You're not talking outside? Good! Don't talk inside, either. If you're quiet outside but fighting in your mind, it's just the same as if you fought with other people, isn't it?*

I've been deaf to this lesson all along, even with great help. Last month at Sea Ranch, I had a lesson in awareness. Bowing along after lunch I was really getting into a thought of repentance. I got rhapsodic and emotional about it. Tears of joy flowed. I felt waves of shame and sadness for my past selfishness and ignorance. My repentance was a sloppy, tear-jerker from a T.V. soap opera. Suddenly, out of nowhere, a big water-balloon flew from a passing car and smacked the ground behind me. My robe and sash were soaked. I was dumb-founded. Here I was being so sincere. How come I got a water balloon?

If I had looked at it with a straight mind, I would have understood. The water balloon spoke Dharma for me. I was indulging in emotion and attaching to states. The Buddhadharma is not that way. National Master Ch'ing Liang vowed,

> *My nature will never be defiled by states of love and emotion.*

The Buddha's eighteen special dharmas—4) no thoughts of (anything being) different, and 5) unfailing concentration—describe the proper state.

Even though I was using effort, it was deviant vigor. Emotion moves the mind and disturbs living beings. It does not lead to "the unsurpassed place of level equality" which the Bodhisattva in the Second Practice promises to attain.

National Master Ch'ing Liang speaks directly in the *Hua Yen Su Ch'ao Prologue*,

When emotion is produced, wisdom is cut off.

But, I wasn't able to return the light and apply the teaching to myself until today. We have reached the end of our twenty-seven month journey beside the Pacific Ocean. This week we turn East on the Boonville-Mt. View Road and head for the City of Ten Thousand Buddhas. Today I vow to leave behind my emotional desires. I vow to cut off my seeking for fame and flavor and specialness and the offenses of false speech that they create. I want to return to proper mindfulness and still concentration. I want to "dwell in the unsurpassed place of level equality" with no thoughts of difference. I want to benefit all beings with this work.

1) I vow never again to use words, gestures, expressions, or postures out of the causes, conditions, methods or karma of emotion or desire.

2) I vow to speak only Buddhadharma, true principle, and words in service to the Triple Jewel, according to the rules of the Bodhisattva's Second Ground of Wisdom.

3) I vow never again to seek the desires of fame or flavor.

I vow to transform my nature by cultivating these ten hearts:

1) A true and real heart

2) A straightforward, direct heart

3) An unmixed, undefiled heart

4) An upright, proper heart

5) A level and equal heart

6) A clear and cool heart

7) A humble and respectful heart

8) A heart of faith and joy in the profound, unsurpassed, subtle and wonderful Dharma

9) An able-to-endure heart

10) A heart of Great Kindness, Great Compassion, Great Joy, and Great Giving

Disciple Kuo Chen (Heng Sure)
bows in respect

Following the rules

September 10, 1979

Boonville Road

Dear Shr Fu,

> *The Bodhisattva vows that all beings dwell peacefully in purified Buddhalands... that they dwell in the ultimate path and in places of peace and happiness.*
>
> *Avatamsaka Sutra*
> *Ten Transferences Chapter*

A young woman spoke to us after lunch today: "My mother has escaped from Vietnam. No one has heard from her. She may be lost at sea. I hope that you will think of her in your prayers."

We were deeply moved by this girl's sorrowful request. Why do we study and practice the Buddhadharma? Because we have found pure goodness within it. Buddhadharma is the best medicine on earth. It can cure the suffering of afflictions. If everyone behaved according to these ancient, universal rules, all wars would stop and suffering would vanish.

For example, the Bodhisattva on the First Ground makes great vows. Afterwards his heart changes. He obtains the ten kinds of minds, or attitudes.

1) *The Mind of Benefit.* Who benefits from wars? Demons. Undertakers. Corpse-eating worms. Bomb-builders.

2) *A Soft, Pliant Mind.* The mind that does not force itself on others, much less does it want to fight a war.

3) *A Mind that Accords.* "Will you monks please be careful up ahead, maybe walk past our construction vehicles and bow on the other side where it's safe?" asks a road-crew foreman. "Yes, we will, Mister. No problem."

4) *A Mind that is Tranquil.* "You @#$%^&*@#$%^&* better tell me what you're doing, or I'm going to break your heads!" Heng Ch'au replies with a sincere smile, "We are Buddhists, making a pilgrimage. We bow and pray." "Oh yeah? Buddhists? I thought you was those (X). Oh well, good luck to you."

5) *A Mind that is Subdued.* I say to myself, "I would sure like to polish off that plate of tofu, but I'm nearly full. Principle says to stick to the Middle: not too much, not too little. Principle is the truth, my thoughts are false. I'll be patient and subdue my greed. Well, look at that. The host who brought this offering and stayed to share it ate the tofu. If I had grabbed the extra food, he would have gone hungry. Good old principle! Can't beat it!

6) *A Mind that is Still.* "Better take off my scarf. No, wait. Concentrate. Don't think about yourself. Hey, the wind's coming up. I'd better put on my hat. No, wait. Don't move. Concentrate. Oh, time to meditate. Quiet, monkey-mind! Be still!"

7) *A Humble Mind.* My good fortune in getting a complete and healthy human body is one in a billion. If I break the rules, I can find myself in a cow's body, or as a swarm of green grasshoppers on a lonely dirt track here in Point Arena, all in the wink of an eye. Only through the great kindness of the Buddhas and Bodhisattvas, my parents and elders, have I been able to meet the Dharma. My greed and anger are as large as Rocky Mts. My offenses are as many as the sands of Arizona and New Mexico. My deviant views would fill up empty space if they had shape and substance. How can I be lazy and not sweat to cultivate repentance and reform? How could I dare to show anger at any being?

8) *A Moistened Mind.* The drought of 1976-1977 turned Southern California into a yellow, crackling mirage. Everything was thirsty. Every plant was brittle and thorny. All the animals

were scrawny and scaly. There was no fertility, no forgiveness in the land. This is my state of mind when I am greedy, when I seek self-benefit. When I am angry and harsh, my mind is just that way. As soon as I remember to moisten my mind and heart with the water of great compassion and kindness, it turns into May of 1979 in Marine County. Wildflowers fill the fields, fat cows graze, sleek Morgan colts gallop in herds across the ridges, shorebirds sing and fish jump in the lagoons. A moistened mind is a happy, growing place.

9) *An Unmoving Mind.* "You crazy goofs, get up from there!" says a young man from a passing car.

"You are our good advisor. You remind me of my boundless offenses of flattery and climbing. I vow to dwell in the heart of level equality towards all beings. I bow to you in gratitude. We will become Buddhas together."

10) *An Unturbid Mind.* We read Buddhist Sutras. We don't keep up with the news. We don't hear advertising. We don't listen to recorded music. We eat plain food. We repent of past offenses and guard against desires. We are learning to respect the rules, "subdue ourselves and return to principle." Subduing the self creates a solid security that is inherent in the ancient rules. Returning to principle, we discover their deep harmony within ourselves. It feels like coming across the buoy channel markers in a fog. You know that soon you will be in port. The old rules tell us how the universe really is before thought and debate, before words and speech. The Buddha's Way is the ancient road back home. It feels like the first view of the landing lights on the airport runway after a rough-weather plane ride.

As an unruly, freedom-loving young man, I reacted defensively at first to the notion of "rules." Disciplining body and mind sounded like courts, cops, lawyers and prison. But respect for the real and worship for them in thought, word and deed, brings true freedom. That's the Buddhadharma's great gift to us all.

Heng Ch'au and I have the feeling that the True Principles of the Buddhadharma are the "deep contours" of the original mind. We all share them, that's why the Dharma is the language of the heart. We met a Sioux Indian in Stinson Beach, who said, "You guys are neat. My teacher is the medicine man of the Rosebud Sioux. He says that when you're neat, you never have troubles. You just slip right on through all situations."

Who is the Buddha? He's a living being who came to be so "neat" at following the rules that he disappeared inside them. He lost himself by perfecting his conduct according to the teachings.

What is the Dharma? The rules. How to live, how to walk, talk and think, as we make our way back to the Original Home.

What is the Sangha? It's the lucky people who have found the trail through the dense forest of confusion. People who give up what's false in order to protect what's true.

Why do we bow? Universal Worthy's Ten vows instruct us to. His Ten Kings of Vows are foremost among the rules.

We bow to worship and revere all Buddhas. We bow to praise the Thus Comes Ones. We bow as an offering to them and to all beings. We repent of all the times in the past we've broken the rules. There are six more vows.

We bow to the King of Kings of all the rule-books, the *Flower Adornment Sutra*. It is the map of the universe. Nature's own blueprint. Like Virginia, from Morro Bay, said when she heard about the precepts, "Boy, when you follow the rules, it really takes a load off your back, doesn't it?"

Disciple Kuo Chen (Heng Sure)
bows in respect

What we give away is ourselves

September 17, 1979

9 Miles above Boonville

Dear Shr Fu,

> *(When the Bodhisattva gives...) he does not expect a reward, he does not seek fame or reputation, he is not greedy for benefit... he gives only to gather beings in.*

San bu yi bai is a constant lesson in giving. We have been greatly given to. Our feelings have been deeply moved by the giving we have witnessed and by the boundless gifts we have received.

Why are Buddhas and Bodhisattvas greatly happy? Because of one basic quality: the kind of giving that they can do. On the other hand,

> *Greed kills,*
> *Desire is death.*
> *Selfishness ends the world.*

This is what we've learned on the pilgrimage. As pilgrim monks, we have seen lots of "true-life adventures" and of all the good and bad deeds we have witnessed, the scenes that will live longest in our hearts are the acts of kindness, compassion, joy, and giving.

Kindness: Sunday morning, Sea Ranch. A police car stops, turns and slowly creeps back around the curve 200 yards ahead to where our car is parked. Suddenly, a white pick-up truck guns its engine and squeal away, the cop in hot pursuit. A break-in prevented, two grateful monks. Another debt of kindness to repay.

Compassion: Mendocino City, road crew grades the highway. The dust turns the air to pea soup each time the sweeper passes. We can't breathe. It blots out the sunlight. Then a big caterpillar bulldozer stops. The driver says to Heng Ch'au, "I want to apologize for all the dust and noise we're making. I hate to bother anyone in their worship. Do you plan to be here long? We'll be working and making lots of dust." Heng Ch'au gives him a handout sheet. As he takes it, he says, "You fellas from that place out of Ukiah? I hope to see *that* some day. See ya later. God Bless." From then on, the sweepers lift their brushes as they pass the bowing.

Joy: Foggy morning in Gualala. Big white truck passes, slows, stops. Tall, bearded man in heavy work boots approaches. His face is full of light. Is he crying or happy? He bows slowly, holds an apple in both hands above his head. He's happy. He stands, hands the apple to the monk, then joins his palms and says, "Thank you brother." He turns and disappears into the fog.

Giving: Labor Day, 1977. Monks, nuns, and laypeople get up at 3 a.m. and drive seven hours to Santa Barbara, arriving just on time to bring food, goods, and high-voltage cheer to us. The vibes are pure white, *yang*, and vitalizing. Their reward? No reward. A long, hot drive back to San Francisco in Labor Day traffic. They gave us Dharma, wealth, and fearlessness. Everyone was happy. This is the kind of selfless work that Buddhas and Bodhisattvas do. It teaches us how to give.

Giving Away the Fruit
The Open-handed harvest

On our altar are three round, red fruits: a crimson tomato, a red Delicious apple, and a scarlet nectarine. They came from people in the Point Arena area. People offer the produce from their gardens with happiness. Each time, there is a touch of magic in the giving. "These came from our labor on this land. I want to share the fruit of my work with you, because I believe in what you do."

The Bodhisattva's path of transference make possible a rare kind of giving. The gift is pure goodness, *yang*-light blessings, merit, and virtue. The Sutra calls it "good roots." All Buddhas took the transference of their good roots as the foundation of their cultivation.

What we give away when we cultivate is ourselves. Since my ego is as big as Mt. Sumeru, I have a lot to give. Offerings to the Buddha, giving to all beings, renunciation of personal benefits, forsaking of evil—all are included in the practice of giving.

But the fruit of this work is never harvested. The Bodhisattva exists only to work. He takes no vacations and expects no rewards. His only satisfaction comes from the gradual growth of his effectiveness. As he gets better at giving, he gets to do more of it. Gwan Shr Yin Bodhisattva bestows happiness from a thousand hands and eyes. His joy at giving is the same as the happiness of the Point Arena gardeners, only multiplied by a thousand. Maitreya Bodhisattva is the "happy Bodhisattva" because his big bag is ever full of gifts to all beings. Kids flock to him. His joy is as full as his belly.

Even the vow to realize the fruit of Buddhahood is an open-handed harvest, not to be grasped or owned.

Sometimes the work of giving up attachments to self seems bitter and hard to bear. A single thought of transference makes it light and joyous. Pure seeds planted in the Buddha's field of blessings nurtured with hard, selfless work, produce a rich harvest to share with all the world.

"I hope you pilgrims will enjoy this produce. It came from our garden" (note left on bag of vegetables and placed on our car).

Disciple Kuo Chen (Heng Sure)
bows in respect

In cultivation, everything is voluntary

September 27, 1979

In the Mountains, 15 Miles West of Ukiah

Dear Shr Fu,

These are some reflections from a couple of days bowing, Thursday, September 20, 1979:

We leave the quiet, solitary mountains and enter the Boonville area. Shaved our heads and ate lunch under some cool redwood trees in a small county park outside of town. The last few days we've been bowing on a steep downhill grade. It takes a little practice to keep from sliding downhill while in a prostration. The sash and robe get caught under our heels and trip us up now and again.

Really happy. I don't know why. I don't want anything. Just want everybody to be happy. At the end of the day all the traffic stops and it's very still. As we passed under an oak tree, the only sound was the falling leaves. Each leaf is different and yet gladly they all return to the one. For all our differences we people are the same. I found myself getting lost in the layers of truth and wisdom of these simple words,

> *Strange, indeed. Strange, indeed. Strange, indeed. All living beings have the Buddhanature, and all can become Buddhas. It's only because of false thinking and attachment that they don't attain the fruit.*
>
> Shakyamuni Buddha

In over two years of bowing, two things clearly stand out: at heart, we are all the same, and everyone wants to cultivate. You can see it in the faces and reactions of all the people we have met on this trip. Some say it with words. Some can't find the words, but find other ways to say it... like a farm family handing fresh vegetables and cold water over their front-yard fence on a hot summer's day with a simple "thank you"; or flowers and incense placed on the roadside with a note, "We are *all* with you"; or a map and a bag of fruit sitting on the car at the end of the day; or a little child giving his allowance money; or a big smile and a wave from a passing logging truck driver. Or in this conversation with a newsman walking with us on Mt. View Road:

Reporter: "I don't know, maybe I'd be a lot better person if I put down my house and cars, wife, and kids; if I just said good-bye to my job and money and all of it... but..."

Monk: "You don't have to do that to be a Buddhist. Just do good wherever you are. If you are a father and a husband, be a really good father and husband. You don't have to be a monk or a nun. Anyone, anywhere can cultivate."

Reporter: "That's nice to know. So I could still do it as I am?"

Monk: "Yeah, sure. In cultivation, everything is voluntary..."

Reporter: "But if you didn't follow the rules—you know, by keeping the precepts—then that wouldn't really be being a Buddhist, would it? I mean, what's the point if you don't really want to practice. You'd just be like a lot of other religious people who say one thing but do another... like killing, for example. Buddhism should be different, I feel. I mean, what you have that's really unique is that you actually go and do it! That's rare."

We walked on quietly for awhile. Then he said, "You know, the longer I think about it, the more I see you've got something here, with Buddhism. It makes a lot of good sense if you stop to look at it. But isn't it back-breaking work?"

Monk: "Not if you follow the rules and you are sincere and single-minded. Then it's easy. Doing what you *don't* want to truly do is what's back-breaking."

Reporter: "Maybe so. Sometimes, when I'm really absorbed in my writing and photography... hot on a good story, I can go for hours without a break and never notice. It stops being work and becomes the same as, I don't know, the same as no work...Well, anyway, I like to jog and have naturally pretty much stopped eating meat. Don't miss it and feel a lot better all around. I ate a vegetarian meal once about five years ago—it was at your monastery, in fact, in San Francisco, I believe. It was delicious! Research scientists have found cancer causing agents in even deer meat now."

He watched the bowing for a while. He wanted to stay and cultivate. He asked to see the *Avatamsaka Sutra* and wanted to know what it was about.

"What are some of the things it says, and could I look at it and touch it? Is that permitted?" he asked respectfully. Maybe he saw himself cultivating on the highway and using his journalistic skills, to write pieces steeped in the *Avatamsaka* for the betterment of mankind that came from his heart and not from the pressure of deadlines and a paycheck.

We have met so many people like this man who have the same wish and are nearly bursting with the urge to "put it all down and really go and do it." All these people feel like our family. We hope they all have their wish come true.

> *The Bodhisattva, Mahasattva, equally contemplates all beings just as if they were his own children. He wants to cause them all to get a body which is purely adorned and to accomplish the world's supreme peace and happiness, the happiness of the Buddhas' wisdom, and peacefully dwell in the Buddhadharma, thus being of benefit to all beings.*
>
> *Avatamsaka Sutra*
> *Ten Transferences Chapter*

The reporter took off his sunglasses and reached out with a big handshake. "Today I've been really convinced of something, but I couldn't say exactly what. You folks are regular, on-the-level. Take care, good trip."

Peace in the Way

***Disciple Kuo T'ing (Heng Ch'au)
bows in respect***

* * *

*When the nature is in samadhi,
     the demons are subdued and everyday is happy.
False thoughts not arising,
     everywhere is peaceful.
When the mind stops and thoughts are cut off—
     that is true nobility.
With selfish greed ended forever—
     that is the true field of blessings.*

Venerable Master Hua

Thirteen miles from home

September 28, 1979

Milepost 7.97, Boonville Road

Dear Shr Fu,

We're thirteen miles from home. The scenes and experiences of the last two-and-a-half years are spinning in my mind like leaves in the wind. Have I changed? What have I learned? Yes, I have changed. No, I haven't really changed, I'm more the same than ever. How is this?

The biggest change inside have come from learning to respect and follow the rules. It's called "Offering up your conduct according to the teachings." Every time I put my whole heart behind true principle and the Master's instructions, I change. Every time I follow my own ideas or break precepts, I tumble off the road like a car in the ditch. The Buddhadharma I have absorbed stands pure and solid in my mind, amid all the debris of false-thinking and bad habits. True principles guide our steps through the narrow paths of the mind, the same way highway signs keep drivers on the alert. "Rough Road," "Falling Rocks," "Slippery When Wet or Frosty."

> *When Bodhisattvas see deeds which the Thus Come One has warned us about, (deeds which are) stained with afflictions, they completely forsake them. If they see deeds which accord with the Bodhisattva Path and*

which the Thus Come One has praised, they completely cultivate them.

Avatamsaka Sutra
Fourth Bodhisattva Ground

Principle: "Don't attach to states. There is nothing good in the Triple World. Suffering and bliss don't exist at all."

State: Giving rise to Greed and Delusion.

We're meditating in the car after sunset, parked beneath the redwoods on a deserted mountain top. There are five minutes to go before evening ceremonies begin. Because I nodded and dozed while meditating, I haven't completely "smelted" the energy in my body, there's still a lot of fire circulating as I sit. Just a few minutes more will do it. Oh, there's the bell. Too late. Bummer. Now I won't be able to sleep until I smelt after the Sutra. I've got to sit with these burning legs all through the ceremonies. I'll probably boil over. Heng Ch'au has caused me a lot of pain. It's his fault!

Mistake: Anger and Broken Rules.

Because I attached to greedy thoughts for a body-state, I got angry. During Sutra lecture, despite my vow of silence, I shot out my steam at Heng Ch'au, criticized him and spoke harsh speech.

Retribution:

As soon as the angry words left my mouth, I felt all my Dharma-protectors quickly retreat. Heng Ch'au says my inner light went out just like a candle. I felt cold and numb. During the night I had a dream of a demon who stole my energy. I woke up spent and unhappy.

Why? Harsh speech is one of the Ten Evil Deeds. So is greed. So is anger. So is stupidity (deviant views).

The single thought of attaching to a state of bliss during meditation broke the rules and led to the chain of delusion, karmic error and retribution.

If I had let the state go, followed instructions, and been patient with my body, then everything would have been fine.

I should have returned the light and recognized my own mistakes. I slept when it was time to sit and then tried to cover the error and force the schedule.

If I had admitted my error, I would have been right on the Middle Way. I behaved instead like a living being and wound up angry. Bodhisattvas practice kindness and humaneness. They do not blame others.

Yen Yuan asked Confucius, "What does it mean to be humane?"

"Subdue yourself and return to principle," answered Confucius.

On Tuesday, we found a card on our car window. At first glance, it was Mastercharge. It was promotion for a Christian sect made up to look like the familiar orange and yellow credit card. It said, "Give Christ charge of your life." We reflected that this was a good idea, as long as Christ represented universal principles like kindness, compassion, joy and giving.

But reliance on any individual is still an attachment. The Buddha teaches total self-reliance. Ananda asked the Buddha, "When the World Honored One enters Nirvana, whom shall we take as our teacher?"

The Buddha answered, "Take the precepts as your teacher."

In other words, don't rely on others, follow the rules. This is the road to ultimate freedom. What are the rules? Simply the Dharma. Foremost is faith. Next is giving. Then comes morality. Patience, vigor, concentration, and wisdom are all Dharma-rules.

As for faith and giving, two weeks ago, as we climbed the coast ridge on our way East to the City of Ten Thousand Buddhas, it was *really* hot. The air was thick with smoke from forest fires, and the road burned our hands, knees and foreheads. We made sunhats out of bandanas and bowed along thinking cool thoughts of faith and renunciation.

Earth Store Bodhisattva lives in the hells all the time! We didn't have it so rough. He's vowed to stay there until all hell-dwellers are liberated. That's real giving. Mindfulness of Earth Store kept us going. He gave us faith and strength. I recalled the story of Desert Pete from an old Kingston Trio song. Desert Pete kept a well for thirsty travellers in the desert. By the well was a small bottle of water and a note. The note read, "Don't drink the water in the bottle, use it to prime the pump. There's lots of water down below but the pump won't work unless it's primed. Be patient, friend, and you will get your reward."

The chorus went,

> *You've got to prime the pump, you must have faith and believe. You've got to give of yourself before you're worthy to receive. Drink all the water you can hold, wash your face, cool your feet, leave the bottle full for others. Thank you kindly, Desert Pete.*

Desert Pete understood the principle of giving "when you give up one part, you get ten thousand parts in return." And he taught and transformed many thirsty travellers in this way. Each time we offer up our conduct in faith to true principle, we get ten thousand parts in return. It never fails.

Autumn has come. It's county fair time and the road is full of happy faces. This is a year of bountiful harvest. The Buddhadharma has come to the West. America has a new city of light and goodness. Our hearts are full and grateful.

Disciple Kuo Chen (Heng Sure)
bows in respect

You may walk the heavenly road

October 14, 1979

Ukiah

Dear Shr Fu,

Heng Ch'au and I had talked about what we wanted to do when we arrived at the City of Ten Thousand Buddhas and decided to keep bowing. Our work isn't done and bowing suits our natures so well, but we didn't know if the Master would allow us to continue.

"Heng Sure," said Heng Ch'au. I turned, and there on the sidewalk stood the Master in a blaze of yellow-gold robes. Just like that, on State Street in Ukiah, on Saturday afternoon outside a motel.

"When you reach the City of Ten Thousand Buddhas, if you wish to, you may bow up and down the streets. It's not the case that you must bow straight into the Ten Thousand Buddha's Hall and your trip is over and that's that. Bow around the Buddha Hall if you like," he said.

"This accords exactly with our own wishes," I answered.

What a chance to do the inner work of *san bu yi bai*, the concentration and single-minded bowing to Ten Thousand Buddhas, without all the broken beer bottles! No logging trucks, no bullies, no narrow roads, no poison oak, whizzing motorcycles, bars and drunks, mountain slopes, cold-water shaving, weather-delays, rubber-legs and leather-palms, etc. We have a chance to bow in Heaven.

On August 1, in Sea Ranch, the Master said, "There is a road in Heaven, but first you must accomplish the road here on earth.

When you have walked that road to completion, then you may walk the heavenly road."

I thought he was speaking figuratively in the sense of "when one is a human being to perfection, the Buddha's Way accomplishes itself." I didn't guess that there was actually a road in Heaven for us to bow on!

Some people feel that cultivation is bitterness and suffering. Heng Ch'au and I have come to appreciate the opposite. Cultivation brings us more happiness than we have known, while as the Sutra says,

> *Of all the happiness in the mundane world, there is none which is not suffering.*

> *Avatamsaka Sutra*
> *Ten Transferences Chapter, Part One*

On *san bu yi bai* we have learned to take for granted the daily coping of trying to live the life of contemplatives by the side of California's highways. Yesterday the Master granted our wish to practice the Dharma in a pure place, an adorned Bodhimanda City! A chance to concentrate with all the "dust-fatigue" removed, a chance to bow in Heaven with a single mind.

As Heng Ch'au said, "In Pt. Mugu Air Force Base they wouldn't let us bow around their missile display. (By the gate to that base near L.A. there is a roadside memorial park with a small forest of full-sized, tactical missiles on display. We bowed around it one morning until the MP's chased us away.) But now we will be able to bow around the Buddhas as much as we please." How wonderful!

Disciple Kuo Chen (Heng Sure)
bows in respect

* * *

"At the place of seeking nothing, there are no worries."

P.S.: As I re-read my letter, I really feel ashamed. My selfishness has not changed much since this trip began. What did I expect, going out to bow on the public thoroughfare—red carpets? At the first chance to escape the world, I grab for it. Without a second thought for the suffering of all the beings who will never get to hear of the City of Ten Thousand Buddhas, I jump for joy at the prospect of abandoning the world. This is not the Bodhisattva Way.

Another example: I am greedy for Buddhahood. That is just like anyone who seeks selfish benefit in the world. My heart was closed to giving, to kindness and compassion, all coming from my own selfish greed. I was unhappy. Heng Ch'au tried his best to relax my mind. He reminded me of Gwan Shr Yin Bodhisattva's Forty-two Hands and Eyes—unsurpassed expedient means for giving happiness and relieving suffering. He said, "Rain down lotus flowers, don't shoot bullets."

I saw then how I practice the forms of great compassion, but the heart of selfless giving has not truly come to life inside. I'm really ashamed. If I can't concentrate out here, how will the streets of the City of Ten Thousand Buddhas be different? If I haven't learned to give myself away in the heart of the suffering Saha World, a vacation in Heaven will certainly only add to my selfishness. That is what my letter reflects: I still have thoughts of abandoning the world.

The big lesson yesterday: Bodhisattvas practice compassion everywhere.

Manifesting according to kind,
transforming all the gods,
With similar work and benefits,
gathering those with affinities.

Forgetting self for others, truly no self.
Vowing all beings become Worthy Sages.

Although I've come to the foot of Wonderful Enlightenment Mountain, I still have a long way to go before I reach the genuine City of Ten Thousand Buddhas.

Disciple Kuo Chen (Heng Sure)
bows in respect

Bowing is to get rid of selfishness

October 14, 1979
Ukiah, California

Dear Shr Fu,

There is an atmosphere of kindness and compassion that surrounds the Ven. Abbot. After each roadside visit a little of it rubs off on us. Following each visit I am deeply aware of having witnessed true empathy, and I always feel shame at my own harshness and striving. Yesterday the Master visited and although few words were spoken I learned a great deal.

I watched the Master rub Heng Sure's head and soothe his worried mind outside a little motel on the edge of town. I saw compassion. As I stood and watched, I began to realize how hard and insensitive I have been to the person I vowed to protect and take care of on this trip.

Everybody wants to be a Buddha. Everybody suffers. The Bodhisattva Who Regards the Sounds of the World helps everyone end suffering and become a Buddha. How? Compassion, Great Compassion. Gwan Shr Yin Bodhisattva's compassionate heart is so full and rich, a thousand hands and eyes blossom from it to help and support living beings everywhere.

We have heard a lot of the world's sounds over the last two-and-a-half years. And because of greed, anger, and stupidity, even the sounds that seem like happy sounds conceal the sounds of suffering. Living beings are unfilial and hurt each other, often without knowing, and so the sounds of suffering are everywhere. We hear them in angry yells, in empty whiskey and beer bottles, in hunters' rifles, in rush hour horns, squealing tires of a pick-up truck, a crying child, a laughing cocktail party, passing sirens, in the smell of hamburgers at a Drive-in, a lost sheep, a nursing home, a football game, in the roar of a motorcycle, and on and on. We are forever apart from those we love and can never get away from those we don't like. No one ever gets what they seek. And so all suffer. Birth, sickness, old age, and death and the "blazing skandhas." It's all suffering. Until this trip, I never saw this so clearly.

> *Of all the happiness in the world, there is none which is not suffering.*
>
> *Avatamsaka Sutra*
> *Ten Transferences Chapter*

So, is there no happiness, then? Yes, cultivating the Way is happiness. But it doesn't look like happiness. Some say cultivating looks bitter and boring. Yet, things are not what they seem: cultivation looks like suffering, but it's sweet; worldly happiness looks sweet, but it is bitter and boring.

I've been really uncompassionate. The sounds of the world are the cries of suffering. Our faults are just our afflictions and pain. Faulting others while covering our own faults and flaws hurts us. It is like being sick: sick people need pity and care, not rejection and criticism. Faults are the same. They are the sounds of suffering and cries for help of living beings. Bodhisattvas of great compassion listen to all the sounds of the world and only hear, "Help me! I want to be a Buddha, but I can't find my way. I hurt. Please, help me, please..." And in every face, friendly or unfriendly, beautiful or ugly, the Bodhisattva sees the face of a future Buddha.

This was why I came to Gold Mt. Monastery and became a Buddhist: I was deeply inspired to tears upon seeing an image of Gwan Yin Bodhisattva on a poster and reading the words:

> *A thousand eyes see all,*
> *A thousand ears hear all,*
> *A thousand hands keep and support*
> *   living beings everywhere.*

But it's so easy to get lost in selfishness and forget the vision. It is so easy to get caught up in the small of "every man for himself." Seeing the Master's kindness and compassion, I realized how I had once again let the measure of my own heart shrink. It was time to unroll my spirit and let it fill the Dharma Realm with kindness, compassion, joy and giving. Non-dual means being one with everyone.

> *Disciples of the Buddha, the Bodhisattva's heart of kindness is vast and big, measureless and non-dual. It is without blaming, without opposing (adversaries), without obstacles, without troubling. It pervasively reaches all places exhausting the Dharma Realm and the realm of empty space throughout all worlds. And in this same way, he dwells in compassion, joy, and giving.*
>
> *Avatamsaka Sutra*
> *Third Ground of Emitting Light*

October 15, 1979.

As soon as I made this resolve to be more compassionate, obstacles arose. That night, I found myself dreaming of being trapped in a windy cave and suffocating in attachments and sticky relationships. I couldn't get free. Everywhere I turned, my desire and selfishness sucked me deeper and deeper down through dark tunnels. I said, "I should be bowing with Heng Sure now, not running off anywhere. I don't belong in this cave." That old stifling trapped feeling and heaviness I knew so well as a layman came over me again. I was smothering in my own attachments and ignorance. I started to cringe, "How could I go back to this again when I was free and happy?! No, no, I don't want to go back anymore...!" I yelled in this dream.

Just then, I was awakened from the dream by a "crazy" old man outside the car. We are on a deserted road near a lumber yard and vineyard behind the airport. It's 2:00 a.m. The man is looking in at me through the car window muttering nonsense and crazy talk. I shout to him half awake, "What!?" He is wearing a long robe or overcoat and carrying a big, wooden walking stick that reaches above his shoulders. He wanders off when I shout to him.

Later, I find myself succumbing to the same nightmare and I shout in my dream, "No, no, help me..." I hear a tapping on the window and wake up to find the old man peeking in and rapping his big cane on the window. He's saying something like, "gotta get out of here, gotta get out of here. But I don't know how to get out..."

"Shhh..." I whisper to him. It's 3 a.m. now.

"Yeah, okay, I'll be quiet... but how do I get out of here?" he mumbles and tapping his stick on the ground slowly walks back into the fog. I don't know who he was, but he saved me twice. Was he "crazy" or just compassionate?

Bowing is the best and the hardest thing I've ever done. Best, in that it chips away at my mountain of pride, putting me close to the level ground where I belong. Hardest in that my ego wants to be King of the Mountain and resists bowing with all its might.

> *Push over Mount Sumeru,*
> *The mind ground is flat.*
> *Jealousy and arrogance*
> *   are ultimately invisible.*

Verse by Venerable Master Hua

Cultivators who don't really know their own minds face paradoxes. We know the teachings are right and cultivating the Way is the only thing worth doing, and yet, we resist doing it, oppose instructions, and wriggle out through every crack. The front door to Heaven is wide open, but we won't walk in. The Hells have no door, but we drill right in. Bad habits from beginningless time stick like a shadow and haunt us like a ghost. Each time we give in to the ghost we regret it. No matter where we run off to, or how long, we always find ourselves returning to the Buddhadharma like gravity pulls all things back to earth. Seeking enlightenment and accomplishing Buddhahood is our natural instinct. If I think about cultivation I can get immobilized with the second thoughts of my prattling mind. If I follow the path with heart and just *do it*, then it's wonderful beyond words. So it's said,

> *What is spoken is false;*
> *What is practiced is true.*

When the pilgrimage ends at the City of Ten Thousand Buddhas, we're going to keep on bowing. Isn't that stupid! Everybody asks us, "What are you going to do when you get there?" They all assume we can't wait to stop this "crazy bowing thing" and get back to "normal". If we told people we were going to bow up and down and all around the streets of the City of Ten Thousand Buddhas, they might respond as did this person: "You're nuts! Totally stupid weirdos. What's the point?!" A young man stopped his car after trying to run us off the road and just screamed, "Arrgh, yeoowoo freaks! I can't stand it!" Later he came back, mellowed out to say, "At first I figured you were weird, but there's something to this, ya' know? I mean, I myself would never do it, mind you, but I admire your dedication. It takes guts, or something," shook hands and quietly drove away.

The whole point of the bowing is to get rid of selfishness. All the disasters and calamities and suffering in the world come from selfishness. To truly help the world, the Ego has to die a little first.

Bowing is a wonderful chance to die. If we are sincere, maybe we can bow to the vanishing point.

> *When you reach the point that the mountains are levelled and the seas disappear, and you doubt that there's a way at all, then suddenly, there beyond the dark willow and the bright flowers is another village.*

Peace in the Way

Disciple Kuo T'ing (Heng Ch'au)
bows in respect

* * *

> *He also makes the following reflection, "I should, among all living beings, be a leader, be supreme, be most supreme, be wonderful, be subtly wonderful, be superior, be unsurpassed, up to and including being one with the wisdom of all wisdom upon whom others can rely."*

Avatamsaka Sutra
Ten Grounds Chapter

Arrival at the City of Ten Thousand Buddhas
on a foggy morning.

November, 1979

The Venerable Master rubs the crown of Heng Sure's head upon the monks' arrival at the City of Ten Thousand Buddhas, the destination of their bowing pilgrimage.

Upon arrival at the City of Ten Thousand Buddhas at the completion of the bowing pilgrimage, Heng Sure joins the Venerable Master on stage for a welcoming gathering.

Heng Chau and Heng Sure flank the Venerable
Master at welcoming ceremonies upon completion
of the bowing pilgrimage.

The Venerable Master listens carefully to the speeches given by Heng Sure and Heng Chau during welcoming ceremonies that celebrate the culmination of their three-step-one-bow pilgrimage.

Buddhist Text Translation Society Publication

Buddhist Text Translation Society
International Translation Institute

http://www.bttsonline.org

1777 Murchison Drive,
Burlingame, California 94010-4504 USA
Phone: 650-692-5912 Fax: 650-692-5056

When Buddhism first came to China from India, one of the most important tasks required for its establishment was the translation of the Buddhist scriptures from Sanskrit into Chinese. This work involved a great many people, such as the renowned monk National Master Kumarajiva (fifth century), who led an assembly of over 800 people to work on the translation of the Tripitaka (Buddhist canon) for over a decade. Because of the work of individuals such as these, nearly the entire Buddhist Tripitaka of over a thousand texts exists to the present day in Chinese.

Now the banner of the Buddha's Teachings is being firmly planted in Western soil, and the same translation work is being done from Chinese into English. Since 1970, the Buddhist Text Translation Society (BTTS) has been making a paramount contribution toward this goal. Aware that the Buddhist Tripitaka is a work of such magnitude that its translation could never be entrusted to a single person, the BTTS, emulating the translation assemblies of ancient times, does not publish a work until it has passed through four committees for primary translation, revision, editing, and certification. The leaders of these committees are Bhikshus (monks) and Bhikshunis (nuns) who have devoted their lives to the study and practice of the Buddha's teachings. For this reason, all of the works of the BTTS put an emphasis on what the principles of the Buddha's teachings mean in terms of actual practice and not simply hypothetical conjecture.

The translations of canonical works by the Buddhist Text Translation Society are accompanied by extensive commentaries by the Venerable Tripitaka Master Hsuan Hua.

BTTS Publications

Buddhist Sutras. Amitabha Sutra, Dharma Flower (Lotus) Sutra, Flower Adornment (Avatamsaka) Sutra, Heart Sutra & Verses without a Stand, Shurangama Sutra, Sixth Patriarch Sutra, Sutra in Forty-two Sections, Sutra of the Past Vows of Earth Store Bodhisattva, Vajra Prajna Paramita (Diamond) Sutra.

Commentarial Literature. Buddha Root Farm, City of 10 000 Buddhas Recitation Handbook, Filiality: The Human Source, Herein Lies the Treasure-trove, Listen to Yourself Think Everything Over, Shastra on the Door to Understanding the Hundred Dharmas, Song of Enlightenment, The Ten Dharma Realms Are Not Beyond a Single Thought, Venerable Master Hua's Talks on Dharma, Venerable Master Hua's Talks on Dharma during the 1993 Trip to Taiwan, Water Mirror Reflecting Heaven.

Biographical. In Memory of the Venerable Master Hsuan Hua, Pictorial Biography of the Venerable Master Hsü Yün, Records of High Sanghans, Records of the Life of the Venerable Master Hsüan Hua, Three Steps One Bow, World Peace Gathering, News from True Cultivators, Open Your Eyes Take a Look at the World, With One Heart Bowing to the City of 10 000 Buddhas.

Children's Books. Cherishing Life, Human Roots: Buddhist Stories for Young Readers, Spider Web, Giant Turtle, Patriarch Bodhidharma.

Musics, Novels and Brochures. Songs for Awakening, Awakening, The Three Cart Patriarch, City of 10 000 Buddhas Color Brochure, Celebrisi's Journey, Lots of Time Left.

The Buddhist Monthly–Vajra Bodhi Sea is a monthly journal of orthodox Buddhism which has been published by the Dharma Realm Buddhist Association, formerly known as the Sino-American Buddhist Association, since 1970. Each issue contains the most recent translations of the Buddhist canon by the Buddhist Text Translation Society. Also included in each issue are a biography of a great Patriarch of Buddhism from the ancient past, sketches of the lives of contemporary monastics and lay-followers around the world, articles on practice, and other material. The journal is bilingual, Chinese and English

Please visit our web-site at **www.bttsonline.org** for the latest publications and for ordering information.

The Dharma Realm Buddhist Association

Mission

The Dharma Realm Buddhist Association (formerly the Sino-American Buddhist Association) was founded by the Venerable Master Hsuan Hua in the United States of America in 1959. Taking the Dharma Realm as its scope, the Association aims to disseminate the genuine teachings of the Buddha throughout the world. The Association is dedicated to translating the Buddhist canon, propagating the Orthodox Dharma, promoting ethical education, and bringing benefit and happiness to all beings. Its hope is that individuals, families, the society, the nation, and the entire world will, under the transforming influence of the Buddhadharma, gradually reach the state of ultimate truth and goodness.

The Founder

The Venerable Master, whose names were An Tse and To Lun, received the Dharma name Hsuan Hua and the transmission of Dharma from Venerable Master Hsu Yun in the lineage of the Wei Yang Sect. He was born in Manchuria, China, at the beginning of the century. At nineteen, he entered the monastic order and dwelt in a hut by his mother's grave to practice filial piety. He meditated, studied the teachings, ate only one meal a day, and slept sitting up. In 1948 he went to Hong Kong, where he established the Buddhist Lecture Hall and other Way-places. In 1962 he brought the Proper Dharma to the West, lecturing on several dozen Mahayana Sutras in the United States. Over the years, the Master established more than twenty monasteries of Proper Dharma under the auspices of the Dharma Realm Buddhist Association and the City of Ten Thousand Buddhas. He also founded centers for the translation of the Buddhist canon and for education to spread the influence of the Dharma in the East and West. The Master manifested the stillness in the United States in 1995. Through his lifelong, selfless dedication to teaching living beings with wisdom and compassion, he influenced countless people to change their faults and to walk upon the pure, bright path to enlightenment.

Dharma Propagation, Buddhist Text Translation, and Education

The Venerable Master Hua's three great vows after leaving the home-life were (1) to propagate the Dharma, (2) to translate the Buddhist Canon, and (3) to promote education. In order to make these vows a reality, the Venerable Master based himself on the Three Principles and the Six Guidelines. Courageously facing every hardship, he founded monasteries, schools, and centers in the West, drawing in living beings and teaching them on a vast scale. Over the years, he founded the following institutions:

The City of Ten Thousand Buddhas and Its Branches

In propagating the Proper Dharma, the Venerable Master not only trained people but also founded Way-places where the Dharma wheel could turn and living beings could be saved. He wanted to provide cultivators with pure places to practice in accord with the Buddha's regulations. Over the years, he founded many Way-places of Proper Dharma. In the United States and Canada, these include the City of Ten Thousand Buddhas; Gold Mountain Monastery; Gold Sage Monastery; Gold Wheel Monastery; Gold Summit Monastery; Gold Buddha Monastery; Avatamsaka Monastery; Long Beach Monastery; the City of the Dharma Realm; Berkeley Buddhist Monastery; Avatamsaka Hermitage; and Blessings, Prosperity, and Longevity Monastery. In Taiwan, there are the Dharma Realm Buddhist Books Distribution Association, Dharma Realm Monastery, and Amitabha Monastery. In Malaysia, there are the Prajna Guanyin Sagely Monastery (formerly Tze Yun Tung Temple), Deng Bi An Monastery, and Lotus Vihara. In Hong Kong, there are the Buddhist Lecture Hall and Cixing Monastery.

Purchased in 1974, the City of Ten Thousand Buddhas is the hub of the Dharma Realm Buddhist Association. The City is located in Talmage, Mendocino County, California, 110 miles north of San Francisco. Eighty of the 488 acres of land are in active use. The remaining acreage consists of meadows, orchards, and woods. With over seventy large buildings containing over 2,000 rooms, blessed with serenity and fresh, clean air, it is the first large Buddhist monastic community in the United States. It is also an international center for the Proper Dharma.

Although the Venerable Master Hua was the Ninth Patriarch in the Wei Yang Sect of the Chan School, the monasteries he founded emphasize all of the five main practices of Mahayana Buddhism (Chan meditation, Pure Land, esoteric, Vinaya (moral discipline), and doctrinal studies). This accords with the Buddha's words: "The Dharma is level and equal, with no high or low." At the City of Ten Thousand Buddhas, the rules of purity are rigorously observed. Residents of the City strive to regulate their own conduct and to cultivate with vigor. Taking refuge in the Proper Dharma, they lead pure and selfless lives, and attain peace in body and mind. The Sutras are expounded and the Dharma wheel is turned daily. Residents dedicate themselves wholeheartedly to making Buddhism flourish. Monks and nuns in all the monasteries take one meal a day, always wear their precept sash, and follow the Three Principles:

> *Freezing, we do not scheme.*
> *Starving, we do not beg.*
> *Dying of poverty, we ask for nothing.*
> *According with conditions, we do not change.*
> *Not changing, we accord with conditions.*
> *We adhere firmly to our three great principles.*
> *We renounce our lives to do the Buddha's work.*
> *We take the responsibility to mold our own destinies.*
> *We rectify our lives to fulfill the Sanghan's role.*
> *Encountering specific matters,*
>   *we understand the principles.*
> *Understanding the principles,*
>   *we apply them in specific matters.*
> *We carry on the single pulse of*
>   *the Patriarchs' mind-transmission.*

The monasteries also follow the Six Guidelines: not contending, not being greedy, not seeking, not being selfish, not pursuing personal advantage, and not lying.

International Translation Institute

The Venerable Master vowed to translate the Buddhist Canon (Tripitaka) into Western languages so that it would be widely accessible throughout the world. In 1973, he founded the International Translation Institute on Washington Street in San Francisco for the purpose of translating Buddhist scriptures into English and other languages. In 1977, the Institute was merged into Dharma Realm Buddhist University as the Institute for the Translation of Buddhist Texts. In 1991, the Venerable Master purchased a large building in Burlingame (south of San Francisco) and established the International Translation Institute there for the purpose of translating and publishing Buddhist texts. To date, in addition to publishing over one hundred volumes of Buddhist texts in Chinese, the Association has published more than one hundred volumes of English, French, Spanish, Vietnamese, and Japanese translations of Buddhist texts, as well as bilingual (Chinese and English) editions. Audio and video tapes also continue to be produced. The monthly journal Vajra Bodhi Sea, which has been in circulation for nearly thirty years, has been published in bilingual (Chinese and English) format in recent years.

In the past, the difficult and vast mission of translating the Buddhist canon in China was sponsored and supported by the emperors and kings themselves. In our time, the Venerable Master encouraged his disciples to cooperatively shoulder this heavy responsibility, producing books and audio tapes and using the medium of language to turn the wheel of Proper Dharma and do the great work of the Buddha. All those who aspire to devote themselves to this work of sages should uphold the Eight Guidelines of the International Translation Institute:

1. One must free oneself from the motives of personal fame and profit.
2. One must cultivate a respectful and sincere attitude free from arrogance and conceit.
3. One must refrain from aggrandizing one's work and denigrating that of others.
4. One must not establish oneself as the standard of correctness and suppress the work of others with one's fault-finding.
5. One must take the Buddha-mind as one's own mind.
6. One must use the wisdom of Dharma-Selecting Vision to determine true principles.
7. One must request Virtuous Elders of the ten directions to certify one's translations.
8. One must endeavor to propagate the teachings by printing Sutras, Shastra texts, and Vinaya texts when the translations are certified as being correct.

These are the Venerable Master's vows, and participants in the work of translation should strive to realize them.

Instilling Goodness Elementary School, Developing Virtue Secondary School, Dharma Realm Buddhist University

"Education is the best national defense." The Venerable Master Hua saw clearly that in order to save the world, it is essential to promote good education. If we want to save the world, we have to bring about a complete change in people's minds and guide them to cast out unwholesomeness and to pursue goodness. To this end the Master founded Instilling Goodness Elementary School in 1974, and Developing Virtue Secondary School and Dharma Realm Buddhist University in 1976.

In an education embodying the spirit of Buddhism, the elementary school teaches students to be filial to parents, the secondary school teaches students to be good citizens, and the university teaches such virtues as humaneness and righteousness. Instilling Goodness Elementary School and Developing Virtue Secondary School combine the best of contemporary and traditional methods and of Western and Eastern cultures. They emphasize moral virtue and spiritual development, and aim to guide students to become good and capable citizens who will benefit humankind. The schools offer a bilingual (Chinese/English) program where boys and girls study separately. In addition to standard academic courses, the curriculum includes ethics, meditation, Buddhist studies, and so on, giving students a foundation in virtue and guiding them to understand themselves and explore the truths of the universe. Branches of the schools (Sunday schools) have been established at branch monasteries with the aim of propagating filial piety and ethical education.

Dharma Realm Buddhist University, whose curriculum focuses on the Proper Dharma, does not merely transmit academic knowledge. It emphasizes a foundation in virtue, which expands into the study of how to help all living beings discover their inherent nature. Thus, Dharma Realm Buddhist University advocates a spirit of shared inquiry and free exchange of ideas, encouraging students to study various canonical texts and use different experiences and learning styles to tap their inherent wisdom and fathom the meanings of those texts. Students are encouraged to practice the principles they have understood and apply the Buddhadharma in their lives, thereby nurturing their wisdom and virtue. The University aims to produce outstanding individuals of high moral character who will be able to bring benefit to all sentient beings.

Sangha and Laity Training Programs

In the Dharma-ending Age, in both Eastern and Western societies there are very few monasteries that actually practice the Buddha's regulations and strictly uphold the precepts. Teachers with genuine wisdom and understanding, capable of guiding those who aspire to pursue careers in Buddhism, are very rare. The Venerable Master founded the Sangha and Laity Training Programs in 1982 with the goals of raising the caliber of the Sangha, perpetuating the Proper Dharma, providing professional training for Buddhists around the world on both practical and theoretical levels, and transmitting the wisdom of the Buddha.

The Sangha Training Program gives monastics a solid foundation in Buddhist studies and practice, training them in the practical affairs of Buddhism and Sangha management. After graduation, students will be able to assume various responsibilities related to Buddhism in monasteries, institutions, and other settings. The program emphasizes a thorough knowledge of Buddhism, understanding of the scriptures, earnest cultivation, strict observance of precepts, and the development of a virtuous character, so that students will be able to propagate the Proper Dharma and perpetuate the Buddha's wisdom. The Laity Training Program offers courses to help laypeople develop correct views, study and practice the teachings, and understand monastic regulations and ceremonies, so that they will be able to contribute their abilities in Buddhist organizations.

Let Us Go Forward Together

In this Dharma-ending Age when the world is becoming increasingly dangerous and evil, the Dharma Realm Buddhist Association, in consonance with its guiding principles, opens the doors of its monasteries and centers to those of all religions and nationalities. Anyone who is devoted to humaneness, righteousness, virtue, and the pursuit of truth, and who wishes to understand him or herself and help humankind, is welcome to come study and practice with us. May we together bring benefit and happiness to all living beings.

Dharma Realm Buddhist Association Branches

The City of Ten Thousand Buddhas
P.O. Box 217, Talmage, CA 95481-0217 USA
Tel: (707) 462-0939 Fax: (707) 462-0949
Home Page: http://www.drba.org

Institute for World Religions (Berkeley Buddhist Monastery)
2304 McKinley Avenue, Berkeley, CA 94703 USA
Tel: (510) 848-3440

Dharma Realm Buddhist Books Distribution Society
11th Floor, 85 Chung-hsiao E. Road, Sec. 6, Taipei, Taiwan R.O.C.
Tel: (02) 2786-3022 Fax: (02) 2786-2674

The City of the Dharma Realm
1029 West Capitol Avenue, West Sacramento, CA 95691 USA
Tel: (916) 374-8268

Gold Mountain Monastery
800 Sacramento Street, San Francisco, CA 94108 USA
Tel: (415) 421-6117 Fax: (415) 788-6001

Gold Wheel Monastery
235 North Avenue 58, Los Angeles, CA 90042 USA
Tel: (323) 258-6668

Gold Buddha Monastery
248 East 11th Avenue, Vancouver, B.C. V5T 2C3 Canada
Tel: (604) 709-0248 Fax: (604) 684-3754

Gold Summit Monastery
233 1st Avenue, West Seattle, WA 98119 USA
Tel: (206) 284-6690 Fax: (206) 284-6918

Gold Sage Monastery
11455 Clayton Road, San Jose, CA 95127 USA
Tel: (408) 923-7243 Fax: (408) 923-1064

The International Translation Institute
1777 Murchison Drive, Burlingame, CA 94010-4504 USA
Tel: (650) 692-5912 Fax: (650) 692-5056

Long Beach Monastery
3361 East Ocean Boulevard, Long Beach, CA 90803 USA
Tel: (562) 438-8902

Blessings, Prosperity, & Longevity Monastery
4140 Long Beach Boulevard, Long Beach, CA 90807 USA
Tel: (562) 595-4966

Avatamsaka Hermitage
11721 Beall Mountain Road, Potomac, MD 20854-1128 USA
Tel: (301) 299-3693

Avatamsaka Monastery
1009 4th Avenue, S.W. Calgary, AB T2P OK8 Canada
Tel: (403) 234-0644 Email: ava@nucleus.com

Kun Yam Thong Temple
161, Jalan Ampang, 50450 Kuala Lumpur, Malaysia
Tel: (03) 2164-8055 Fax: (03) 2163-7118

Prajna Guanyin Sagely Monastery (formerly Tze Yun Tung)
Batu 5½, Jalan Sungai Besi,
Salak Selatan, 57100 Kuala Lumpur, Malaysia
Tel: (03) 7982-6560 Fax: (03) 7980-1272

Lotus Vihara
136, Jalan Sekolah, 45600 Batang Berjuntai,
Selangor Darul Ehsan, Malaysia
Tel: (03) 3271-9439

Buddhist Lecture Hall
31 Wong Nei Chong Road, Top Floor, Happy Valley, Hong Kong, China
Tel: (02) 2572-7644

Dharma Realm Sagely Monastery
20, Tong-hsi Shan-chuang, Hsing-lung Village, Liu-kuei
Kaohsiung County, Taiwan, R.O.C.
Tel: (07) 689-3717 Fax: (07) 689-3870

Amitabha Monastery
7, Su-chien-hui, Chih-nan Village, Shou-feng,
Hualien County, Taiwan, R.O.C.
Tel: (07) 865-1956 Fax: (07) 865-3426

Verse of Transference

May the merit and virtue accrued from this work,
Adorn the Buddhas' Pure Lands,
Repaying four kinds of kindness above,
And aiding those suffering in the paths below.

May those who see and hear of this,
All bring forth the resolve for Bodhi,
And when this retribution body is over,
Be born together in the Land of Ultimate Bliss.

Dharma Protector Wei Tuo Bodhisattva